CAPITALISM AND
COMMUNICATION

The Media, Culture & Society Series

Series editors: John Corner, Nicholas Garnham, Paddy Scannell,
Philip Schlesinger, Colin Sparks, Nancy Wood

The Economics of Television
The UK Case

Richard Collins, Nicholas Garnham and Gareth Locksley

Media, Culture and Society
A Critical Reader

edited by
Richard Collins, James Curran, Nicholas Garnham,
Paddy Scannell, Philip Schlesinger and Colin Sparks

CAPITALISM AND COMMUNICATION

Global Culture and the Economics of Information

Nicholas Garnham

edited by
Fred Inglis

SAGE Publications
London • Newbury Park • New Delhi

First published 1990

SAGE Publications Ltd
28 Banner Street
London EC1Y 8QE

SAGE Publications Inc
2111 West Hillcrest Drive
Newbury Park, California 91320

SAGE Publications India Pvt Ltd
32, M-Block Market
Greater Kailash – I
New Delhi 110 048

British Library Cataloguing in Publication data

Garnham, Nicholas
    Capitalism and communication: global culture and the
    economics of information. – (The Media, Culture and
    Society series).
    1. Society. Role of mass media. Research
    I. Title   II. Series
    302.23

    ISBN 0–8039–9257–7
    ISBN 0–8039–8258–5 pbk

Library of Congress catalog card number 90-61353

Filmset by Mayhew Typesetting, Bristol, England
Printed in Great Britain by Dotesios Printers Ltd,
Trowbridge, Wiltshire

Contents

To Caroline
in loving appreciation of my
sternest but most supportive critic

Acknowledgements

I took the decision to publish this collection of essays because I was persuaded by a number of people, not only of their continuing relevance and coherence, but also of the usefulness of making available in one place work originally produced in a wide scatter of publications, some not readily available, and over more than a decade.

I have taken this opportunity to write a new introductory chapter placing the essays in what I see as their contemporary intellectual and political context.

Much of the empirical detail in these essays has inevitably dated since they were written. I have not in general attempted to update them, where the details are used to illustrate an argument and where the argument has not, in my view, been invalidated by more recent developments.

In some cases updating was required so I have made minor amendments to Chapter 8 and added a new postscript to Chapter 11. I have also taken the opportunity of republication to add a concluding section, on 'The Problem of Time', to Chapter 2, a section which, for reasons of length, had to be dropped when the essay was originally published.

These essays were first published as follows:

'Contribution to a Political Economy of Mass Communication', *Media, Culture and Society*, Vol. 1, 1979; 'Film and Media Studies: Reconstructing the Subject' in *Film and Media Studies in Higher Education*, ed. C. Gledhill, British Film Institute, 1981 and in *Film Reader 5*, Film Division, Northwestern University, 1982; 'The Myths of Video' in the *CILECT Bulletin*, II; 'Bourdieu and the Sociology of Culture', *Media, Culture and Society*, Vol. 2, 1980; 'Politics and Mass Media Study in Britain', *Media, Culture and Society*, Vol. 1, 1979; 'The Media and the Public Sphere', in *Communicating Politics*, eds P. Golding, G. Murdock and P. Schlesinger, University of Leicester Press, 1986; 'Public Service versus the Market', *Screen*, Vol. 24, No. 1, 1983; 'Telecommunications Policy in the United Kingdom', *Media, Culture and Society*, Vol. 7, 1985; 'Public Policy and the Cultural Industries', in *The State of the Art or the Art of the State*, Greater London Council, 1984 and in *Cultural Studies*, Vol. 1, No. 1, 1987; 'The Economics of the US Motion Picture Industry' as a report by the Division of Cultural Action of the European Commission, 1980.

I would like to thank the publishers in each case for permission to republish.

1

Media Theory and the Political Future of Mass Communication

Underpinning all the discussion that follows is first an academic argument concerning the nature of cultural and media studies; it aims to answer the question, what should we be studying, how and why? Secondly, there is a political argument concerning media and cultural policy. That is based upon necessarily normative assumptions as to both the proper and potential role of media and cultural institutions and practices in society, and upon a tactical or strategic judgement as to the appropriate form and place of intervention.

Finally, as exemplified by the book itself, there is a view of the link between intellectual inquiry and political action and thus of the role of intellectuals in our time. These essays are written out of the conviction that more is at stake in one's engagement in academic debates than academic demarcation disputes, careerism or matters of scientific nicety, and that secondly the academic field is itself an object in our field of inquiry and subject to the same analysis and critique as that directed at other cultural institutions and practices.

I write this against the background of an intellectual field from which recently dominant Marxism, in the midst of a deep intellectual crisis, has widely withdrawn and in which its place has been taken by versions of either post-modernism or classic liberalism (the rediscovery of the market and of political rights). In the political field the social democratic consensus that dominated western European politics since 1945 has begun to break up and neo-conservative and neo-liberal challenges to its characteristic policies and institutional forms have struck a powerful chord with voters.

The disciplinary approach developed in these essays is that of the political economy of communications and culture. In developing that approach I am concerned to oppose three specific tendencies within cultural and media studies. First, and above all because it was and still is dominant in the field, that tendency which privileged the text and laid its analytical focus on questions of representation and ideology. This tendency developed out of literary and film studies and carried its textuality into versions of structuralist and post-structuralist Marxism and on into post-modernism. It took with it the bacillus of romanticism and its longing to escape from the determining material and social constraints of human life, from what is seen as the alienation of human essence, into a world of unanchored, non-referential signification and the free play of desire. The dionysiac mind-set of this tendency and its deep roots within western European culture are, I think, clear. It is also perfectly designed as an ideology of intellectuals or cultural workers for it privileges their special field of activity, the symbolic, and provides for cheap research opportunities, since the only evidence required is the unsubstantiated views of the individual analyst.

Second, I am concerned to oppose a pluralism, derived from political science and in particular US political science, which sees the media and other cultural institutions as a given, perhaps technologically determined, field upon which a swirling and varying set of social interest groups compete for power. If the textual tendency evacuates the terrain of explanation by giving up on reference, this tendency has no concept of the structured and differential nature of social power or of the sources of that power. It pays for its proper respect for human agency with a weak to non-existent concept of social structure. In so doing it idealizes the institutions of both bourgeois democracy and the capitalist mixed economy and has a tendency to fall prey to their associated ideologies of freedom of the press and free flow of communication as the transparent mechanisms through which interest group politics are eternally played out.

Against this background I think it is important to restate, as clearly as I can, what I see as the nature of the project of media and cultural studies, as exemplified by these essays. What, in short, is at stake intellectually and politically?

First I want to oppose the tendency inherent in the academic division of labour, to autonomize this field of study and thus both to exaggerate the special significance of the social phenomena under investigation (the study of the media *per se* tends to the trivial) and to cut the field off from the main stream of social science. The media are only worth studying in so far as they focus key problems within the general project of the social sciences. This project has come down to us from the Enlightenment and at a time when this heritage is under widespread attack intellectually from Nietzschean post-modernists, and politically from neo-conservatives, it is important to restate its basic lineaments.

II

The Enlightenment project can be seen as a response to three developments. First the break with the doxa of Christianity and with its associated theodicy posed the question of the explanation for, and legitimation of, a given social structure and heirarchy of power. If the structures of social life and the distribution of material surpluses and political power were made by humans rather than created by God, then they could be unmade and remade by humans. Furthermore the challenge to theodicy placed the critique of ideologies at the heart of the project of human liberation. Humans were seen as enslaved not just, or even most importantly, by physical coercion and material deprivation, but by false ideas or systems of belief.

Secondly the acceleration of social change associated with the early development of capitalism raised the question of history, of the nature of the dynamic processes involved and of the value to be attached to the notion of progress.

Thirdly the voyages of exploration and the development of colonialism raised the question of the differences between social structures and cultures. Linked to the idea of progress it thus placed on the agenda the possibility of alternative social futures. Here the use of images of other, non-European landscapes and cultures in the construction of utopias within the western European imagination – in part the re-realization of the Garden of Eden, in part the use of other possible worlds as critiques of existing western European societies and social practices – is striking. One has only to think of Shakespeare's *The Tempest*, Defoe's *Robinson Crusoe* or Swift's *Gulliver's Travels*. It also posed the question of totality by raising the question of the relationship between social structure and culture, as for instance in Montesquieu's *The Spirit of the Laws*.

In breaking with religious explanations it placed the responsibility for human action and human salvation in human hands and sought the answer to the questions it posed in the concept and practice of human reason. It was reason which linked the project of understanding the world to the project of changing it. Social science and progressive politics developed in intimate relationship out of this link. In my view they both still depend upon it. Thus both projects are inconceivable without an allegiance to rationality. This is a term one now uses, I realize, at one's peril. What I mean by it is a system of inter-subjective communication based: first, on a shared and realist epistemology – that is, an assumption that there is a material world external to our cognitive processes which possesses specific properties ultimately accessible to our understanding; second, on shared rules of discourse such that there are propositions which we can all agree, on the basis of the presented evidence and the observance of common rules of argumentation, to be either true or false; third, on the assumption that humans share enough common characteristics to make it possible for them to agree about the accuracy of external descriptions of their interests and the reasons for their actions, as well as being potentially capable of arriving at a common set of judgements as to the rightness or wrongness of any given action in the light of an agreed set of common interests.

A social science which cuts its links with this rationalist project of human liberation either sinks to the trivial level where mere intellectual games are played, although always in this arena the games are at someone else's expense, or it joins the ranks of those who, throughout history, have perfected and wielded the technologies of domination, whether physical or symbolic, in the service of ruling elites. A politics which rejects rationality in favour of any form of relativism is reduced to an eternal power struggle of all against all, in which there is no place for the normative except as ideology.

The core problem for this Enlightenment project was to ground the universality of human reason in the face of both the observable differences between human cultures and associated value systems and of the manifest clash of human interests. How were different definitions of the project of human liberation to be reconciled? In whose name could social scientists and politicians design and implement a new society?

There are two responses to this problem which are of relevance to my argument here. The first is Kant's, who argued for what I will call a consensus theory of social, or as he put it moral, truth. Not in the sense that moral truth was any old set of values which a particular group agreed about at any one time, but that, as he argued, human beings shared the same set of fundamental moral interests. Just as they could arrive, through the use of a set of fundamental epistemological presuppositions and on the basis of the evidence of commonly possessed faculties of perception, at agreement as to the truth of a proposition about the material world, so through a process of empathy and unconstrained debate they could arrive at a similar common agreement on a desirable moral order. Although for Kant himself this moral order was already given and to be discovered rather than produced by consensus-forming debate, it is this position which ultimately underlies the concept of the public sphere and of the political centrality of the values of free communication within the western political tradition.

III

The next and crucial step on the road to the political economy of communications was then taken by Marx. He argued that the concept of human interest and of universal rationality had to be grounded materially and historically. Crucially he argued that the creation of a social order which reflected a common human interest and was the realization of human liberation depended upon two historical conditions. Firstly it was dependent upon a process of historical material development which ensured liberation from material scarcity, and secondly it was dependent upon the creation of a class whose interests were universalizable in the Kantian sense; that is who had an interest in changing the existing structure of social power and, because of the massive spread of proletarianization and the role of the proletariat within the mode of production, had the power to do so. For my purposes here I would want to stress that Marx shared with Kant the presupposition as to the universality of human moral reason linked to a consensus theory of truth, in the sense, as outlined above, of the truth that would be agreed to by free human beings as the result of an unconstrained process of rational debate, and as the normative basis for both human science and political liberation. The difference between them lies in Marx's stress on the historical conditions necessary for their realization.

For the purposes of my argument here the crucial aspects of the Marxist development of the Enlightenment project are the linkage between the development of the material conditions for human liberation on the one hand and what I might call the symbolic conditions for the formulation and realization of the project of human liberation on the other. It is these symbolic conditions which are sometimes referred to as the problem of ideology. Thus what I have called the political economy of communications and culture links the analysis of capitalism, both as an overall social formation and as a specific mode of production, to the normative definition and realization of human liberation at three levels. Firstly the relation between the mode of production of material life in general and the specific set of material practices by means of which symbolic forms are created, circulated and appropriated. Secondly the relation between capitalism as a social system and the set of ideas about the world possessed by human agents within that system. Thirdly the relation under capitalism between human ideas and human actions.

Marx held to a concept of human rationality and to a philosophical realism that maintains that a world exists exterior to human beings with defined properties which can in their turn be captured in those systems of representation through which we interpret that world, in such a way that human beings can come to a common and true understanding of that world through the evidence of their senses as communicated through the languages at their disposal. But it is central to his theory of ideology that this process of understanding is neither simple nor unproblematic. This is both because of the complexity of the world to be analysed and because of the mediated relationship between phenomena themselves, and between observing human agents and those phenomena. Thus the Marxist theory of ideology depends on a rationalist theory of truth against which ideology can be measured as false and at the same time acknowledges a possibility of false consciousness in the sense of systematic error in a world in which increasingly the knowledge of the world we require for action is not based upon evidence directly available to our senses. Hence the centrality of mediated forms of communication in the process of social life and its analysis.

A political economy of communications and culture, therefore, fully accepts the arguments of the textualists as to the centrality of the process of the construction and exchange of meaning in a social world made by intelligent, reflexive human agents. Where it parts company decisively with the post-modernist current, is in continuing to hold to the idea that discourse is capable of expressing a truth about a world external to that discourse, and further, that discourse has a determinate relation to the actions of human agents, actions about which it is possible to make normative judgements. We can say meaningfully of such actions that they are good, bad, or mistaken.

But crucially a political economy of communications and culture stresses that all mediated forms of communication involve the use of scarce material resources and the mobilization of competences and dispositions which are themselves in important ways determined by access to scarce resources; that the understanding we have of the world, and thus our ability to change it, will be in their turn determined by the ways in which access to and control over those scarce resources is structured.

It is important to stress, since it often causes misunderstanding, that I here use the word determination in the 'soft' sense used by Raymond Williams (1977: 83–9), not as fixing a simple causal relationship, but as a setting of limits. It does not predetermine human action in any unilateral sense, but it does make some courses of action more likely than others, if only because it makes some more difficult than others, and also acknowledges that there are, at any one time, certain absolute, often material, limits to the range of human action. Determination also implies that humans learn from their historical experience in ways which create habits and thus inertia, and in ways which provide warnings against certain courses of action and thus make such actions less likely in the future. I am thinking here of what appears to be to the deep-seated and, in my view, perfectly rational human aversion to risk and therefore to many forms of change. It is here that I part company with many Marxist colleagues and with that tradition which has placed its stress on dominant ideology as the explanation for the maintenance of the social status quo. Since in my view it is revolutionary change that has to be explained, the problem of the dominant ideology simply is not posed.

What I would want to stress in its place is the problem of reproduction, one of the problems central to the classic tradition of political economy from Smith via Ricardo to Marx. For them the maintenance and continuation of a system of material production, a system upon which all other human endeavour rests, could not be taken for granted. In agricultural subsistence economies, human civilization and the very survival of the given human group were always at risk from famine and other natural disasters, but the units of production were small and those of production and consumption almost identical. Societies were made up of a very loosely connected network of small, self-sufficient groups. In exchange economies, on the other hand, the social fabric is made up of a much more complex set of interrelationships and interdependencies between individuals and groups. The development of extensive and intensive divisions of labour, the necessarily more complex and widespread system for distributing both human labour and production inputs and outputs resulting from that division of labour, and the mediation of most relations by an abstract monetary medium of exchange, all mean that the problem becomes one of constructing and maintaining a complex system of social coordination which is vulnerable to crisis and breakdown because of its very complexity. Thus a political economic approach distinguishes itself from a neo-classical or marginalist approach first by placing its emphasis on production or supply rather than consumption or demand as the determining moment. It never takes the social construction and maintenance of the given system of material production for granted. It recognizes that system for the unstable human achievement that it is, and thus stresses the problems of disequilibrium, the constant threats to the smooth working and continuity of the system, rather than assuming equilibrium.

But this very complexity also makes both analysis and planned interventions into the operation of the mode of production increasingly difficult. This is in itself a form of determination. In an intelligent critique of my own work Robins and Webster (1988) characterize it as an 'economic analysis in terms of price and profit', and argue that it is not sufficiently social and political to serve as a basis for the analysis of what they see as the true significance of the contemporary 'communications revolution', namely the 'recomposition of the microstructures – and of the experiences – of everyday life'. Since I believe this to be a serious mischaracterization of my position it is worth explaining why. Prices and profits are certainly one important indicator of economic determination within a capitalist exchange economy. They are signals within a system which guide the actions of agents within that system and are one means by which relative valuations are expressed with determinate effects on human behaviour, both individual and, precisely because it is a system, collective. Thus in a monetary-based exchange economy coordination is managed by means of a universal system of exchange equivalents the effects of which impose themselves upon the human agents and withdrawal from which is in effect impossible without starvation. The first and crucial argument of a political economy is that it is through the specific form this system of exchange relations takes under capitalist conditions that the 'systems of micro power' – to use Robins's and Webster's phrase – predominantly operate, either directly, because based upon access to scarce material resource or indirectly, because concerned with the understanding and management of human relations dominated by those processes of economic exchange. Such an analysis does not claim that all forms of social power are economic, but postulates a hierarchy of determinations and a related hierarchy of analytical priorities. Thus a political economy is always concerned with analysing a structure of social relations and of social power. But it is particularly concerned to analyse the peculiarities of that system of social power called capitalism.

This is a social system within which human relations are increasingly mediated through a monetary-based exchange system and within which the system of material production is based upon a historically specific relation between capital and labour. This means that, because capital controls access to the physical means of production, the majority of people, no longer involved in a subsistence economy, are dependent, either directly or indirectly, first for their physical survival, and second for access to the resources required for the symbolic exchanges of cultural practice on wages and thus upon entering into a wage contract.

The price obtained for labour under this contract is determined by a general system of relative values over which the individual has little control: for instance, the relative productivity of a Japanese as opposed to a British car-worker. The conditions of the contract are determined by the relative and unequal power of the contracting parties which is derived from a historically given set of property relations – the private ownership of capital and the legal protection of property rights – and from a historically specific, but always contested, economic distribution of the surplus as between capital and labour.

Secondly a political economy claims that the very possibility of scientific analysis of the social system is dependent upon the fact that it is a system the probabilistic outcome of which cannot be determined unilaterally by the agents whose interactions create it. Thus the social process is only susceptible to scientific analysis in so far as it is both abstract and systematically determinant. It is only worth analysis because it is the result and cause of the real actions of real human agents.

Such an analysis only goes as far, however, as telling us how the system works and what are its determinate effects. It makes no normative claims. The normative side of political economy stems from the fact that as well as prioritizing production of the economic surplus, it places the question of the distribution of that surplus at the heart of its analysis. By contrast neo-classical economics uncritically assumes a specific, historically given distribution of the surplus between capital and labour as exogenous, and on that basis can assume that an equilibrating market will optimize sub-distribution within both production and consumption of this already divided surplus. Political economy, on the other hand, starts with the assumption that the historically observable unequal distribution of the surplus product, from an essentially collaborative enterprise, as between capital and labour requires explanation, is historically contingent and is the result of the specific structure of the mode of production. That is to say a different set of production arrangements would produce a different pattern of distribution and the existing structure cannot be assumed to be optimal.

The approach to the study of the media exemplified by these essays, which I am calling a political economy of communications and culture, rejects methodological individualism and starts from the Aristotelian assumption that human beings are essentially social. It is not just that individual humans depend for their nurture, and thus the human species for its reproduction, on a relatively stable network of human interrelationships. It is precisely because they are communicating animals that, as Hegel argued in his analysis of the master/slave relationship, their very identity as individuals is created in relation to an other.

These structures of social relations within which human beings exist as human beings are created and sustained by the exchange of meaning or symbolic forms. It is this general social process of the production, circulation and appropriation of symbolic forms that is the field of study of media studies as I conceive it.

Human social actors enter into this process along three dimensions:

1 interaction with the material environment – the process designated within Marxist theory as labour;
2 interaction with other human actors for the purposes of social co-ordination;
3 interaction with the self – the identification and maintenance of self-identity through projection.

These dimensions have recently been designated by Habermas as, respectively, culture, society and personality. It is no accident that they correspond to Kant's tripartite epistemological division.

The first classic question facing the study of communications then becomes the nature of the interrelationship between these dimensions within the general process of social reproduction. What do I mean by social reproduction? It is the process of what Anthony Giddens has called 'structuration', whereby the actions of intelligent human actors pursuing their own interests as they see them, and in particular their own physical survival and the biological survival of their social group, are coordinated through space and time within a determinate social structure and process of intergenerational development or breakdown.

We are dealing with a structured process because the human interactions involved are doubly determined by an inertia derived both from the structured set of material resources available and from the inherited set of meanings and cultural codes which the actors have at their disposal for understanding their situation and planning their future-directed strategies. Moreover, and this presents a challenge to analysis, these material and cultural resources are imbricated within sets of organized practices which I will call institutions.

Historically social formations have been characterized by increasingly complex divisions of labour and by increased spatial extension such that reproduction depends, along each dimension of the cultural process, upon an increasingly mediated cultural process. Specialized technologically based institutional forms and practices have been developed to extend the process of cultural interaction through time and space beyond face-to-face interaction. Thus culture comes to be grounded no longer upon direct experience and upon the individual's natural information processing and communicative endowments, but upon access to and control of the scarce material and cultural resources mobilized by these specialized institutions. It is the study of the form taken by this set of institutionalized cultural processes within capitalist social formations that is the domain of the political economy of communications and culture.

In the face of this development the classic questions have been and remain:

1 What determines access to or control of these scarce material and cultural resources?
2 What determinate effect does that structured access and control have upon social structure and process in general?

In analysing these processes of determination we are always faced with three distinct levels of analysis and their problematic interrelationship. There is first the level at which symbolic form is produced and circulated such that a set of potential appropriations is made available. There is then the level of appropriation at which the form is interpreted as meaning by an individual within a social setting. There is then the level at which this meaning is or is not translated into social action, an action which is, at the same time and always, itself a symbolic form.

One does not have to share all of the Frankfurt School's epistemological suppositions and social biases, to agree with their way of posing the cultural question as an integral part of the historical materialist analysis of capitalism, an analysis which I would argue is essentially normative in that it is concerned with the conditions for and historical possibilities of the exercise of human freedom.

The fact that the process of the production, distribution and appropriation of meanings takes a specific form within the capitalist mode of production has its effect along all three dimensions at all three levels of analysis. If we understand capitalism as a social formation determined by the domination of social interaction by a process of material production characterized by generalized relations of commodity exchange, the private ownership of the means of production, the provision of labour as a commodity and the pursuit of capital accumulation through competition, we need to analyse how that social formation determines who can say what to whom within the process of cultural production, and then to identify the meanings appropriated as well as how those meanings are translated into social action. I am not arguing any simple notion of economic determinism. I am arguing rather for a hierarchy of determination within a mode of production such that the possibilities at each succeeding level are limited by the resources made available by the logically preceding level. These determinations operate at different levels of generality. Thus we need to remember that a system of commodity exchange is itself based upon an institutionalized system of cultural production with a symbolic form, money. Indeed Habermas, following Talcott Parsons, identifies money along with power as one of the two basic media of communication which have historically ensured the development of what he calls the system-world and the associated rationality of modernity.

Here I touch on a classic and central question for our field, namely the relationship between a social formation and the symbolic forms which it produces, what the Annales school of historians refers to as *mentalité* or Raymond Williams as 'a structure of feeling'. Does such a general structure exist? To what extent is its structure and dynamic specific to the symbolic realm itself and how does it represent a non-symbolic social structure and process? For the purposes of our present discussion can we posit a capitalist structure of feeling which limits the creative and interpretative possibilities for individuals forced to represent and interpret their social and material environment within that symbolic structure?

Let me now turn to the core of the argument, namely to the analysis of the capitalist mode of cultural production, to the process referred to by the Frankfurt School as the industrialization of culture.

At this level we need much more research than we have on the nature of the production processes involved. Here, I shall join the tradition of industrial economics to the analysis of cultural fields proposed by Pierre Bourdieu.

We have a scattering of studies of the cultural production process, but they have not been linked, as they need to be, to parallel work on the nature of the firm and intra-corporate organization or on the labour process. Such work suffers from a tendency to succumb to the superficial glamour of the media world and to take media workers' own evaluations of the specially creative nature of their work at face value. While we can posit a general connection between an industrial, capitalist mode of cultural production and the cultural system it produces (for instance the general effects of advertising finance as opposed to public finance), little work has been done on the ways within a particular media industry or production site that the labour process and the technologies of production and distribution determine the actual structure of the symbolic forms themselves, or the ways in which the particular organization of cultural markets determines the range of such forms circulated and the social groups to whom they are made available. Bourdieu has demonstrated, in studies of elite cultural fields, how the career strategies of individual cultural workers and the social status fights between groups of cultural consumers interact within a context of general class struggle to structure cultural fields. The work I have called for would enable us to show the mechanisms by which this structuring takes place within those cultural fields the time and space of which are determined by the mass media.

This analysis of market structure will take account of the specific problems of attempting to produce and distribute symbolic forms as commodities, as well as include the determinants of consumer behaviour under market conditions. It will need, for instance, to study the inter-action between the homogenizing forces of global market dynamics on the one hand and the limits placed on that process by the local linguistic or cultural specificities of consumer demand. It will need to study the relation between the private and public sectors in cultural production and between market and non-market provision.

Discussion of Bourdieu's approach points us towards another neglected area of research – namely, the life of intellectuals understood as those with a specialized function within the general division of labour for the production and distribution of symbolic goods. How are they selected and trained, what are their class origins, how are they organized, what are their specific ideologies and how do all these factors affect what they produce? Much work on cultural production from a broadly political economic perspective – certainly much work on ideology within the Marxist tradition – has taken the actual work of the producing and distributing institutions and of those who work within them as unproblematic. It has simply assumed a straightforward and unquestioned relay between a general capitalist or industrial mode of production on the one hand and a certain cultural output and ideological effect on the other.

In recent years increased attention has rightly been given to the moment of consumption but, with the exception of earlier, largely US work within 'gate-keeper' theory, the bibliography on the producers of culture is scandalously empty. In its place we find, even in academic circles, a version of history as the actions of great men in a semi-journalistic hagiography or demonology (depending on the writer's taste) of the media barons such as Murdoch, Maxwell or Berlusconi. Both the current debate on the likely effects of the expansion and increased commercialization of media channels, as well as the wider debate about the nature of an information society and the social role and importance of 'information workers', urgently demand that this gap be filled.

There has been no considered work done on the adoption of new production technologies within the UK newspaper industry on the nature of the newspapers produced. Nor has there been any work done on the effect on TV programme production of the increased use of an 'independent' production sector rather than of the broadcasters' in-house production facilities and staff. We know almost nothing systematic about the people who produce the advertising that now so dominates our visual and verbal landscape.

This analysis of the structure and process of cultural production needs to recognize that it relates to the system of material production in general in two distinct ways which, while mutually determining, nonetheless require separate analysis. All systems of production integrate the moment of demand and consumption into their economic cycle of accumulation. In the case of cultural production there are two distinct types of demand. First, which has been overwhelmingly the focus of analysis, there is final consumer demand for products and services consumed in the domestic and leisure environments and serving the function of social coordination and self-identity. This demand needs to be understood within the general structure of consumer demand in an economy increasingly dominated not by subsistence or functional material needs but by psychological and symbolic needs. This is a field increasingly structured by interaction between status competition and the search for self-definition on the part of the consumer on the one hand and 'niche marketing' and flexible specialization in production on the other. It is a field where *all* commodities become symbolic forms, representations of the social whole and of the consumer's perception of his or her place within it. Here Bourdieu's analysis, even if one rejects his view of cultural markers as entirely arbitrary together with his pessimistic functionalism, is nonetheless central. If we are to reject his analysis of the interrelation between social class position and modes of cultural appropriation and the role of cultural production as symbolic violence in the legitimized service of the status quo, we need to put a more convincing explanation in its place rather than simply avoid the problem. Otherwise we are permanently prone to the danger of falling back into the indeterminism and individualism of ethnomethodology, into the relativist irrationalism of most post-modernist discourse theory or alternatively into forms of schematic and crudely reductionist economic determinism.

Furthermore, cultural production directly services the wider system of material production. This link is neglected. The neglect stems from that romantic tradition of analysis which continues to mark so much of our cultural analysis and which sees cultural practice as a residual and marginal social practice consigned to the fields of 'leisure' and the 'private' cut off from the 'real' world of earning a living. The most obvious way in which cultural production services the wider system of material production is through advertising. The existence of advertising media and their audiences constructed through the cultural practices of newspapers, magazines and broadcasting have been essential to the development of modern consumer capitalism. Precisely because of the process described above, whereby the circulation of symbolic values becomes integral to the circulation of commodities, advertising is growing in importance.

But from their earliest days newspapers also served a more directly business function by providing direct market intelligence to their readers. This function has massively expanded recently with the growth in trade magazines of all sorts and of specialized, on-line information services. The recent development of Reuters is emblematic of the process by which the institutions of cultural production are being integrated into the system of material production. Reuters has moved in the last decade from being a small company supplying, on the basis of cooperative ownership, international news to its subscriber newspapers, to become a large and dynamic provider of specialized financial information services and transactional services to the international financial sector. Its original news service now represents a small and rapidly declining part of its business. The sale of information becomes an increasingly important market exchange in inter-corporate competition. These processes not only change the operation of cultural institutions, as the example of Reuters shows. They also have a growing effect on what information is made available at what price and to whom. But we can also see the institutions of cultural production being called on to play a growing role in corporate organization and in relations between capital and labour. Labour disputes are beginning to be fought out not at mass meetings or on the picket line but through video and print in a battle between union leaders and management for the hearts and minds of workers. In the US we are now witnessing the construction of a major broadcasting industry devoted to the production of programmes by corporations solely for their internal use – training, employee relations and so on. In the UK the so-called 'independent' television production sector, including production companies and facilities houses, earns the bulk of its income from corporate video. Increasingly the channels of communication are developed and built largely for business communication and the line between advertising and all other media content blurs through the development of product placement, sponsorship and public relations. This whole process of growing and private corporate involvement in cultural production and politics needs much more study than it has received.

I have argued so far that access to and control over the means of cultural production within a capitalist social formation is determined by the specific economic characteristics of the sector and by its direct functional interrelationship with the wider system of material production. This, in its turn, then determines in ways to be analysed, the type and range of symbolic forms circulated. One cannot avoid, in any discussion of the fields of media and cultural studies today, the questions of the status of the text and its interpretation. All forms of inter-human communication are mediated through, and all forms of human knowledge constructed within, languages. By languages I mean socially constructed and therefore shared systems by means of which individuals can represent to others in a strongly coded form perceptions or mental states such that they can in some sense be shared.

Of course this process involves a two-fold problem of translation, and we are thus not talking about systems of one-to-one correspondence or of perfectly transparent communication. All mediations involve slippage. There is slippage in the process of both meaning construction and meaning interpretation. We are all aware, even in our use of natural language in everyday face-to-face interaction, of the inadequacy of our expression before what we are trying to express. How much truer this is in loosely coded, iconic forms of communication as well as in the more highly mediated and socialized forms of media production. It is also true that we often only come to know what we mean in the process of the construction of meaning itself. On the side of interpretation we are all aware of the possibilities of misunderstanding, the constant opaqueness of communication. However, I would want to stress, against those currents in contemporary thought which stress the indeterminate nature of interpretation and the unboundedness of inter-textual semiosis, the role of a shared intentionality in communication. We undertake communicative action with the intention of communicating a given meaning or reciprocally of understanding the other as though they were attempting to convey such an intentional meaning and that through a process of communicative iteration the problems of slippage inherent in mediated communication are reduced such that the parties to a communicative action can agree that they understand one another. Part of this process of mutual intentionality and understanding is a mutual recognition of the boundedness of given texts – a conversation, a narrative, an image or a piece of music exists within a socially shared frame that determines the appropriateness of an interpretation. We of course bring to both the construction and interpretation of those framed texts our knowledge of other texts and of the non-textual world, but that knowledge includes our knowledge of the frames. Moreover as against the more extreme versions of text-based approaches interpretation is not only determined within the text itself, but by the fact that communicative action is usually designed to result in some form of action *tout court*. The test of the successful accomplishment of any communicative action lies not within the process of semiosis, but in the world of social action.

Thus political economy stresses that media texts structure the meanings available to consumers in determinate ways which are open to analysis. A newspaper article or TV programme is the way it is and carries one set of meanings, and by so doing excludes another set, because of the way in which production is organized. To put it crudely, the budget available and the given structure of the division of labour affects what you can say and how you can say it. In addition, the interpretative frames that are used to extract meanings from media texts are themselves determined by the wider socioeconomic structure. Whether and in what way you feel a communication is directed at you and the consequences you can draw from it will be determined by your pre-existing, pre-constructed social identity. One's readiness to accept or reject, to take seriously or otherwise any given media representation depends upon the specific 'taste public' into which you have been socialized. It may also depend upon your possession of more general, but also socially differentiated, interpretative skills, most obviously literacy. The ways in which the resulting meanings are translated into social action will then also be determined both materially by the range of institutionalized practices made available within a given social structure and hermeneutically by the range of legitimized practices available.

I want to end by looking at one last classic question within the problematic I have been outlining. I mentioned earlier the essential normative dimension to the Frankfurt School approach, and I argued that one of the dimensions of the cultural process was interaction with other human beings for the purposes of social coordination. This is the realm of the political and of the ethical where the purpose of symbolic interaction is the defining of social means and ends. Central to the study of the mass media from the beginning has been the question of how mass democracies can and should be governed.

This problem has been handled within the Frankfurt School tradition within the conceptual framework of the public sphere. The theory of the public sphere, as articulated in particular by Habermas in his *The Structural Transformation of the Public Sphere*, develops through concrete historical analysis the insight of Adorno and Horkheimer's *Dialectic of Enlightenment* that the development of capitalism created both the historical material conditions for the realization of the Enlightenment dream of human liberation, and at the same the conditions for the suppression of that liberty through the development of the rationalizing processes of the capitalist exchange economy. Habermas argued that, just as the participatory democracy of the Athenian agora depended upon the material base of slavery, so it was the development of competitive market capitalism that provided the conditions, initially in eighteenth-century Britain, for the development of both the theory and practice of liberal democracy. It did so by making available to a new political class, the bourgeoisie, both the time and material resources to create a network of institutions within civil society, such as newspapers, learned and debating societies, publishing enterprises, libraries, universities and polytechnics and museums, within which a new political power, public opinion, could come into existence. This public sphere possessed the following key characteristics. It was protected from the power of both Church and State by its access to the sustaining resources of a wide range of private individuals with an alternative source of economic power. It was in principle open to all in the same way that access to the market was open to all, because the cost of entry for each individual was dramatically lowered by the growth in scale of the market. The public sphere thus took on the universalistic aspects of the Hegelian State, membership of the public sphere being coterminous with citizenship. All participants within the public sphere were, as with the competitive market, on terms of equal power because costs of participation were widely and evenly spread and because social wealth in general, within the bourgeoisie, was evenly distributed. It was distinct from the private interests that governed civil society, on the other hand, because, in the Enlightenment tradition, it obeyed the rules of rational discourse, political views and decisions being open, not to the play of power, but to that of argument based upon evidence, and because its concern was not private interest but the public good. Habermas went on to argue that the public sphere, this space for a rational and universalistic politics distinct from both the economy and the State, was destroyed historically by the very forces that had brought it into existence. The development of the capitalist economy in the direction of monopoly capitalism led to an uneven distribution of wealth, to rising entry costs to the public sphere and thus to unequal access to and control over that sphere. In particular the rise of advertising and public relations has exemplified these trends since they represent the direct control by private interests or State interests of the flow of public information in the interest, not of rational discourse, but of manipulation. At the same time these developments in the economy led to related developments by the State, which itself became an active and major participant in the economy, thus coming to share the private interests there pursued. At the same time the State was called in, by those class forces that wished to defend and expand the public sphere against the encroaching power of private capital, to itself provide its material support, through for instance the provision of public education, public libraries, systems of public cultural subsidy. In addition, the growth of the State's role as a coordinator and infrastructure provider for monopoly capitalism led to the massive development of State power as an independent administrative and bureaucratic interest, distinct from the rationalist determination of social ends and of the means to those ends in that political realm guaranteed by the existence of the public sphere. Thus the space between civil society and the State which had been opened by the creation of the public sphere was squeezed shut between these two increasingly collaborative behemoths. In Habermas's words:

> The liberal model of the public sphere . . . cannot be applied to the actual conditions of an industrially advanced mass-democracy organized in the form of the social welfare state. In part the liberal model has always included ideological components, but it is also in part true that the social pre-conditions, to which the ideological elements could at one time at least be linked, had been fundamentally transformed. (Habermas, 1979)

However, Habermas wishes to distinguish between the set of principles upon which the bourgeois sphere was based and which, in the fight against feudalism, it brought into existence, on the one hand, and the set of specific historically concrete institutions which embodied those principles on the other. For Habermas, while the specific forms in which they are embodied will vary, the principles are the indispensable basis of a free society. These principles are general accessibility, especially to information, the elimination of privilege and the search for general norms and their rational legitimation.

This framework in particular relates communication as an activity central to political process and structure on the one hand and communication as an economic activity on the other. The Marxist tradition has been rightly criticized for placing too great a stress on labour at the expense of an insufficient stress on the political dimension of social structure and development. It is, however, in my view also correct to say that other traditions of political thought have tended to suppress the necessarily material dimension of political practice. This is particularly true of its communicative dimension. Within the western European tradition of democratic theory freedom of expression and information has always been central to the concept of citizenship. Equality of access to the information upon which rational political decisions should be based, and to the debates on choices of both means and ends, has been seen as an essential attribute of the exercise of political freedom. The difficulty with this still dominant and liberal version of freedom of communication, as indeed with its wider politics, is its neglect of positive as opposed to negative freedoms and its overwhelmingly individualist interpretation of freedom. This limitation has made it incapable of adequately confronting concentrations of economic power based upon private property and the political and communicative power which results.

Rights to information and expression, and access to scarce economic resources were extended to the new technologies of communication via the concept of freedom of the press without any serious examination, within democratic political theory, of the problems raised by access to the necessarily scarce communicative resources involved. Theory remained based upon a model of information circulation founded on the use of natural language in the face-to-face situation. The political rights involved were simply extended to corporations as legal persons. This has been particularly true in the United States where the First Amendment has indeed served as a real defence of individual freedom of expression, and as a foundation for a genuinely more open political system than in other liberal bourgeois democracies, but is increasingly being used to block or dismantle any regulation of private corporate power over the social communication process. Recently, for instance in the cable TV industry, the freedom of expression of an isolated individual citizen was equated with the output of a multinational media conglomerate.

The importance of examining this problem from within the conceptual framework of the public sphere is that such a framework takes in this problem of the provision of the material resources necessary for political participation. Thus a truly competitive market is seen as potentially providing access to these resources by individual citizens free of state control, and concentration in these markets in general is seen as one side of the refeudalization of the public sphere and the creation of a manipulated public opinion rather than one enjoying the free play of rational debate. On the other hand the State is also seen as problematic and its increased intervention in the form of Welfare, in response to both working-class political pressure and the infrastructural needs of an advanced capitalist economy, is another form of feudalization.

This analysis of the role of both private capitalist accumulation and the State in the destruction and possible re-creation of the public sphere is important in my view to current policy research in the cultural field, where the modes of operation, respective spheres of influence and mutual relations of State and market are being rapidly redefined. The simple reiteration of unexamined notions of freedom of the press or public service is a demonstrably inadequate response to the degenerations of democratic theory and practice which result. In particular there is growing tension between the globalization of the communications and cultural market at the economic level and the role of the nation-state at the political level. We need to rethink the concept of citizenship in the modern world in relation to a re-examination of the locus and powers of the institutions of representative democracy and their appropriate regulatory relationship to the system of cultural production. Such a reworking of what I have called the Enlightenment project is unlikely to be fruitful unless we work against the grain of the idealizing tendency of most cultural analysis and recognize, and place at the centre of our analysis, the determining, and at some level unavoidable, weight of an increasingly global economic system.

References

Adorno, T. and Horkheimer, M. (1973) *Dialectic of Enlightenment*.

Habermas, J. (1979) 'The public sphere', in A. Mattelart and S. Siegelaub (eds), *Communication and Class Struggle*, vol. 1. New York: International General.

Habermas, J. (1989) *The Structural Transformation of the Public Sphere*. Boston: MIT Press.

Robins, K. and Webster, F. (1988) 'Cybernetic capitalism: information technology and everyday life', in V. Mosco and J. Washo (eds), *The Political Economy of Information*. Madison: University of Wisconsin Press.

Williams, R. (1977) *Marxism and Literature*. Oxford: Oxford University Press.

PART I

METHODOLOGY AND THE MASS MEDIA

2

Contribution to a Political Economy of Mass Communication

The major modern communication systems are now so evidently key institutions in advanced capitalist societies that they require the same kind of attention, at least initially, that is given to the institutions of industrial production and distribution. Studies of the ownership and control of the capitalist press, the capitalist cinema, and capitalist and state capitalist radio and television interlock, historically and theoretically, with wider analysis of capitalist society, capitalist economy and the neo-capitalist state. Further, many of the same institutions require analysis in the context of modern imperialism and neo-colonialism, to which they are crucially relevant.

Over and above their empirical results, these analyses force theoretical revision of the formula of base and superstructure and of the definition of productive forces, in a social area in which large scale capitalist economic activity and cultural production are now inseparable. Unless this theoretical revision is made, even the best work of the radical and anti-capitalist empiricists is in the end overlaid or absorbed by the specific theoretical structures of bourgeois cultural sociology. (Williams, 1977: 136)

Williams's note is hidden in a book of literary theory. It is thus perhaps hardly surprising if few in media and cultural studies made the theoretical revision for which he called. Indeed, in the years since I first wrote this essay, media and cultural studies have moved ever further, not only from political economy but from notions of social determination in general, to focus on discourse within a relativist, largely ahistorical and individualistic frame of analysis.

In the light of actual economic and political developments this is ironical, not to say perverse, because the need to elaborate a political economy has never been more intensely practical. It has become even more urgent and relevant since my essay was originally written, if only because governments throughout the developed world have placed the future of their communication and information industries at the top of their political agendas in the formation of economic and industrial policy.

Symptoms of these changes can be seen in the general move towards what has been dubbed 'deregulation' in the broadcasting and telecommunications sectors. In the UK in the 1980s we have witnessed a stream of government reports and legislation, accompanied by extensive and continuing debate, on the provision of telecommunications infra-structures and services, on over-air broadcasting, on cable TV and direct broadcasting satellites, on subscription television and spectrum alloca-tion. Similar activity can be seen in other member states of the European Community, in the USA and Japan, and in international fora such as the ITU and GATT, as countries and regional blocks jockey for competitive advantage in a developing global information economy. At the economic level symptoms are the almost daily announcement of takeovers, mergers and strategic alliances in a process of increasing international consolida-tion in the publishing, audiovisual and telecommunications industries. It is easy in such a situation for the analyst to be inundated and confused by a mass of empirical data. Our only hope of understanding the process and thus intervening successfully within it is to establish a theoretical distance.

II

Before turning to concrete examples of the problems a political economy of mass communication tries to analyse, it is necessary, precisely because of the dominance of idealism within the analysis of culture and the mass media, to make an unavoidable theoretical digression in order to base subsequent discussion firmly within the necessary historical materialist perspective. In asking for a shift within mass-media research towards historical materialism, one is asserting an order of priorities which is both a hierarchy of concrete historical and material determinants in the real world as well as an order of research priorities. That is to say, we are faced with the problem of understanding an actual historical process which itself concretely exhibits structurally ordered determinants within which material production is ultimately determinant. It is this which makes our theory materialist. At the same time there are a limited number of researchers with limited material resources (among which I include time) who must choose, from within the complex totality of the historical social process, to examine those aspects of the process which are likely to lead to the clearest understanding of the dynamics of that process and through that understanding to its human control. It is this question of choice which underlies Marx's own mode of abstraction. Thus, in opposition to that Althusserian/Lacanian current which has been so dangerously dominant within recent British Marxist research in the area of mass media, one asserts, not that the problem of subjectivity for instance is of no interest, but that it is of less interest than that of class or capital accumulation.

That is to repeat the axiom that the economic is determinant under capitalism. Capitalism is a mode of social organization characterized by the domination of an abstract system of exchange relations. Further, the particular relationship between the abstract and the concrete, or between ideas and matter, which is appropriate to historical materialism as a mode of analysis of capitalism, stems from the real relation between the abstract (exchange relations) and the concrete (individual lived experience, real labour, etc.). In a social formation in which social relations were not abstracted into a relation of exchange a different theoretical relationship between the abstract and the concrete would hold.

Moreover, the abstract should not be opposed to the concrete, just as the phenomenal forms should not be opposed to the real relations. One is precisely a form of the other. The exchange relation has a concrete material reality in the form of money, bills of exchange, credit cards, banks, etc., but its mode of operation and with it the reproduction of the capitalist social formation depends upon its abstraction, the fact that it works 'behind men's backs' and thus 'can be determined with the precision of natural science'. It can only be determined with such precision so long as it is a supra-individual social process. This is both a methodological and historical postulate. The necessary condition for a capitalist social formation is the existence of a more or less universal domination of social relations by the exchange relation, i.e. a market economy. Wherever such domination is challenged (and we do not see, and never have seen, in this sense, an 'ideal' capitalist social formation) by explicit political action, by human will and reason, the logic of capital is challenged. It is for this reason that the State is a necessarily contradictory form.

This leads us to the concept of ideology which so dominates our field of study and to the central problem within cultural theory, namely the base/superstructure relationship. The central postulate of historical materialism is that man as a biological organism must undertake a constant material exchange with nature and it is this exchange that is named labour. Within history the labour/nature relationship has become increasingly mediated through specific modes of production, thus making the links more difficult to analyse. Because of this difficulty the possibility of error and thus of ideology enters. But it remains a material fact that, ultimately, material production in this direct sense is determinate in that it is only the surplus produced by this labour that enables other forms of human activity to be pursued. Thus the superstructure remains dependent upon and determined by the base of material production in that very fundamental sense.

Clearly, the greater the surplus to immediate physical needs the greater the autonomy of the superstructure, and indeed its greater variation and diversity within superstructural organization. In this important sense the superstructure of culture is and remains subordinate, and the crucial questions are the relationship between, on the one hand, the mode of extraction and distribution of the material surplus (class relations) and, on the other, the allocation of this material surplus within the superstructure, for instance the problem of public expenditure. But while, historically, the superstructure has become more autonomous, there still remain direct, narrow material constraints upon individuals even within developed, industrial societies. Everyone has to eat and sleep and be maintained at a given body temperature in determinate temporal cycles. Thus, as Marx himself noted, every economy is an economy of time, which is why labour-time is so crucial an analytical concept. Cultural reproduction is still directly governed by these material determinants in the sense that the time and resources available to those who have to sell their labour power to capital, within labour-time constraints largely imposed by capital, remain limited, and they still use the most significant proportion of their available time and material resources in order to stay alive.

It is at this primary level, both theoretically and actually, that social being determines social consciousness. Thus economism, the concern for immediate physical survival and reproduction within the dominant relations of exchange, is an immediate and rational response to the determinants of social being. What E. P. Thompson has recently dubbed 'the bourgeois lumpen intelligentsia' (1978: 195) too easily forgot this, both because their material conditions of existence are often less immediately determinate and also because of a guilty conscience concerning the relationship of exploitation in which they personally stand vis-à-vis productive labour.

III

No political economy of culture can avoid discussion of the base/superstructure relationship, but in so doing it needs to avoid the twin traps of economic reductionism and of the idealist autonomization of the ideological level. The central problem with the base/superstructure metaphor, as with the related culture/society dichotomy, is that being a metaphor of polarity, essentially binary in form, it is unable adequately to deal with the number of distinctions that are necessary, in this instance between the material, the economic and the ideological. These should be seen not as three levels. They are analytically distinct, but coterminous moments both of social practices and of concrete analysis. There is a sense in which the base/superstructure metaphor always does imply a notion of expressive totality, a totality in which either the superstructure is expressive of an economic base, or in the tautological sense by which all phenomena of a social formation are expressive of that social formation. The notion of expressive totality can be used either deterministically or relationally. It is clear that the analysis in *Capital* is of the latter type. What is being analysed is not, as Mandel (1975) has stressed, a social formation in equilibrium but in disequilibrium: a still incomplete process of capitalist development, a development which is marked not by the determinacy of capitalist economic forms (an expressive totality in that sense) but on the contrary by a series of shifting relationships between the economic and other instances, each interacting with the other in a process of uneven and contradictory development. The totality of the social formation at any historic moment is only expressive of the actual state of those shifting interrelationships.

Thus the meaning of any analytical category such as base and superstructure, expressing as it does a relationship, will shift as the historical reality it is used to explain shifts. We could say that the purpose of a political economy of culture is to elucidate what Marx and Engels meant in *The German Ideology* by 'control of the means of mental production', while stressing that the meaning they gave to the term was quite clearly historical and therefore shifting, and was never meant to be frozen into some simple dichotomy as it has so often been in subsequent Marxist writing. Further, the political economy of mass media is the analysis of a specific historical phase of this general development linked to historically distinct modalities of cultural production.

In his discussion of base and superstructure in *Marxism and Literature*, Williams points out that although, in stressing the determinacy of the base against bourgeois idealism, one version of Marxist cultural theory has been accused, both by bourgeois and Marxist critics, of 'vulgar materialism', 'the truth is that it was never materialist enough'. And he continues:

> What any notion of a 'self-subsistent order' suppresses is the material character of the productive forces which produce such a version of production. Indeed it is often a way of suppressing full consciousness of the very nature of such a society. If 'production', in capitalist society, is the production of commodities for a market, then different but misleading terms are found for every other kind of production and productive force. What is most often suppressed is the direct material production of 'politics'. Yet any ruling class devotes a significant part of material production to establishing a political order. The social and political order which maintains a capitalist market, like the social and political struggle that created it, is necessarily a material production. From castles and palaces and churches to prisons and workhouses and schools; from weapons of war to a controlled press: any ruling class, in variable ways though always materially, produces a social and political order. These are never superstructural activities. They are the necessary material production within which an apparently self-subsistent mode of production can alone be carried on. The complexity of the process is especially remarkable in advanced capitalist societies, where it is wholly beside the point to isolate 'production' and 'industry' from the comparable material production of 'defence', 'law and order', 'welfare', 'entertainment' and 'public opinion'. In failing to grasp the material character of the production of a social and political order, this specialised (and bourgeois) materialism failed also, but even more conspicuously, to understand the material character of the production of a cultural order. The concept of the superstructure was then not a reduction but an evasion. (Williams, 1977: 92–3)

Williams's stress here on the materiality of the cultural process is a necessary correction to both bourgeois idealism and its post-Althusserian Marxist variants. But this formulation also suffers from a misleading reductionism by failing to distinguish between the material and the economic. It is in fact a materialist rather than a historical materialist formulation. The absence of this necessary distinction is contained in the apparently insignificant but crucial phrase 'in variable ways though always materially', for it is precisely the specific articulations of these variable ways that define the shifting meaning of what Marx and Engels called 'control of the means of mental production', shifts which it is the central purpose of a political economy of mass communication to map and analyse. Certainly a licensed press and a commercial, 'free' press are both material, but the economic differences between these two forms of 'political' control are precisely what differentiates a capitalist from a pre-capitalist form. Similarly, the difference between the economic structure of private and public education constitutes, within the same materiality, the substance of political struggle. While the materiality of politics, i.e. its maintenance out of the total social surplus of material production, is a general, universal phenomenon, the ways in which that surplus is extracted and distributed, and the relation of that economic form to the political, are historically distinct and specific, so that, at present, the matter of subsidies to political parties or to the press becomes an object of political struggle to change economic forms and by so doing to change political structures.

Similarly, while Williams is correct to stress the materiality of all social practices it cannot be said, from an economic perspective, that it is wholly beside the point to isolate 'production' and 'industry' from the material production of 'defence', etc., when what is often in question when considering the relation between these various social practices is not their shared materiality, but on the contrary their significantly different economic articulation. For instance there is a sharp variance between those practices carried on by private capital for profit, such as the publication of a newspaper, and those practices carried on by the State outside direct commodity production, such as the BBC or the State education system. To collapse all this into a general category of 'material' production is precisely an 'evasion', both of the differing and developing economic articulations between various forms of material production and also of the amount of cultural production and reproduction that takes place within the industrial sphere as narrowly defined. Such reproductions occur throughout the organizations of the labour process with its industrial psychologists, its labour relations experts, its time-and-motion study experts, its production engineers and its personnel managers, in the structures of employer paternalism and in the organization of the market itself. To take one example of such an articulation, one might hypothesize that the relationship between the male predominance in newspaper readership as compared with the composition of TV audiences was not unconnected with the contrast between the culture of

work as against the culture of home, and has important political consequences.

This confusion between the material and the economic is common, and
it is worth dwelling briefly on the nature of the distinction. In so far as
historical materialism is materialist, it is based upon the postulate that
Williams outlines. But in so far as it is historical, it is concerned to
analyse the specific and shifting modes of this fundamental material relation, all of which are forms of that relation. In particular, it is
postulated that any form of extended social relationship depends upon
the extraction and distribution of material surplus, and the means by
which this is achieved is thus the central determining characteristic of any
social formation. Such modes of social production and exchange are
cultural, hence the very real problem of making a society/culture
differentiation without narrowing the definition of culture to include
only those elements of social interaction which involve a secondary level
of abstraction, namely the representation of concrete, material relations
in *symbolic* forms. Thus we must distinguish two types of form. The first
is a social form which is a series of material relations that, in so far as
they operate unconsciously, can be abstractly analysed and determined
with the precision of natural science. The second is a cultural form
which, while it entails a material support, is not itself material and has
an essentially mediated divide between these distinct formal realms, the
existence of which allows ideology to enter, because it allows denial and
the lie, both of which depend upon a relationship which is not determinant. However, this autonomy is bought at the cost of a loss of real or
material effectivity. Cultural forms become effective only when they are
translated into social forms which do have material effectivity. Thus
there is a constant dialectic at the cultural level between autonomy and
effectivity, and it is at the level of social effectivity that material production is ultimately determinant.

However, at the level of social forms, the economic is a specific
historical form of the social relations of production and distribution. It is
the form these relations take in a social formation within which commodity
exchange is dominant. Thus, it is possible to argue that the economic is
superstructural in relation to the material base or structure, that it could
in fact be seen as the dominant level of the superstructure. For what Marx
argues in *Capital* is that the real historical transition to capitalism involves
a move from a system of social relations and domination based upon the
direct physical control of landed property and people to one based upon
increasingly indirect control through commodity exchange and, in
particular, through the exchange of the commodity of labour power, and
that this real historical process is a process of social abstraction which thus
requires appropriate theoretical abstraction for its analysis. It is because
the economic is the most abstract and fundamental form of the social relation within capitalism that it is primary, but it is so as a historically specific
representation of a predeterminate material relationship.

It is the real existence of this abstract economic level of extended commodity production that allows for the development of an increasing division of labour and thus for the development of the superstructural forms of capitalism. Thus the relative autonomy of the superstructure is a real and increasingly central characteristic of capitalism, but it is itself determined at the level of the economic and ultimately it is a form, at two levels of mediation, of a material relation which remains determinant in and through the economic.

IV

From this perspective available historical materialist theories are inadequate to deal with the practical challenges they face largely because they offer reductionist explanations which favour either a simple economic determinism or an ideological autonomy. Thus we are offered the following:

1 An unproblematic acceptance of the base/superstructure model drawn from a partial reading of *The German Ideology* which, unargued, simply states that the mass media are ideological tools of ruling-class domination either through direct ownership or, as in the case of broadcasting, via ruling-class control of the State. Such a position neglects both the effects of subordinating cultural production and reproduction to the general logic of capitalist commodity production and the specificities of the shifting relationships between economic, ideological and political levels. Miliband, in *Marxism and Politics*, expresses a classic version of this theory:

> Whatever else the immense output of the mass media is intended to achieve, it is *also* intended to help prevent the development of class-consciousness in the working class and to reduce as much as possible any hankering it might have for a radical alternative to capitalism. The ways in which this is attempted are endlessly different; and the degree of success achieved varies considerably from country to country and from one period to another – there are other influences at work. But the fact remains that 'the class which has the means of material production at its disposal' does have 'control at the same time of the means of mental production'; and that it does seek to use them for the weakening of opposition to the established order. Nor is the point much affected by the fact that the state in almost all capitalist countries 'owns' the radio and television – its purpose is identical. (Miliband, 1977: 50)

2 In partial reaction against this classic Marxist explanation of the role of the mass media, we are offered an elaboration of the relative autonomy of the superstructure. All such theories in their effort to reject economism or, as Althusser puts it, 'the idea of a "pure and simple" non-overdetermined contradiction', to a greater or lesser extent have also removed economic determinacy. In such theories 'the lonely hour of the "last instance" never comes' (Althusser, 1969: 113). This general position has rightly developed the insights of the Frankfurt School into the

importance of the superstructure and of mediation, while neglecting a crucial component of the Frankfurt School's original position, namely the fact that under monopoly capitalism the superstructure becomes precisely industrialized; it is invaded by the base and the base/superstructure distinction breaks down via a collapse into the base rather than, as is the tendency with the post-Althusserian position, via the transformation of the base into another superstructural discourse.

> In our age the objective social tendency is incarnate in the hidden subjective purpose of company directors, the foremost among whom are in the most powerful sectors of industry – steel, petroleum, electricity and chemicals. Culture monopolies are weak and dependent in comparison. They cannot afford to neglect their appeasement of the real holders of power if their sphere of activity in mass-society is not to undergo a series of purges. (Adorno and Horkheimer, 1977: 351)

The truth of this original insight is demonstrated monthly as firms in the cultural sector are absorbed into large industrial conglomerates and brought under the sway of their business logic. Indeed, the real weakness of the Frankfurt School's original position was not their failure to realize the importance of the base or the economic, but insufficiently to take account of the economically contradictory nature of the process they observed, and thus to see the industrialization of culture as unproblematic and irresistible. Those who have come after, while criticizing the Frankfurt School for its absence of concrete class analysis, an absence stemming precisely from their insufficiently nuanced analysis of the economic level, have, in developing their theories of the effectivity of the superstructure, compounded the original error.

The most distinguished exponent of the post-Althusserian position in Britain, Stuart Hall, in his essay 'Culture, the media and the ideological effect' (1977) recognizes that there is a decisive relationship between the growth of the mass media and 'everything that we now understand as characterising "monopoly capitalism"'. At the same time he refuses an analysis of this decisive relationship, claiming that 'these aspects of the growth and expansion of the media historically have to be left to one side by the exclusive attention given here to media as "ideological apparatuses".' Murdock and Golding (1979) rightly criticize Hall and claim that, on the contrary, the ways in which mass media function as 'ideological apparatuses' can only be adequately understood when they are systematically related to their position as large scale commercial enterprises in a capitalist economic system and if these relations are examined historically. Hall's failure to do this leads him to explain the ideological effect in terms of ideologically predetermined communicators or encoders choosing from an ideologically predetermined set of codes. Hence there is a systematic tendency of the media to reproduce the ideological field of society in such a way as to reproduce also its structure of domination. That is to say, he offers the description of an ideological process, but not an explanation of why or how it takes place, except in tautological terms.

Moreover, he is led by his mode of analysis, as his critics point out, to favour a specific and atypical instance of media practice, namely public service broadcasting, and indeed within that an atypical form, namely informational broadcasting. His mode of analysis does not allow him to deal, for instance, with an important and developing moment within the press caused by a contradiction between the crucial under-pinning idea of a 'free press' and the economic pressures towards monopoly. He cannot analyse the relationship between the ideological effect of broadcasting and the fact that it is perceived by its audience to be under State control as opposed to the biased privately owned press.

3   A further elaboration of the post-Althusserian position, popular within film studies, leads in its elaboration of a theory of autonomous discourses to an evacuation of the field of historical materialism, whatever its materialistic rhetoric, placing its determinacy in the last instance on the unconscious as theorized within an essentially idealist, indeed Platonist, problematic. Such idiocies need detain us no further.

4   Finally, Dallas Smythe (1977), identifying the excessive stress on the autonomy of the ideological level within western Marxism as its 'blind spot', redirects our attention away from the mass media as ideological apparatuses and back to their economic function within capitalism. But in so doing, he proposes an extreme reductionist theory. For Smythe, any political economy of mass media must be based upon an analysis of its commodity form, and for him the commodity form specific to the mass media is the audience. That is to say, for Smythe, the crucial function of the mass media is not to sell packages of ideology to consumers, but audiences to advertisers. Now it is undoubtedly important to focus atten-tion upon the ways in which the mass media manufacture and sell audiences as one moment in the complex circuit of capital that structures the operation of the mass media economically. Moreover, to stress this moment as the crucial one and to concentrate on the mass media's directly functional role for capital as advertising vehicles is undoubtedly a more plausible reflection of reality in the North American context than it would be in Europe. However, Smythe's theory misunderstands the function of the commodity form as an abstraction within Marxist economic theory, and thus neglects the relationship between specific forms of the commodity, in this case the audience, and the commodity form in general. As a result his theory lacks any sense of contradiction, failing to account for the function of those cultural commodities directly exchanged, failing to account for the role of the State, failing sufficiently to elaborate the function for capital of advertising itself and, perhaps most crucially of all, failing to relate the process of audience production by the mass media to determinants of class and to class-struggle (Levant, 1978; Murdock, 1978; Smythe, 1978).

V

What problems is it, then, that a political economy of mass communication attempts to analyse? The research perspective, whose theoretical and historical basis I have briefly outlined, attempts to shift attention away from the conception of the mass media as ideological apparatuses of the State, and sees them first as economic entities with both a direct economic role as creators of surplus value through commodity production and exchange and an indirect role, through advertising, in the creation of surplus value within other sectors of commodity production. Indeed, a political economy of mass communication in part chooses its object of study precisely because it offers a challenge to the Althusser/ Poulantzas theorization of the social formation as structured into the relatively autonomous levels of the economic, the ideological and the political. For the major institutions of mass communication, the press and broadcasting, although displaying notable differences of articulation, at the same time display close interweaving within concrete institutions and within their specific commodity forms of the economic, the ideological and the political. When we buy a newspaper we participate simultaneously in an economic exchange, in subjection to or reaction against an ideological formation and often in a quite specific act of political identification. We also know from historical analysis of the development of the press that the nature of the political involvement is, quite specifically, economically conditioned. Similarly, TV news is economically determined within commodity production in general, performs an ideological function and explicitly operates within politics.

While accepting that the mass media can be politically and ideologically overdetermined at many conjunctures, a political economy, as I understand it, rests upon ultimate determination by the economic (a level that itself always remains problematic and to be defined in the process of analysis).

Indeed, one of the key features of the mass media within monopoly capitalism has been the exercise of political and ideological domination through the economic (Curran, 1977). What concerns us in fact is to stress, from the analytical perspective, the continuing validity of the base/superstructure model while at the same time pointing to and analysing the ways in which the development of monopoly capitalism has industrialized the superstructure. Indeed Marx's own central insight into the capitalist mode of production stressed its generalizing, abstracting drive; the pressure to reduce everything to the equivalence of exchange value.

Before going on to examine the economic level and its specific articulations within the cultural sphere, let us look at the relationship between the material conditions of production (not, as we have seen, to be confused with the economic far less the capitalist modes of such production, which are specific forms) on the one hand and ideological forms on the other. That is to ask, how do we relate Williams's correct stress upon the materiality of cultural production to Marx's famous distinction 'between the material transformations of the economic conditions of production, which can be determined with the precision of natural science, and the legal, political, aesthetic or philosophic – in short – ideological forms in which men become conscious of this conflict and fight it out' (Marx, 1962).

Marx underlines the importance of the distinction between the two levels, a distinction focused upon the difference between the *unconscious* forces governing material production 'beyond our will', etc., and the conscious form of ideology. (If we follow the Althusserians and make ideology an unconscious process this crucial distinction is lost.)

There are here two distinctions to be made. I think we can liken ideological practice to what Marx called the 'real labour process'.

> Looking at the process of production from its real side, i.e. as a process which creates new use-values by performing useful labour with existing use values, we find it to be a *real labour process*. As such its element, its conceptually specific components, are those of the labour process itself, of any labour process, irrespective of the mode of production or the stage of economic development in which they find themselves. (Marx, 1976)

The processes of consciousness and of representation, for instance in language, are real processes by which human beings socially appropriate their environment (nature), which continue to exist within specifically capitalist modes of ideological production, and indeed upon which these capitalist modes rest.

The materiality of such ideological production *qua* ideology rests upon the fact that consciousness is a human transformation of 'real' experience; it is in that sense 'practical knowledge'. Clearly, therefore, the relationship of any particular instance of ideological production to the totality of social experience will depend upon an analysis of the experiential position of the human consciousness in question, e.g. the conventional and simple definition of class consciousness as based upon the direct experience of a given position within the capital/labour relationship. Of course in any complex society such direct experience becomes highly mediated. But its translation into forms of representation is nonetheless a process of consciousness which is different from, and in its forms has no necessary correspondence with, the economic processes to which it relates or of which it is a representation. Indeed as a representation it is by definition distinct from those processes which it represents.

Moreover ideological forms can never be simply collapsed into a system of exchange values, precisely because they are concerned with difference, with distinction; they are by definition heterogeneous; whereas exchange value is the realm of equivalence.[1]

VI

> In order to study the connection between intellectual and material production it is above all essential to conceive the latter in its determined historical form and not as a general category. For example, there corresponds to the capitalist mode of production a type of intellectual production quite different from that which corresponded to the medieval mode of production. Unless material production itself is understood in its specific historical form, it is impossible to grasp the characteristics of the intellectual production which corresponds to it or the reciprocal action between the two. (Marx, 1959: 82)

We need to lay stress on and distinguish two distinct but related moments in a historical materialist analysis of intellectual production.

1 Culture as a superstructural phenomenon in relation to non-cultural modes of material production, i.e. on the one hand, the dominant or hegemonic cultural production paid for out of capitalist *revenue* and, on the other, a subordinate working-class or oppositional culture paid for out of wages. Cultural production in this sense and its articulations with the sphere of material production involves one specific interpretation of the meaning in *The German Ideology* of 'control of the means of mental production', i.e. through the direct payment of ideologists and the necessary maintenance of the physical instruments of their ideological production. It is within that analytical perspective that we need to analyse the historical development of the 'historically specific needs' of the working class and their sustenance of 'organic intellectuals' and of specific instruments of cultural production such as trade unions.

2 Culture as part of material production itself, directly subordinate to or at least in a closely determined articulation with the laws of development of capital. This is both a latter historical phase, part of monopoly capitalism (the phenomenon dubbed 'the industrialization of culture') but it also lives alongside the other moment and in specific instances we need to analyse the interrelationship between these two distinct modes of intellectual production within intellectual production in general.

What, in general, has been lost in Marxist studies of the mass media is the precise historical elaboration of what Marx and Engels meant in *The German Ideology* by 'control of the means of mental production'.

In general it is clear, in *The German Ideology*, that Marx and Engels were concerned with the payment of ideologists, of intellectuals, and of capitalist revenue. It is this perspective that Raymond Williams picks up in the passage already cited. That is to say they rightly saw that superstructural activities require a cohort of mental workers who were not directly and materially productive, and thus whose price of reproduction must be borne by the sphere of material production. Since under capitalism it was capitalists who were extracting this surplus, it was they who could redistribute this surplus into superstructural activities of their choosing, and by so doing exert direct economic pressures on the ideologists who were their hired servants.

The creation of surplus labour on the one side corresponds to the creation of minus labour, relative idleness (or non-productive labour at best) on the other. This goes without saying as regards capital itself; but holds then also for the classes with which it shares; hence of paupers, flunkeys, lick-spittles, etc. living from the surplus product, in short, the whole train of retainers; the part of the *servant* class which lives not from capital but from revenue. (Marx, 1973: 401)

This direct relationship remains important and should not be forgotten. The working class also developed, out of its wages, a subordinate or counter-culture with its own 'organic intellectuals' such as paid trade union officials, cooperative organizers, journalists, etc., but the surplus available for this purpose was exiguous both really and comparatively, so that this direct ideological power was decisively weighted in favour of capital. It remains so. Compare a small organization like Counter Information Services with the public relations and research investment of a major company. Look at the way in which large companies manipulate the legal system by their ability to sustain expensive, long-drawn-out actions. Look at the way media research itself has been and is significantly influenced by the flow of funds from vested commercial interests.

There now exists, of course, as the division of labour has developed further, a more mediated version of this employment of ideologists out of revenue. This is the object of Bourdieu's analysis: the creation of a subordinate fraction of the capitalist class who possess cultural capital (Bourdieu and Passeron, 1977). Just as younger sons of the aristocracy went into Church and army, so now a section of the capitalist class occupies key positions in the cultural sector. The class origins of ideological workers remain an important but neglected aspect of media analysis. This does not of course mean that such people necessarily reproduce ruling-class ideology (Engels and William Morris are obvious counter-examples). It does mean that there is a structural tendency to do so.

Neglect of this aspect of the direct economic control of ideologists is reflected in current discussion of the ideological role of the media where there is much sophisticated discussion of professionalization, of hierarchies of discourse, of hegemonic and subordinate codes, etc., discussions which often serve to mask a reality which is ever-present to those actually working in the media: losing one's job. This reality is of course often internalized by both employee and employer in the form of the ideologies of professionalism or managerialism, but it remains no less potent for that, indeed, is the underpinning which professionalism requires. Once again, this was a fact that Adorno and Horkheimer did not make the mistake of forgetting:

Under the private culture monopoly it is a fact that 'tyranny leaves the body free and directs its attack at the soul'. The ruler no longer says, 'You must think as I do, or die'. He says, 'You are free not to think as I do, your life, your property, everything shall remain yours, but from this day on you are a stranger among us'. Not to conform means to be rendered powerless, economically and therefore, spiritually – to be 'self-employed'. When the outsider is excluded from the concern, he can only too easily be accused of incompetence. Whereas today in material production the mechanism of supply and demand is disintegrating in the superstructure it still operates as a check in the ruler's favour. (Adorno and Horkheimer, 1977)

The second moment, upon which increasingly in the actual historical development the former moment has come to depend, is the actual control by capital of the means of cultural production. This moment was underdeveloped at the time when *The German Ideology* was written but it is now crucial for an analysis of cultural reproduction under monopoly capitalism.[2] Within the sphere of cultural production the development of specifically economic, industrial forms was in part possible because at the other moment working-class powers of cultural resistance were weakened. A good example of this is Williams's suggestion that the popular success of ITV and of the general invasion of American commercialized cultural forms was a reaction on the part of the working class to the liberating overthrow of a particular hegemonic cultural formation represented by the BBC. It is in particular on the implications of this second moment that I wish to concentrate, i.e. the effects of the imposition of capital logic upon cultural production.

I have indicated there has been a tendency to see such an imposition as ideologically non-contradictory. One must stress at the outset that this is not so. Because capital controls the means of cultural production in the sense that the production and exchange of cultural commodities become the dominant forms of cultural relationship, it does not follow that these cultural commodities will necessarily support, either in their explicit content or in their mode of cultural appropriation, the dominant ideology. Indeed as Terry Lovell has noted and as, once again, Adorno and Horkheimer made clear, the cultural commodity possesses an inherent contradiction, a contradiction which may be profoundly subversive.[3] Before turning to the general implications of the proposition that one definition of the control of the means of mental production is the takeover of large areas of cultural production and reproduction by capitalist commodity production, what the proposition leads one to question is that stress on intentionality which we find in theories such as that of Miliband. It is quite clear in Marx's analysis of *Capital* that he wished to distinguish firmly between the logic of capital and the intention of individual capitalists, even at the economic, let alone the ideological level.

The fact that baking, shoemaking, etc. are only just being put on a capitalist basis in England is entirely due to the circumstances that English capital cherished feudal preconceptions of 'respectability'. It was 'respectable' to sell Negroes into slavery, but it was not respectable to make sausages, shoes or bread. (Marx, 1976: 1014, footnote)

It is perhaps worth noting in passing that this characteristic of British capital still operates with respect to the media, which carry a certain bohemian, mountebank and marginal reputation. Hence the characteristics of the particular capitalists who started ITV, for instance, or who developed the British film industry in the 1930s or the role of colonial capital via Beaverbrook and Murdoch in the British press. Such attitudes still affect the Tory Party in its ambivalent reaction to commercial broadcasting.

> The function fulfilled by the capitalist is no more than the function of capital – viz. the valorization of value by absorbing living labour – executed *consciously* and *willingly*. The capitalist functions only as personified capital, capital as a person, just as the worker is no more than *labour* personified. (Marx, 1976: 989)

Capitalists, for analytical purposes, are not unified subjects. A given person or group can only be described as capitalist in those moments when each is acting in conscious and willed accord with the logic of capital accumulation. Thus there may well be many such conscious, willed actions, never mind unconscious actions, that are contradictory to the logic of capital. There may therefore be a clear divergence between the functions of capital within the material process of mental production and the conscious, willed intentions of the capitalist or of their ideologues. We cannot predict *a priori* which at any time will be predominant, e.g. how long a Harmsworth, a Beaverbrook or a Thomson will keep a loss-making newspaper going for reasons of social prestige or political power, although there are always outer limits to such possibilities.

There is then (and this cannot be sufficiently stressed) no necessary coincidence between the effects of the capitalist process proper and the ideological needs of the dominant class. On the contrary the entire thesis of capital points to the opposite conclusion.

This, for instance, affects assumptions concerning the relationship between capital and the State. To take one example, the proportion of the budget of the Central Office of Information that has to be devoted to paid access to the media, i.e. the use of paid advertising for Government propaganda or information, has risen in the last decade from 20 to 50 per cent. Such evidence can be interpreted in two ways. The first, that there is an observable conflict between the ideological needs of the State and the accumulation process within the media sector (leaving aside the question of whether the State is in fact the representation of capital or of the dominant class, and therefore whether such a conflict would represent a contradiction between the economic and ideological needs of that class in general, or whether it would represent a contradiction between the ideological needs of capital in general versus the economic needs of a class fraction who control the media sector). Alternatively, this evidence can be interpreted to show the increasing sway of capitalist logic over the political and ideological level, forcing it to work increasingly through direct exchange relations within the economic.

This question of intentionality within ideological production is, of course, central to the media debate within both the bourgeois and Marxist problematic. One argument runs the Frankfurt School way, that the mass media are important because monopoly capitalism has moved from direct coercion of the working class to ideological coercion as its preferred method of domination, and the mass media or Ideological State Apparatuses are crucial in this process.

But do we in fact require this shift onto the terrain of ideology in order to explain the absence of direct coercion? Marx, on the contrary, saw the avoidance of such coercion as central to the economic mechanism of capitalism. That is to say the abstraction of exchange value, the wage-form, etc., were in themselves quite powerful enough to explain the dominance of capital, and indeed that this non-coercive dominance was both historically necessary and progressive. Bourdieu has developed this general proposition.[4]

> Thus at the level of material production, of the life process in the realm of the social – for that is what the process of production is – we find the *same* situation that we find in religion at the ideological level, namely the inversion of subject into object and vice-versa. Viewed *historically* this inversion is the indispensable transition without which wealth as such, i.e. the relentless productive forces of social labour, which alone can form the material base of a free human society, could not possibly be created by force at the expense of the majority. (Marx, 1976: 990)

VII

Let us now turn back to look at intellectual production as a process of capitalist production and at the implications for our modes of social communication of the subsumption by capital of the real forms of ideological production.

This needs to be looked at historically. Unlike the capital logic or capital derivation school we must not see capitalism as a mode of production which arrives *sui generis* and then sprouts a social formation like dragon's teeth. It is rather a specific form which grew within a pre-existing social formation and is involved in a process of expansion and conquest of non-capitalist sectors, a process which is incomplete and contradictory. This process of expansion involves both the subsumption of other areas of material production and pre-capitalist forms of economic organization and also of non-economic activity under the sway of the economic in its capitalist form.

When examining mass communication within predominantly capitalist social formations we must not make the mistake of assuming that they are therefore necessarily capitalist. We cannot make the easy elision Miliband makes between those sectors controlled by private capital and those controlled by the State. Nor can we assume that all non-State sectors are in fact capitalist. Indeed the relationship between pre-capitalist and capitalist forms within the media sector is a significant feature both economically and ideologically, thus the relationship between notions of creative freedom, freedom of the press, the fourth channel debate, community broadcasting, etc. This relationship significantly determines the forms of the struggle within the media over the labour process.

Artisanal modes of labour organization ranging from individual craft production, such as the authorship of a book, to the small group, such as the independent film company or record producer, remain common and important within the cultural sphere. Such residues have been the focus for struggle against the logic of capital, and have produced a powerful anti-economist cultural ideology. Nonetheless in certain instances such artisanal organization may be functional for capital so long as capital controls the means of mass reproduction of the authorial product and its mass distribution, because it ensures the necessary production of a range of cultural artefacts from which capital can choose without having to bear the risks and overheads which are borne directly by labour. Indeed, the ideology of creative freedom can be used by capital to keep its labour force divided and weak, and with no control over the strategic moments of the total labour process. Thus, for instance, while the Open Broadcasting Authority will be fought for by cultural workers under the banner of creative freedom and against the apparent interests of capital in the form of ITV, such small-scale freelance production, if it were to be realized, would be more functional for capital in general than an extension of the present structure, because it would open British broadcasting more fully to advertising and to the pressures of the international market.[5]

Nor must we make the mistake of assuming an easy equation between private ownership and capitalism.

> Where capital still appears only in its elementary forms such as commodities . . . or money, the capitalist manifests himself in the already familiar character of the owner of money or commodities. But such a person is no more a capitalist in himself than money or commodities are capital in themselves. They become translated into capital only in certain specific circumstances and their owners likewise become capitalist only when these circumstances obtain. (Marx, 1976: 976)

What then are these circumstances? The central characteristic of capital is growth or accumulation.

> In itself the sum of money may only be defined as capital if it is employed, spent, with the aim of increasing it, if it is spent expressly in order to increase it. In the case of the sum of value or money this phenomenon is its destiny, its inner law, its tendency, while to the capitalist, i.e. the owner of the sum of money, in whose hand it shall acquire its function, it appears as intention, purpose. (Marx, 1976: 976)

Thus to examine the specifically capitalist mode of media production we need to see the ways in which capital uses the real process of media production in order to increase its value, and grow, and the barriers which are placed in the way of this process either by the inherent contradictions of the process itself or by external forces.

In order to accumulate, capital must bring living labour into the production process by exchanging in the sphere of circulation through the wage bargain. It must combine this living labour in a determinate manner with objectified labour as a means of production (raw materials and instruments) in the production of a commodity in the exchange of which surplus value will be realized.

In a fully constituted capitalist mode based upon relative surplus value and competition between capitals this process of growth requires ever-increased productivity and ever-widening markets.

Historically the sphere of mental production or non-material production continues to present important barriers to this process, and the forms and dynamics of the mass media can in part be understood as resulting from a continuous attempt to surmount those barriers.

We thus start from the historical materialist assumption that the development of capitalism or the capitalist mode of production is a contradictory process, and not yet complete. The contradictory nature of the process is in part intrinsic. It is situated in the conflict between capital and labour, the conflict between capital accumulation and the socialization of the forces and relations of production, the conflict between the drive to accumulate through the extraction of relative surplus value and labour power as the creator of surplus value, a contradiction expressed in the tendency of the rate of profit to fall.

In part the contradictions are extrinsic, that is to say related precisely to the relationship between developing capitalism and the non-capitalist areas of the social formation. The necessary expansion of the valorization process is not a process of automatic expansion; it comes up against social and political barriers; it needs to conquer physical barriers, e.g. communication and transport; it requires the necessary accumulation of capital.

We see these contradictions in the field of mass media:

1 in resistances both actual and ideological to the industrialization of the artisanal modes of cultural production;
2 in the conflicts between national and international capitals, sometimes mediated through the State and sometimes direct, e.g. in the split in the Tory Party over the original introduction of commercial broadcasting – or in the developing struggle over national versus supranational control of European satellite broadcasting – or in the existence of quotas on the importation of foreign film and TV material;
3 growing Third World demand for a New World Information Order.

The problem with cultural and informational goods is that, because their use value is almost limitless (they cannot be destroyed or consumed by use) it is extremely difficult to attach an exchange value to them. They are classic public goods. What we are considering is what Marx called 'non-material production'. Marx discusses such production in the context of a discussion of the distinction between productive and non-productive labour. In brief, Marx clearly foresaw difficulties in subsuming non-material production under capitalism. He identified two possible forms of such production:

(1) It results in commodities which exist separately from the producer, i.e. they can circulate in the interval between production and consumption as commodities, e.g. books, paintings and all products of art as distinct from the artistic achievement of the practising artist. Here capitalist production is possible only within very narrow limits. Apart from such cases as, say, sculptors who employ assistants, these people (where they are not independent) mainly work for merchants capital, e.g. booksellers, a pattern that is only transitional in itself and can only lead to a capitalist mode of production in the formal sense. Nor is the position altered by the fact that exploitation is at its greatest precisely in these transitional forms.

(2) The product is not separable from the act of producing. Here too the capitalist mode of production occurs only on a limited scale and in the nature of the case it can only operate in certain areas (I want the doctor not his errand boy). For example, in teaching institutions the teacher can be no more than wage-labour for the entrepreneur of the learning factory. Such peripheral phenomena can be ignored when considering capitalist production as a whole. (Marx, 1976: 1047–8)

This passage would be worth lengthy analysis. At this stage I would only like to point to the following.

1 The relevance of the first example for the debate between Marcuse and Benjamin concerning the role of the aura of a work of art and the effect on that aura of the attempt to subject culture production to the forces of capitalist production.[6]
2 The need to look, with reference to the observation concerning the degree of exploitation in this field, at the evidence of the persistent low pay of cultural workers and the extent to which even the most advanced sectors of capitalist cultural production depend upon drawing relative surplus value from sectors which still operate a pre-capitalist artisanal mode of economic organization.[7]
3 The need to examine the relationship between Marx's belief that capitalist production of cultural goods was possible only within very narrow limits, the phenomenon of Baumol's disease (Baumol and Bowen, 1976) and the ever-increasing pressure on the State to intervene in the cultural sector.
4 Similar considerations are raised by Marx's second example where the product is not separable from the act of producing, imposing strict limits to productivity and thus raising relative costs.

The economic contradictions that arise from the nature of cultural commodities take different forms within different sectors of the media and at different historical moments.

Five main ways have been adopted in an attempt to circumvent the problem.

1 Copyright. This is in effect an attempt to commoditize information by turning the author into a commodity. But this only works if either you make the commodity scarce and stress its uniqueness (as in the economics of the art market), or if you control supply, by control of access to the means of reproduction such as printing presses and film laboratories. However, if such control is used to over-price it will encourage the development of pirating alternatives. This is now a major problem internationally for the cultural industries in records, books, films and even TV programmes.

2 Control of access to consumption through a box-office mechanism at the point of sale or through economic control of the channels of distribution, such as newspapers and cinema. The problem here is that such control is resistant to economies of scale and, as the theatre found when faced by the cinema and the cinema when faced by broadcasting, is highly susceptible to competition from more efficient technologies of reproduction and distribution. However, as broadcasting demonstrates, the massive economies of scale produced by these more efficient means of distribution by destroying the box office, and thereby making access open, create major problems at the moment of exchange.

3 Built-in obsolescence, through the manipulation of time. This was the great achievement of the newspaper which, by creating rapidly decaying information, created thereby a constant need to re-consume. But this manipulation of time has its limits, since consumption time is physically limited. (The central importance of time within the economics of the mass media is the subject of my subsequent post-script to this chapter.)

4 The creation, packaging and sale, not of cultural and informational goods to direct consumers, but of audiences to advertisers.

5 State patronage. The inherent tendency towards the socialization of cultural and informational goods has always given the State an important role in this field from the days of direct patronage of cultural workers by King, Aristocracy and Church via the early subsidy of newspapers by governments and political parties, through public libraries and public education, to the key contemporary example of broadcasting.

In brief, therefore, the specific nature of the commodity form within cultural production leads to a constant problem of realization and thus to a two-way pressure either towards advertising finance or towards State finance. We find these pressures quite clearly at the moment in the growing controversy over sponsorship in sport and the arts.

These pressures raise two questions: in what ways are advertising and State intervention in this sphere functional for capitalism? What are the effect of such pressures upon cultural production itself?

VIII

Since all cultural forms are material in the sense that they take time which will only be available after the needs of physical reproduction are satisfied, the material requirements of the cultural process must be extracted as surplus from direct material production. As we have seen this can be done by paying for cultural production directly out of revenue. But as Marx remarked of capitalism in general, it has found it more efficient as a means of control to extract surpluses directly by means of economic processes. Thus the developments of the capitalist mode of production and its associated division of mental and manual labour have led to the development of the extraction of the necessary surplus for the maintenance of cultural production and reproduction directly from the commodity and exchange form. But this process will take place only to the extent that:

1 there is surplus capital searching for opportunities for valorization;
2 the anticipated rate of profit in the chosen sphere of cultural production is at least as high as that available elsewhere.

Where these conditions do not exist cultural processes will have to continue to be undertaken by the direct transfer of resources, i.e. by the expenditure of surplus. This may take place under the following conditions.

1 By capitalists as individuals or groups funding such activities, e.g. the classic model of arts patronage. Such a form may be sustained within the contemporary capitalist social formation by means of tax concessions. It may be channelled through charitable foundations, etc.

Such funding leads to direct ideological control, legitimated as the cultural extension of private property, namely personal taste. This can give rise to significant political battles, e.g. the debate about costs of the national heritage.

Examples within the field are the direct subsidy of newspapers by political parties or by politically ambitious individuals, e.g. Beaverbrook, Goldsmith, Maxwell, Morgan-Grampian.

2 Via the State. Here electronic communication is the key case. The exact mix in the field of both telephonic and broadcast communication between the State and capital needs examination state by state. As any superficial examination will show, key differences between western Europe and the United States give the lie to any simple capital logic explanation of how the particular economic and institutional forms, within which electronic communication has developed, have arisen.

The explanation of such differences and the present conjunctural relations between national capitals and the State, between states and between international capital and states in this area would have to take account of the following.

1 The structures of national capitals.
2 The existing State structure, e.g. the federal structures of the USA and Germany as opposed to the centralized structures of Britain and France.
3 The strategic requirements of the State, e.g. the State-inspired creation of RCA as the first step in a long history of the US government's explicit geopolitical involvement in communication, the clearest case of which is satellites, such a policy requiring intervention to restructure national capitals.
4 The balance of forces between capital and the State's assessment of both economic and strategic requirement. Thus at the foundation of the BBC we see an interaction between the needs of the nascent British electronic industry, which the State wished to foster both for strategic and economic reasons, and the industry itself, which was interested only in the sales of hardware, and was able to shift the expense and ideological problems of programme production on to the State. Furthermore, the State needed to take account both of the economically and politically powerful British press, which was opposed to competition for advertising and of a culturally conservative and elitist ruling-class fraction.[8]

To sum up, the development of the material process known as the superstructure depended upon the availability of a surplus in the sphere of direct material production, i.e. the sphere of the extraction, shaping and consumption of nature. Historically the shape of that superstructure is determined by the social relations of production, because it is these social relations that determine the distribution of that surplus. For example, Athenian democracy as a form of political practice depends directly materially upon the slave economy that supported it by making time available for political activity to a non-productive class. Such directly material considerations remain important. In a planned economy such as the Soviet Union direct choices have to be made between (for instance) producing more shoes or the paper for more newspapers. Such considerations may be acute in the planning of media systems in Third World countries; indeed it is the influencing of such decisions in the interest not of the indigenous economy or social formation but of a foreign high surplus economy that is one of the matters at issue in the media imperialism debate. It is a less obvious form of the starvation caused in some countries by the development of industrialized agriculture serving a world market. Under capitalism the means of cultural production may be provided: either in commodity form as part of the accumulation process (e.g. records): *or* as part of the realization process of other sectors of the capitalist economy (e.g. advertising): *or* directly out of capitalist revenue (e.g. arts patronage): *or* through the State.

Each of the above means of surplus distribution to the cultural sphere will differentially affect the ways in which the dominant class controls the means of cultural production. Different contradictions will come into play, contradictions which need to be specifically analysed in each case. Not only are these contradictions intrinsic to each subsidiary mode of cultural production but there are also contradictions which arise because of conflicts between them. There is conflict intrinsic to broadcasting, whether state or private, and the press, a conflict in its turn differentially mediated through competition for readers and viewers, *and* through competition for advertising.

IX

While drawing different conclusions as to the significance of the phenomenon, both bourgeois and Marxist economists agree that the current phase of capitalist development is characterized by the following key features:

1 Unprecedented capital concentration in all the key traditional manufacturing sectors accompanied in general by a rising surplus.
2 A resulting problem of valorization which drives surplus capital in search of other areas of investment.
3 An associated development of the so-called service sector characterized by the industrialization of sectors which were either more primitively organized or, as in the sphere of domestic labour, altogether outside the market.

All I wish to do now is point out certain key aspects and examples of this tendency.

This absorption of the sphere of reproduction into full-scale commodity production is characterized by the following.

1 Increased international competition and the resulting take-over of domestic, national publishing companies, advertising agencies, private broadcasting stations, etc. by multinational companies. This competition also leads to increasing penetration by international media products, particularly Anglo-Saxon ones.[9]
2 A sharpening struggle within cultural production over the labour process in an attempt by capital to increase productivity in a sector notoriously resistant to such increases. This struggle has been most marked recently in the newspaper industry, with the Wapping solution being the most notorious and current example in Britain.
3 Increasingly persistent attempts to open up new markets in order to absorb excess capital. The most obvious example of this is the increasing pressure throughout western Europe to privatize public broadcasting.
4 Attempts to open up new markets for both cultural hardware and software by introducing new communication technologies, such as cable TV, satellites, Teletext, etc. Because of the huge infrastructural

investments involved and the comparatively low rate of return on such investments these moves involve close alliances between capital and the State in an attempt to get the taxpayer to carry the cost of the distribution system, while private capital takes the profits from the sale of hardware and from the subsequent development of a consumer durable market in such items as teletex decoders and the products of a software market. The full development of this push into new technologies has undoubtedly been slowed down significantly by recessions in the western economies, but the long-term implications for national cultures, for class cultures and for freedom of expression of all these trends, not only in the Third World where the problem is dramatized as media imperialism, but in the capitalist heartlands, are profoundly significant.

Thus I return to where I started by reiterating that the development of political economy in the cultural sphere is not a mere matter of theoretical interest but of urgent practical political priority. So long as Marxist analysis concentrates on the ideological content of the mass media it will be difficult to develop coherent political strategies for resisting the underlying dynamics of development in the cultural sphere which rest so very firmly upon the logic of commodity production. In order to understand the structure of our culture, its production, consumption and reproduction and of the role of the mass media in that process, we need to confront some of the central questions of political economy in general, the problem of productive and non-productive labour, the relation between the private and public sectors, and the role of the State in capitalist accumulation, the role of advertising within late capitalism. This is the long agenda of this book.

As long ago as 1960, Asa Briggs wrote in his Fisher Memorial Lecture:

> The provision of entertainment has never been a subject of great interest either to economists or to economic historians – at least in their working hours. Yet in 20th century conditions it is proper to talk of a highly organized entertainment industry, to distinguish within it between production and distribution, to examine forces making for competition, integration, concentration and control and to relate such study to the statistics of national income and output, the development of advertising, international economic relations and – not least – to the central economic concept of the market which, in the 20th century, is as much concerned with leisure as it is with work. (Briggs, 1960)

Three decades later that research gap remains, and there has been little coherent effort to understand the process known as 'the industrialization of culture', a process of which, as Briggs put it, 'Massive market interests have come to dominate an area of life which, until recently, was dominated by individuals themselves' (Briggs, 1960).

POSTSCRIPT: THE ECONOMY OF TIME

The special distortions effected upon the cultural industries, treated in all their materiality as aspects of production and accumulation, come out in a historical study of time itself as a feature of the productive and the consuming processes. It is present, of course, as a central issue in Taylorization; it is much more complexly (and uncontrollably) present as cultural superstructure settles into economic base. It becomes more than a contradiction; it is a focus of struggle.

Marx is quite clear in the *Grundrisse* ('Capital is circulating capital', p. 536) that capitalism seen from the point of view of capital is a process which is continuous, circular and through time. That is to say, capital, from the point of view of its own accumulation, is a continuous process of the production of value in a cycle within which the moment of consumption is part of the production process. 'With capital the consumption of the commodity is itself not final; it falls within the production process; it itself appears as a moment of production, i.e. of value positing.'

This is a crucial starting point for any political economy of mass communication because there is a school of thought within Marxism which, as we saw, grounds its distinction between base and superstructure or between the economic and the ideological, implicitly if often not explicitly, upon a fetishized distinction between production on the one hand (the sphere of value creation) and distribution and consumption on the other, placing determinacy within production thus narrowly defined. The opposing school, in arguing against the vulgarity of what they call economism and for the relative or even virtually complete autonomy of the ideological and political levels, adopts the same model but then turns it on its head by arguing for the non-determined nature of consumption.

If one returns to Marx's central notion of process or *flow*, such distinctions become invalid. What one wishes to examine is the ways in which the dynamics of this flow are determined by the differing moments through which they pass and by the physical, spatial and temporal transition through which capital is forced to pass in its process of self-realization.

Within the grand cycle of capital transforming itself through production into a commodity and then realizing itself as money through consumption in order to be retransformed into those commodities needed for production, there is a whole series of capital circulation itself. There is competition between individual capitals as well as the different circulating times within various sectors, some external to capital itself, such as the biological cycle of labour power (nature in the form of the cycle of seasons) or as within agricultural production, or even the much longer cycle of the replenishment of other energy sources. Marx himself constantly uses the metaphor of the human body with the differing circulating times of the skeleton, the flesh, the blood.

It is axiomatic for historical materialism in general and political economy in particular that the dynamics of the whole process can only be understood in terms of the contradictory interaction between moments within the total process. Thus a crisis may be caused by increased difficulties and scarcity in the extraction of raw materials, by limitation of consumption, by political resistance on the part of labour within the labour process, all of which can obstruct the smooth circular flow required for reproduction and accumulation.

Within this framework let us examine the problem of time. As Marx wrote in the *Grundrisse*, 'All economics ultimately reduces itself to economy in time.' Why is time crucial? If we assume a single economy which merely reproduces itself, it is strictly governed by natural, biological time. Generations reproduce themselves within a given time span. Food is reproduced on a seasonal cycle and labour reproduces itself through varying time cycles of energy input and output ranging from a roughly daily cycle of sleep, food and liquid intake through the cycles of biological reproduction to the cycle of life and death itself. At this level the economy is dominated by natural time.

If we now move to an accumulating capitalist economy, the basic natural constraints still apply but within these cycles growth is achieved by accelerated internal cycles of production exchange and consumption paralleling accelerated cycles of biological reproduction, accelerated rates of energy exchange with nature, etc.

Capital accumulation depends upon productivity which is a constant process of attempting to overcome these barriers, of reducing socially necessary labour time, production time and circulation time.

As Marx puts it in reference to circulation time, 'Circulation time thus appears as a barrier to the productivity of labour = an increase in necessary labour time = a decrease in surplus labour time = a decrease in surplus value = an obstruction, a barrier to the self-realisation process of capital' (Marx, 1973: 539).

In examining the dynamics of the accelerated turnover of capital in its process of self-realization we can analyse the separate moments of production (in the sense of the transformation of raw materials into a commodity) and of circulation. Within production such an analysis needs to look at the relationship between forces and relations of production. Within circulation we need to look at what Marx called the locational and temporal moments, referring to the problems both of the actual spatial extensions of the market (the physical transport of goods) and the time expended in commercial transactions (this time refers not to any labour time used in commercial transactions, but to the actual lapsed time expended in transforming a commodity into money and vice-versa, e.g. the time it takes to pass a cheque from one account to another. Costs in these areas were for Marx costs of production; thus labour time employed in these sectors was production of surplus value.) We need to look separately at time lost not in getting a commodity to market or in transforming a commodity into money, but at the process of circulation itself, that is, to time during which capital lies idle, locked up with commodities on warehouse or storage shelves. This Marx regarded as pure loss.

Firstly, and clearly related to the above, we need to look at the time of consumption itself. This is the resistance offered to the flow of capital by the limited capacity of individuals or groups actually to consume the products brought to market.

Marx pointed to capital's need for the constant continuity of this process, but also and at the same time to the ways in which the various phases of the cycle were actually separated in time and space and thus appear disjunctive.

> It is clear from everything said above that circulation appears as the essential process of capital. The production process cannot be begun anew before the transformation of the commodity into money. The *constant continuity* of this process, the unobstructed and fluid transition of value from one form into the other, or from one phase of the process to the next, appears as a fundamental condition for production based on capital to a much greater degree than for all earlier forms of production. On another side, while the necessity of this continuity is given, its phases are separate in time and space, and appear as particular, mutually indifferent processes. It thus appears as a matter of chance for production based on capital whether or not its essential condition, the continuity of the different processes which constitute its process as a whole, is actually brought about. (Marx, 1973: 535)

Marx himself saw the development of credit as the means by which capital in general suspended this chance element. I think it is clear that another major mechanism which has been largely developed since Marx's day is advertising and, of course, State intervention. This brings me to the relationship between this general analysis of the importance of time within the cycle of capital and mass communication.

In examining mass communication from this point of view we need first to analyse separately before subsequently combining:

1 mass communication as a particular capital or capitals involved in commodity production, that is to say the effect of attempts to overcome time constraints within their own capital circuits;
2 mass communication, by means of advertising, as a mechanism of capital in general, or of certain particular capitals, for accelerating, within the moment of circulation, the turnover time of capital in general.

This means first developing the methodology of Chapter 1 of *Capital* and, taking mass communication as itself a sphere of commodity production, analysing those products in terms of cultural needs (as opposed to needs of subsistence).

This has first a historical dimension. That is to say we need to look at the way in which what Marx described as 'the socially posited needs' (which communication, or symbolic cultural interaction, fulfils) were progressively satisfied by capital. Marx describes socially posited needs as 'those which the individual consumes and feels not as a single individual in society, but communally with others – whose mode of consumption is social by the nature of the thing' (1973: 532). Let us see cultural goods as 'socially posited needs' in this sense. Marx refers to such needs within a general discussion of the means by which societies provide means of transport. He argues that since means of transport are forces of production it is in capital's interest to develop these, but that in the early days of capitalism there was either insufficient concentration of capital to undertake the task or there might be insufficient relative return on such investment. In such situations the State either steps in as a representative of capital in general to provide the necessary infrastructure, or alternatively the State on behalf of society in general 'still possesses the authority and the will to force the society of capitalists to put a part of their *revenue*, not of their capital, into such generally useful works' (1973: 531).

For example, in the early days of printing we witness a dual phenomenon. On the one hand the development of a consumer market for books in order to realize the capital invested in the new technology of printing, a process accompanied by acute problems of realization and bankruptcy, on the other hand the State stepping in and effectively subsidizing a sector of the printing trade, the Stationers Company, for ideological reasons. These two aspects of the problem of the development of markets in cultural commodities as part of the realization cycle of capital invested in a new technology, as well as the tension between capital and State, remain centrally important.

The second development in the sphere of printing was the newspaper, which from the start was a response of capital to problems in the sphere of circulation. Newspapers first sold commercial intelligence as a function of the development of overseas trade, and second, sold advertisements as a function of the development of internal national markets. However, we cannot look at the development of advertising as merely functional for capital in general, but also as a response within the printing sector itself to its own problems of realization. Only by selling space to advertisers could they overcome the perennial problem of cultural goods production, multiple consumption. They did so by charging advertisers for those readers who could not themselves be persuaded to pay, and at the same time, by reducing their cover price, achieve those economies of scale which valorized capital investment in new printing technology, and in its turn reduced necessary labour time in production.

However, that capital itself found it difficult to provide the necessary forces of production is evidenced by the long transitional history, a history which in western Europe still continues, where newspapers still find it necessary to receive subsidies from the State or political parties.

Marx himself appeared to foresee a process by which capital steadily took over more and more of what he described as 'the general condition of the process of social production'. As he puts it,

> The separation of public works from the state, and their integration into the
> domain of works undertaken by capital itself, indicated the degree to which
> the real community has constituted itself, in the form of capital . . . the
> highest development of capital exists when the general conditions of the
> process of social production are not paid out of *deduction from the social
> revenue*, the state's taxes – where revenue and not capital appears as the
> labour fund, and where the worker, although he is a free wage worker like any
> other, nevertheless stands economically in a different relation – but rather out
> of capital as capital. This shows the degree to which capital has subjugated all
> conditions of social production to itself, on one side; and, on the other side,
> hence, the extent to which social reproductive wealth has been *capitalised* and
> all needs are satisfied through the exchange form. (1973: 532)

We can see this process at work (as delineated by James Curran) in the
development of the British press in the nineteenth century, a process
which carried the expansion of capital into new markets and new sectors
of which the so-called industrialization of culture is a part, but a process
in which mass advertising joins to general capital accumulation where the
urgent need of fixed capital required an accelerated turnover time.

Before looking at the development of new recording and broadcasting
technology, and the industries based upon them, within the general
development of monopoly capitalism, let me turn now to the constraints
of consumption time. For the requisite increased productivity and
accelerated turnover time of monopoly capital required matching by
increased consumption if the circuit of capital was to be completed. (I
am not here arguing a unicausal underconsumption theory of capitalist
crises, but for the importance of consumption as a moment in the total
process.)

There are two related constraints on consumption – time and money.
While the development of capitalism has in part freed the majority of the
population in industrialized countries from direct dependence upon
natural cycles, nonetheless the reproduction of labour power is still
closely tied to a variety of short-term cycles, from the daily ones of
sleeping and eating to weekly or at most monthly financial cycles. Thus
a majority of the working population needs to exchange its labour power
week by week in order to reproduce itself and its dependents.

Within the total cycle of production and exchange, capital's problems
of realization relate closely to the time constraints within which
consumption must take place. Consumption takes place in real time
whether this is immediate consumption – you can only eat and digest so
much food in a given time – or less immediate consumption such as so-
called consumer durables which have a given lifespan at a normal rate
of usage. One of the causes of capitalist crisis is the different temporal
cycles both within and between production and consumption.

There is a dialectical relationship between available labour time and
available consumption time. Maximum available labour time is limited
within a roughly 24-hour cycle by the workers' need for rest and direct

physical reproduction (eating, fornicating, child care) and, at a historically developed level of capitalist expansion, by the time required for other consumption activities such as shopping, leisure activities in general, media consumption in particular. Lastly, labour time is limited by those activities which are not yet completely within the sphere of exchange such as a range of social intercourse from casual chat to political or union meetings.

Parallel to the development of complete time discipline within the work process itself (in order to make available to the capitalist the maximum potential labour power for a given labour time), the capitalist system also requires the imposition of similar time discipline within that moment of production devoted to consumption. This has taken several forms. There has been planned obsolescence or the accelerated turnover time of consumption. We saw this with mass communication in the development of the commodity 'news', with its imposition of a daily (or in radio, hourly) cycle of consumption. There has been the development of forms of popular cultural commodity, such as the tabloid press, much radio and TV programming that requires minimal consumption time, and may be accompanied by other consumption activities (eating, ironing, do-it-yourself).

These general tendencies have been reinforced by the electronic media, which operate in continuous real-time and thus create instant obsolescence. These processes have been intensified by the more efficient use of non-work time. An example of this is video in the home rather than visits to the cinema, which wastes travel time. We can notice a similar relationship between newspaper consumption and commuting; the filling of otherwise 'dead' consumption time.

Lastly, we have seen the invasion of the private sphere by the industrialization of, for example, convenience foods, releasing women especially both for use as cheap surplus industrial labour, as well as for other consumption activities.

Now the development of mass media into modes of real-time continuous consumption such as 24-hour radio, has led to one of the central contradictions in this sphere, which is an ever-sharpening competition within media and between media and other spheres for a restricted attention span. This competition is constantly raising the real cost to the consumer of each unit of media consumption because of duplication. We have radio *and* a hi-fi for listening to music, but as our total music consumption time cannot easily rise, then we are perhaps doubling our investment for the same consumption.

The consumer resistance that results may manifest itself in various ways: licence evasion; pirating through photocopying and taping; the drift of advertisers to the most effective medium as the cost of each becomes uneconomic.

This resistance leads to a polarization of provision. There ensues increased media provision at the top end of the market, where spare money and spare time make the higher unit costs sustainable, together with increased loss of variety at the bottom end of the market where the fight for ever-larger markets and their associated economies of scale are the only means of survival. This development leads to viewdata and pay cable TV rather than general provision of domestic telephones or adequate investment in existing public service broadcasting.

It is hardly surprising that propagandists of the media industries are the leading prophets of an imminent 'leisure' society. However, what we are in fact getting is, alongside this polarized provision, structural unemployment on similar lines, which does of course make consumption time available, but since it at the same time withdraws consumption resources, is not time that capital can readily exploit for its realization.

In this general context it is important to note the acute relevance of Bourdieu's work on the relationship between amounts of available free time and modes of cultural consumption. Thus elite aesthetic forms presuppose ample time and comfort for their consumption. There is also the close relationship visible in public statistics between amounts of cultural consumption in all categories and income groups, reflecting both greater availability of disposable income for expenditure on more materially peripheral forms of consumption, as well as the shorter and less intense work time enjoyed by upper-income groups.

Lastly, and relating to both these points, we need to note the relevance of the quality as well as the quantity of available consumption time, or what we might term consumption power. This in turn relates to the organization of time within the work process itself where increased intensity of labour produces *tired* consumers. There is good evidence that the electronic media, because of their ease of consumption, partly fill up *recuperation* time.

Thus we need, in parallel with the analysis of the work process, to analyse the *consumption* process in terms of consumption time, consumption power and consumption intensity and, as in analysis of the work process, look at how the mass media structure socially necessary consumption time in ways that are functional to the general reproduction of the capitalist mode of production at the economic level.

We not only need to analyse the role of the mass media within consumption in general, and from the point of view of the consumption time of media products themselves, we also need to link this analysis to the cycle of capital within the media sector. Pushing against the barrier of limited media consumption time we have the pressure from particular capitals in competition with each other and in competition with other consumption time, all driving to accelerate the turnover time of their capital.

As with capital in general, media capital can do this by shortening production labour time and by expanding consumption both spatially and temporally. All these histories can be written.

The history of the British press in the nineteenth century shows a

complex dialectic relationship between developments in paper manufacture, in reproductive technology for both words and pictures, and in the
development of a mass market with its associated distribution system.
Along with these developments the processing of content (by journalists)
also progressed along classic industrial lines, with increased division of
labour within newspaper offices resulting in an increasingly standardized
product.

Following this long, slow development came a second technological
revolution which saw the rapid development of systems by means of
which other symbolic forms beside the written word, such as sounds and
moving pictures, could be industrialized; the gramophone, the cinema,
radio, and finally television.

The gramophone followed printing, of which it is, in a sense, a form,
by producing commodities for direct sale to the consumer. The cinema,
on the other hand, took over the form of realization of the theatre.
Instead of selling actual film, it sold access to performances. It did not
(because it could not) increase its labour productivity at the point of
production; the creation of a fictional film consumes more labour than
the equivalent theatrical performance, but the gains of productivity in the
moment of circulation were prodigious. The strips of film could be
endlessly and cheaply reproduced in a laboratory and were easily and
rapidly transportable to an audience. Moreover, because the marginal
costs of wider circulation were small, greater profits were to be made
from wider circulation than from entering another cycle of production.
Once an investment has been made in cinemas, surplus value is actually
created and realized at the point of consumption, and this process can
be continually repeated without further investment in production itself.
For two commodities are produced: first, the actual film, the copyright
of which can be bought and sold, and second, the actual performance.
The constant reproducibility is only limited by the contradictory need
within cultural consumption for novelty and difference. With cultural
commodities there is a sense in which they are never consumed by each
individual consumer without at once satisfying a need and at the same
time creating one. Cultural consumption is of its very nature a surpass-
ing, a negation; it is the creation of unsatisfiable needs, the source of its
great attraction for capital.

Following the cinema, radio and TV represented not an improvement
in productivity at the point of production, but a massive and final gain
in the speed of circulation. Circulation time was now reduced to zero.
From one point of view radio and TV represented in their sphere the
ultimate logic of capitalist development.

However, once TV had achieved, via global satellite, a commodity
circulation time which was virtually zero, together with an extension
which was virtually total, reaching all consumers within the given
market, the barrier to further growth within the media sector became
insurmountable. This has resulted in an increasingly sharp struggle both

between modes of cultural distribution (press and broadcasting) and *within* modes (TV channels) as well as between conglomerate national or multinational media capital. These battle for a strictly limited consumption time, a competition which is rapidly increasing the unit cost of media consumption.

On the side of private capital this leads to a reinforcement of general tendencies to monopolization so that a given capital can control as wide a span of this consumption time across different modes as possible, while on the part of the State it leads to an increasing need for coherent media policy in order to avoid the wasteful duplication of media investment and to ensure the optimum use of the scarce available consumption time.

Notes

1 For a detailed discussion of this problem see Baudrillard (1972, 1975)).
2 But note Marx's own comments in the *Grundrisse* (1973: 532):

> The highest development of capital exists when the general conditions of the process of social production are not paid out of *deduction from the social revenue*, the state's taxes – where revenue and not capital appears as the labour fund, and where the worker, although he is a free wage worker like any other, nevertheless stands economically in a different relation – but rather out of *capital as capital*. This shows the degree to which capital has subjugated all conditions of social production to itself, on the one side; and, on the other side, hence, the extent to which social reproduction wealth has been *capitalised* and all needs are satisfied through the exchange form. (Marx's italics)

3 See Lovell (1980) and Adorno and Horkheimer (in Curran *et al.*, 1977: 361):

> Nevertheless the culture industry remains the entertainment business. Its influence over the consumer is established by entertainment; that will ultimately be broken not by an outright decree, but by the hostility inherent in the principle of entertainment to what is greater than itself.

4 See Bourdieu (1971: 183–97):

> It is in the degree of objectification of the accumulated social capital that one finds the basis of all pertinent differences between the modes of domination. . . . Objectification guarantees the permanence and cumulativity of material and symbolic acquisition which can thus subsist without agents having to recreate them continuously and in their entirety by deliberate action; but, because the profits of their institutions are the object of differential appropriation, objectification also and inseparably ensures the reproduction of the structure of distribution of the capital which, in its various forms, is the precondition for such appropriation, and in so doing, reproduces the structure of the relation of dominance and dependence. (p. 184)

5 The Open Broadcasting Authority was an early proposed form of what later became Channel 4. For a fuller elaboration of the modes of labour organization within capitalist cultural industries, see Huet *et al.* (1978).
6 See Benjamin (1977) for the positive view, and Marcuse (1972) for the negative view.
7 See Huet *et al.* (1978) for theoretical elaboration, and Krust (1977) for data. See also discussion in Owen, Beebe and Manning (1974), which shows, from a neo-classical perspective, that the so-called economic efficiency of US TV depends upon high unemployment in Hollywood.
8 For a discussion of the relationship between the French State and private capital in the

development of the electronic audiovisual field in general, see Flichy (1978) and Huet
et al. (1978).
9   It should be noted that from this point of view the UK is in a privileged position, since
it is second only to the USA as a media exporter.

References

Adorno, T. and Horkheimer, M. (1977) 'The culture industry' (abridged), in Curran *et al.*
(1977).
Althusser, L. (1969) *Contradiction and Over-determination* London: Allen Lane.
Baudrillard, J. (1972) *Pour une Critique de l'Economie Politique du Signe*. Paris:
Gallimard.
Baudrillard, J. (1975) *The Mirror of Production*. St Louis: Tela Press.
Baumol, W. J. and Bowen, W. G. (1976) 'On the performing arts: the anatomy of their
economic problems', in M. Blaug (ed.), *The Economics of the Arts*. London: Martin
Robertson.
Benjamin, W. (1977) 'The work of art in the age of mechanical reproduction', in Curran
et al. (1977).
Bourdieu, P. (1971) *Outline of a Theory of Practice*. Cambridge: Cambridge University
Press.
Bourdieu, P. and Passeron, J. L. (1977) *Reproduction*. London: Sage.
Briggs, A. (1960) Fisher Memorial Lecture, University of Adelaide.
Clarke, S. (1977) 'Marxism, sociology and Poulantzas's theory of the state', *Capital and
Class*, no. 2, Summer.
Curran, J. (1977) 'Capitalism and the control of the press, 1800–1979', in Curran *et al.*
(1977).
Curran, J. *et al.* (eds) (1977) *Mass-Communication and Society*. London: Edward
Arnold.
Flichy, P. (1978) *Contribution à une Etude des Industries de l'Audiovisuel*. Paris: Institut
National de l'Audiovisuel.
Hall, S. (1977) 'Culture, the media and the ideological effect' in Curran *et al.* (1977).
Huet, A. Ion, J., Lefèbvre, A., Miège, B. and Peron, R. (1978) *Capitalisme et Industries
Culturelles*, Paris: University of Grenoble.
Krust, M. (1977) *Droit au Travail et Problèmes d'Emploi du Travailleur Culturel du Spec-
tacle et de l'Interprétation Musicale dans la Communauté Economique Européenne*.
European Commission.
Levant, P. (1978) 'The audience commodity: on the blindspot debate', *Canadian Journal
of Political and Social Theory*.
Lovell, T. (1980) *Pictures of Reality*. London: British Film Institute.
Mandel, E. (1975) *Late Capitalism*, ch. 1, London: New Left Books.
Marcuse, H. (1972) 'Art as a form of reality', *New Left Review*, 74.
Marx, K. (1959) *Selected Writings in Sociology and Social Philosophy*, ed. T. Bottomore
and M. Rubel. London: Watts.
Marx, K. (1962) Preface to a contribution to a critique of political economy, in K. Marx
and F. Engels, *Selected Works*, vol. 1. London: Lawrence & Wishart, p. 364.
Marx, K. (1973) *Grundrisse*. London: Pelican.
Marx, K. (1976) 'Results of the immediate process of production', in *Capital*, vol. 1.
London: Pelican.
Miliband, R. R. (1977) *Marxism and Politics*. Oxford: Oxford University Press.
Murdock, G. (1978) 'Blindspots about Western Marxism: a reply to Dallas Smythe'.
Canadian Journal of Political and Social Theory, 2(2).
Murdock, G. and Golding, P. (1979) 'Ideology and the mass media: the question of deter-
mination', in M. Barrett *et al.* (eds), *Ideology and Cultural Production*. London: Croom
Helm.

Owen, B., Beebe, J. and Manning, W. (1974) *TV Economics*. London: D. C. Heath.

Smythe, D. (1977) 'Communication: blindspot of Western Marxism', *Canadian Journal of Political and Social Theory*, 1(3).

Smythe, D. (1978) 'Rejoinder to Graham Murdoch', *Canadian Journal of Political and Social Theory*, 2(2).

Thompson, E. P. (1978) *The Poverty of Theory*. London: Merlin Press.

Williams, R. (1977) *Marxism and Literature*. Oxford: Oxford University Press.

3

Film and Media Studies:
Reconstructing the Subject

No-one of even the most fortunate experience can believe that, if an adequate conception were made fully operative, a literacy education would be satisfactory by itself. The more one believes in the relevant discipline, the less one is likely to feel happy about permitting undergraduates to devote the years of an 'Honours' course to literary studies alone. One of the virtues of literacy studies is that they lead constantly outside themselves, and, on the other hand, while it is necessary that they should be controlled by a concern for the essential discipline, such a concern, if it is adequate, counts on associated work in other fields. (Leavis, 1948: 35)

The preceding chapter sets out my view of method in media studies. But as the long introduction emphasizes, this book is intended to make plain the connections between theory and practice – communications theory and political practice. Given that media studies have had their prominent and popular place in higher education for some years, given further how many graduates compete eagerly for posts in the media professions, I need to say something directly about the conduct of the relevant academic courses, and the ways in which I would like to square such study and teaching with the frameworks of inquiry already commended in my first two chapters.

In what I say I shall largely confine myself to higher education, because that is where such experience and expertise as I possess lie, but I think what I have to say is also relevant to secondary education, and this relevance can be brought out in the development of the National Curriculum.

I will start with the assertion that, for all the concrete signs in the universities and polytechnics and around the BFI Educational Advisory Service and SEFT of healthy growth, our field of study is in a mess and is developing in the wrong direction. While I am by no means optimistic about the possibilities of redirection, I think that there is no hope at all unless we recognize what is at present wrong and why, and at least aim in what I see as the desired direction.

The clearest immediate signs of our present troubles are the title and agenda of a subject area which essentially categorizes film studies as an area separate from and worthy of more attention than media studies, rather than as a subsidiary category of the latter. And yet, and here I make assertion number two, film is, by any standards today, of entirely marginal intellectual interest *per se*. It cannot possibly justify itself as the basis for a substantive discipline or field of study. Nor indeed in my view can media studies, except in the sense in which briefly I will attempt to reconstruct it. This seems to be even truer of secondary education than of higher education, and the attempt to do so in secondary education seems to me to play right into the hands of those constructing the present communication studies syllabuses and examinations.

To justify these assertions we need to look briefly at the history of the development of film and media studies and at the relationship of that development to British education and to the development of the mass media themselves. For film studies as at present constructed is a classic case of an ideological formation whereby developments in the media industries have led to the concrete marginalization of a cultural practice (namely film-going), to an accompanying shift in the social base for this mode of cultural consumption and thus to the legitimization of that shift within the educational system. That is to say that film has become available as an object of study precisely to the extent that it has ceased to be a centrally important medium of mass cultural production and distribution. In contrast TV, radio, newspapers and records are central sites of political and ideological struggle and thus cannot be constructed, hard as *Screen* may try, as objects of study in the same way.

Ironically, what we have witnessed over the past decade or so, accompanied at the conscious intellectual level by an overt, if simple-minded, rejection of the Leavisite heritage, has been the retracing of the trajectory of Leavis's notion of English studies upon the terrain of film studies. If one goes back and re-reads Leavis's 'A Sketch for an English School' (1948), one is struck by its multidisciplinary vision and by the way the study of English literature is grounded in the concrete analysis of a whole historical conjuncture. It is in fact a sketch of what is now called cultural studies, and should be read with care by all those designing courses in media studies in Britain today. The way in which that broad vision was narrowed by the pressures of the British educational system is evidenced not only in university English schools up and down the country but also by assorted conceptions of a film studies curriculum within the post-Leavisite tradition.

I would want to argue that film studies in Britain developed very largely out of a tradition of English studies that was already cast in the mould of a decadent Leavisism, and that this decadent Leavisism was itself a significant withdrawal within terms acceptable to the British educational system from the very historical problems that had originally inspired Leavis's work. In part the development of film studies was an attempt to return to the roots of the Leavis tradition and its confrontation with an industrialized and commercialized culture, while maintaining and developing the radical potential of that whole tradition by, at the same time, avoiding and indeed explicitly challenging the elitism of those established notions of cultural hierarchy embedded in the concept of literature, to which Leavis and his followers had been forced back by the pressures of British academia. Thus film studies saw itself as, and indeed was, a radical development. Hall and Whannels' *The Popular Arts* (1964) stands, I suppose, as the classic exemplar of that movement.

However, while challenging the cultural elitism of Leavisite English studies, it nonetheless took over from that tradition, not Leavis's original breadth of cultural analysis, but its aetiolated reduction to Practical Criticism and the Great Tradition, concerns that matched well with the importation of *Cahiers du Cinéma* formalism and 'auteur' theory. The early issues of *Movie* stand as exemplars of that fusion.

As a separate and parallel development, meanwhile, Leavis's original project had been significantly taken over and carried forward by Williams, Hoggart and Hall, developing into the cultural studies tradition as most clearly expressed in the work of the Centre for Contemporary Cultural Studies at Birmingham. Film studies has remained until recently largely aloof from that development, and the fact that that important intellectual cadre has also itself largely ignored film can be taken as further support for my assertion of the marginality of film as a focus of intellectual interest. The manifest gulf between the two fields presents a problem not for cultural studies but for film studies.

> In the circumstances of British intellectual activity in the nineteen-sixties and seventies, the constitution and development of a distinct field of Film Studies has been correlative with a vehement rejection of sociological perspective. (Nice, 1978)

It is at this point that one must point with retrospective scorn at the notion of 'specificity' that came to dominate the development of film studies, bringing with it those damaging tendencies towards intellectual remoteness and coterie inquiry, accompanied by sheer intellectual narrowness manifest in too much of the work in recent years of both the BFI and of SEFT. It is easy to understand why 'specificity' became so central a concept and indeed rallying cry. Within education, precisely because of inherited and established notions of cultural hierarchy and academic respectability, film studies was marginalized as subaltern to English, as a 'soft-option' ingredient within the inchoate mash of liberal studies or as form of evidence at best or visual aid at worst for historians and social scientists.

At the same time the BFI needed to mark out its own institutional territory and, in so doing, to combat a pervasive sense of cultural inferiority and, in terms for instance of its actual funding as compared with the Arts Council, of solid cultural discrimination. These ideological needs for identity and scholarly content led film studies in a delirious rush of pseudo-radicalization from Leavisite practical criticism via *Movie* formalism to the Platonic hotch-potch of Althusser and Lacan that passes for film theory while clogging the pages of *Screen*.

This is neither the time nor the place for an exploration of the reasons for that dismal trajectory of a group of British intellectuals. Why this trajectory and why film studies provide its site are both important questions in their own right. All I would wish to note here is the way in which 'specificity' was given its aura of political radicalism in the ideological form of Althusserianism, which made it easiest to begin absorbing film studies painlessly into the established intellectual hierarchies of academia. It is also worth noting because of its relevance to what I will say later about the way in which the French debate was radically dehistoricized in its passage to England. It was dehistoricized in the sense that it was the very selective purloining of elements in an intellectual tradition and controversy out of the concrete historical context in which those intellectual questions had been argued. Thus there was Althusser, Barthes, Metz and Lacan, but not Sartre, Braudel, Lefebvre, Vilar or Bourdieu. But it was also dehistoricized in the sense that all these debates originally took place within, and developed out of the discipline of history, and especially out of the work of the Annales School, so that concepts like structure, conjuncture, the concern with psychoanalysis, the concern with the mass media themselves all arose out of the attempt to answer concrete questions thrown up in the process of historical research. When wrenched from this context the concerns and the concepts are radically impoverished.

This intellectual development within British film studies would not have been sufficient on its own to accomplish the task of recuperation had it not been paralleled by institutional developments within the BFI, particularly the establishment of the BFI lectureships. The strategy behind these lectureships was based firmly on the concept of 'specificity'. That is to say the notion was that film studies and the BFI would become respectable if universities could be persuaded to develop film studies as a distinct subject area of discipline with associated degrees, research, and so on. In general, debate has not been about the desirability of that aim and the construction of the subject that results, but about details of what should be taught within a syllabus already constructed within the narrow English Literature tradition as text-based. The only dispute has been between post-Leavisite 'auteuristes' and those from the *Screen* position as to the mode of textual analysis to be adopted.

While we are considering the notion of specificity it is important to recognize a parallel development within polytechnics. To begin with, the situation here was healthier than at universities. While the BFI sought the holy grail of respectability by pump-priming university developments, media studies or communication studies were developed autonomously in the polytechnics where such developments were less constrained by the heavy weight of academic tradition. However, the search for respectability via disciplinary specificity is now manifesting itself in the polytechnics in the form of an attempt to construct communication studies as a discipline out of a horrendous mix of information theory, linguistic philosophy, semiology, ethology, group dynamics, etc.

What has been lost in this whole development of film studies, and now of communication studies as well, is the original reason for studying the subject in the first place. Leavis's early work, with its concern for the mass media, must not be seen in isolation. It was part of a general reaction on the part of western intellectuals to the phenomenon subsequently dubbed 'the industrialization of culture' and of their various attempts to come to terms with that phenomenon. Shaped by the specific cultural contexts within which theorists were working, this produced mass society theory in its various guises. In particular it is striking now with the benefit of historical perspective to see the similarities between the contemporaneous analysis and concerns of Leavis and of the Frankfurt School.

But mass society theory is itself a development of that central strand of the western intellectual tradition stemming from Vico and Montesquieu in the eighteenth century, the tradition from which, in their damagingly separate ways, both modern history and sociology developed. Such inquiry took as its field the function of the symbolic realm in the maintenance, change and differentiation of social formations. We see this central concern expressed in such a trio of classic texts as *The German Ideology, Elementary Forms of Religious Life* and *The Protestant Ethic and the Spirit of Capitalism*. It is to this concern that, in my view, media studies has to address itself if it is to be a serious area of study, and in doing so at least as much emphasis will have to be placed upon history and economics as upon the subaltern discipline of aesthetics.

The mass media are concrete historical phenomena socially created as part of the general development of industrial capitalism and their shifting function can only be understood within that context. If study of those media is to amount to anything more than the study of media artefacts in ways that merely reinforce by pandering to the particular cultural tastes of specific social groups (this is the tendency of the avant-gardism of *Screen*), then it needs to tackle the central historical questions surrounding the development of these phenomena.

The first conjunctural focus of such a study needs to be that period in Britain from about 1880 through to the First World War (and associated periods in the United States and western Europe, although the exact temporalities will differ), when technologies of reproduction, the gramophone, film, high-speed printing and photogravure, were mobilized and institutionalized as part of a shift in the general economic structure from competitive, industrial capitalism to monopoly consumer capitalism. The actual forms of that development are rooted in the economic developments and classic struggles of the nineteenth century as a whole. To understand the continuing significance of that historical shift media studies students need to be familiar with the general theoretical problems concerning the development of capitalism; they need the appropriate intellectual tools with which to analyse a mode of production and distinguish between forces and relations of production, between production and exchange within the circuit of capital. An understanding of these historical processes would help such students to avoid conceptualizing film in the narrow way that, in general and implicitly, film studies now does; namely as a form that involves the projection of sounds and images reproduced on celluloid before an audience in a cinema and which thus leads to the constitution of television studies as a separate field and media studies as yet another. Instead the form at present studied by film studies would be seen as part of a historical continuum of the production and distribution of dramatic performances using different recording techniques, different modes of production and distribution and differing associated modes of economic organization, whether or not with significantly different social functions and effects remaining to be established.

Within this general process the shift from modes of production historically associated with film to those associated with broadcasting would serve as the second conjunctural focus for any study of the mass media, introducing the central theme of the role of the State in monopoly capitalism and leading both to problems surrounding international media and the analysis of media and cultural imperialism within the general context of an economic analysis of imperialism as well as to debates over the so-called post-industrial society or information society and the role of new communication technologies.

Another focus of any media studies course needs to be the historical study of the development of the division of labour and of the division of mental and manual labour within that more general development, and such study needs to look closely at the problem of the labour process. Students need to be familiar with the debates concerning the social position and function of that social group variously referred to as intellectuals, as cultural workers or as ideologists.

This brings me to the vexed question of ideology. In recent years film studies has marched, with media studies in tow, under the banner of ideology, but the concept of ideology that it has employed to give itself the illusion of radicalism has been fatally flawed because severed from the historical context which gives it its meaning and its analytical purchase on the problems of the mass media. The concept of ideology, as it developed in nineteenth-century social thought and as employed by Marx and Engels, was used to describe and analyse a phenomenon produced by the general development of capitalism, namely the increased complexity and interdependence of the social totality and thus the increasing abstraction and necessary generalization of the modes of mediation within that totality. The crucial and central form of this process, which gives capitalism its name and which makes the economic level the centre of any social analysis, was the generalization of commodity production and exchange, itself mediated through the abstract exchange of money. The core of Marx's concept of ideology is an extremely simple proposition: that the more complex and interrelated a social totality becomes, (a) the harder it is for individuals to analyse and understand the totality of which they are a part and (b) the more they are dependent for their knowledge of that totality not on direct experience, but on experience mediated in symbolic form. Because of these two related factors there is a greater possibility of intellectual error and – since the essence of symbolic forms is their capacity to lie – a greater possibility of manipulation.

It is at this point that we must return to the more general economic and social analysis, for it is by bringing together the concept of ideology in the ontological sense outlined above with the detail of given relations of production, and of class struggles around those relations, that we can approach problems of ideological domination and opposition and of the role of the mass media therein.

While for any media studies course the problem of ideology is central, it is a problem that can only be adequately studied within and subsidiary to a study of those historical developments of the social formation that produced both the problem and the concept of ideology, and the mass media as exemplary sites for its study.

The study of ideology, within film and media studies, because severed from its concrete historical moorings has concentrated upon ideology either as an epistemological or as an ontological problem. The Althusserian theory of ideology, laying stress upon the universality of ideology and reducing ideology to a mere practice rather than maintaining the crucial distinction and thus dialectic between consciousness and practice, echoes, for all its rhetoric, the position of the original mass society theorists who criticized the mass media for their denial of authentic, immediate experience. Such a stress on the universal, ontological status of ideology leads to the neglect of the central focus of a historical materialist theory of ideology, namely the difference between ideological formations and the attempt to root the analysis of those differences in the concrete origins of the differing social formations. This neglect then leads to a-social and a-historical theories, whereby the struggle becomes one not against specific ideologies, but against ideology as such and the site of that struggle is projected either back into a Golden Age, as in much mass society theory, or forward to a utopian future or inwards into the unconscious. Whatever the site for their realization these theories bear remarkably idealist similarities.

In order to avoid these traps media studies needs now to forget notions of its own specificity and re-establish its links with the mainland of the social sciences, the queen of which is history in the robes of historical materialism.

References

Hall, S. and Whannel, P. (1964) *The Popular Arts*. London: Hutchinson.

Leavis, F. R. (1948) *Education and the University*. London: Chatto & Windus.

Nice, R. (1978) 'Bourdieu: a "vulgar materialist" in the sociology of culture', *Screen Education*, 28 (Autumn): 24.

4
The Myths of Video:
A Disciplinary Reminder

It is a lowering truth about the climate in film and media studies as I describe it in the preceding chapter that it regularly congratulates itself on the extension of democratic opportunity which its practitioners see as inscribed in new communications technology, and for which they profess themselves enthusiastic apologists.

Nowhere is this more evident than in the claims made for video and instruction in its use at school or polytechnic. Since I too subscribe to the view that the education of a citizen capable of active participation in modern society must include an intelligent, critical grasp of the significance of that society's communications, it is timely to issue a warning or two about the ways in which new technology does nothing at all for freedom.

Light-weight, portable video equipment was originally developed for military purposes. Like so much of our new information processing technology it was a product of a US Defence Budget swollen by the Cold War, the Korean War and finally and most extensively by Vietnam. As in many other technological fields, the private corporations who had received this largesse wished to reap the benefit of their technological advance in the civilian as well as the military market, if only as a hedge against reduced defence expenditure.

In order to widen the market for a tool of limited value, portable video was promoted in the following terms: 'Decentralization, flexibility, immediacy of playback, global transmission pathways, input to two of the senses . . . democratization of technology and flowering of variety, etc.' A host of misconceptions were allowed to cluster around the term video: those who perhaps should have known better on the radical, libertarian, utopian Left swallowed the bait and a far-from-innocent technology became the focus of widespread fantasizing and wish-fulfilment. In the United States, where the notion of technological fix was more deeply embedded in the culture, this may have been excusable. In Europe it was and remains mere naiveté, naiveté closely associated with the fashionable adoption of the surface trappings of American style, the Coca-Cola T-shirts, etc.

The two major misconceptions link video, which is merely an electronic recording system for sound and pictures, with broadcast television on the one hand and with sociocultural animation on the other, with neither of which activities it has any necessary connection.

Let me look first at the equation between video and broadcast television. The argument of those who propound this version of video myth runs somewhat as follows: television is now the major means of mass communication, what Ed Berman of Inter-Action has described as 'the basic mass folk-cult form of this technological age'; the development of cheap and easy-to-use portable video equipment gives the people at large access to the means of production of television and is thus a powerful force for democratic participation in television and, by extension, through television for the democratization of society at large.

This position is based upon a number of fallacies. Network television is *not* primarily dependent upon the technology of electronic recording. It can and for a lot of the time does operate very well with film as its recording medium. Moreover, network television is not primarily either a medium in that technological sense or even a production activity. It is a distributive activity, whose forms and socioeconomic power rest upon its control of broadcasting frequencies. This control in its turn rests upon both State powers and access to large-scale economic resources. The means of production of this 'basic mass folk-art' are frequencies and money, not videotape of whatever gauge. Even if in the relatively distant future the distribution method shifts from over-air broadcasting to cable, access to that network will be similarly controlled but with the key controlling factor shifting in turn from State control of frequencies to control of economic resources, whether public or private. Access, therefore, to portable video technology in no way alters this situation, any more than access to pen, paper or typewriter has led to a more participatory or democratically controlled press. Moreover the illusion that playing around with portapaks is part of the fight for a more democratically controlled mass media system actually inhibits consideration of how such control might be achieved.

The second fallacy underlying the video-as-alternative-TV slogan is the assumption that access to a recording technology also gives one access to a mode of communication. Whether one chooses to use ½-inch portable video, Super 8 film, tape/slide, cartoon, wall-posters or whatever, the use of these modes to communicate about something to somebody takes time, and time is a scarce economic resource. All the experiments in the use of portable video with non-professionals seem to reinforce this view. The work of Challenge for Change, for instance, was dependent upon highly skilled and highly paid full-time 'animateurs' and there is no evidence that without such skilled, expensive full-time intervention such non-professional video work can either start or be sustained. I believe average citizens to be healthily realistic about this. They live in societies with a highly developed division of labour, and provided they will the ends, they are happy that a specialist should provide the means. Everyone is not, does not want to be and indeed should not be a skilled film-maker, TV producer, or, indeed, animateur. Most people have better things to do.

It is claimed that the aim of encouraging the non-professional use of portable video is 'de-mystification of the media'. The aim is indeed laudable, but is it fulfilled? As a mode of communication portable video is extremely inefficient. Its low definition makes it positively painful viewing and listening, even in highly skilled hands. It is extremely difficult to edit and those technological means being devised to improve editing capability immediately cancel its supposed advantages, that is cheapness and ease of access; the necessary equipment is expensive, difficult to operate and maintain, thus requiring centralized, professionally staffed facilities. Moreover, non-professional users will be constantly comparing their results against the professional models and when they fail to match the model, they exhibit reinforced alienation from the means of TV production. Far from de-mystifying the media, nothing so rapidly teaches respect for professional media skills and output as the average person's contact with portable video.

The hope is held out that, operating outside professional constraints and the socializing effects of broadcasting institutions, amateurs will come up with new forms with which to revitalize mainstream TV. But as an evaluator points out of the Australian Open Access scheme,

It is highly unlikely that anyone in the Access movement is going to develop any new and innovative forms of communication. After nearly a year of experience the Access Directors and users still have not gone beyond elementary stages in evolving any style or techniques. When presented with the idea of using an interview as voice-over, they seize on it as being a new original idea. The point I am trying to make, is that these people do not even watch television analytically. They do not even learn themselves. They are totally unaware of – jump cuts, cut-aways, reverse angles, picture framing, sync question in interviews, voice-over, etc., etc. It is not that they reject these filmic devices . . . they are unaware of them.

When faced with this line of criticism the mythologists of video fall back upon 'process' rather than 'product', upon the alternative paradigm which links video to community development and social work rather than to broadcasting and communication.

Now it is true that portable video's one advantage over other inherently more efficient modes of communication such as Super 8 and tape/slide (let alone print) is its instant replay capability. Of course, it should be noted that the equipment needed to replay to more than one person, via monitors, cuts down the portability of the equipment. The equipment is heavy and needs delicate handling so that a vehicle is essential for satisfying use. In practice the equipment is mobile rather than portable. However, the instant replay capability is of unique value in a restricted number of situations, where high-definition sound and vision is not required, such as skill-training and observational situations: how to kick a football, the observation of classroom practice in teacher training, and so forth.

But it is quite wrong to build upon this limited advantage a whole ideology of 'process' and of video's contribution to community development. I would not deny that a skilled animateur can use video, if it is readily available, as one among a range of means. But there is no evidence that video has played any essential part in those experiments in social animation that have been documented. The great advantage of the 'process' defence of video from the point of view of its advocates is that it cannot be tested. But what evidence there is seems to show that 'video' is in no way superior to other communication forms such as drama, community newspapers, radio, etc., and is in general more expensive and less readily available.

The linkage made between video and animation does lead me to some conclusions about the use of video in film and television schools. Ironically, portable video which was supposed spontaneously to demystify the techniques of audiovisual communication has itself become one of the most powerful of mystificatory instruments. It should then be a prime aim of schools in the present climate to demystify 'video'. Indeed they should resolutely refuse to talk about 'video', referring only to videotape as one form among several of recording and replaying audiovisual images. Once this has been done, once 'video' has been put in its place among a spectrum of communication devices, the role of these devices within the broader social context must be rigorously examined. Thus the demystification of 'video' can lead, at the same time, to the demystification of film. By that I do not mean the rejection of technique, far less the propagation of some notion of spontaneous creativity. But most students of film and television do need their attention directed away from the enclosed world of image creation and manipulation and towards social situations and the various modes of intervention which audiovisual modes of communication can make in those situations. It is, unfortunately, widely observable among students of film and TV that they are attracted to the media not by a desire to explore the world, but by a desire to hide from it by using the camera as a shield. Such students could certainly benefit from more training in modes of social investigation and reportage with the minimum of opportunity for concealment behind a barrier of technology. The questions that need stressing in such schools are not so much how to obtain a series of images, important as that remains, but what content and meaning those images will have. What film and TV schools must inculcate is precisely the hardest lesson for them to teach, namely the limited usefulness of film and TV. It is the absence of such humility that makes the propagandists and mythologizers of video so dangerous.

If it is the purpose of a school to train future professional practitioners in TV, it is important not to foster the illusion that portable video can be used to simulate professional conditions. In general, in network TV the work students do on portable video would in fact be done on film. While it is true that miniaturization has now led to the utilization by broadcast TV of electronic news-gathering equipment, we should be clear about how that equipment is used. It is used like a film camera, but one which, by cutting out the processing stage, accelerates the provision of pictures. Thus its usage is part of the ideology and professional practice of hot news, where because minutes are regarded as important, they are paid for highly. The ideology underlying this obsession with speed and immediacy is itself extremely dubious and should not, in my view, be over-emphasized with students, but more importantly its satisfaction depends upon highly sophisticated editing facilities as support, facilities a student is unlikely to have or even need. So news-gathering techniques can almost certainly be better simulated on film.

It is worth adding that the other professional use of such portable equipment is as a portable outside broadcast unit. That is to say what is exploited is the technological capacity to feed live on to air. But utilization of this facility obviously depends upon access to a broadcasting network.

Given the extremely limited usefulness of portable video, why has it become the focus for such dangerous and persistent myth? The reason, I think, is that powerful economic and ideological forces stand to gain from the propagation of these myths. As I pointed out at the start, community action, public education and 'every citizen his own TV producer' all made good advertising slogans to assist the unloading of portable video equipment on the civilian market. These same interests, having saturated this market and in the face of evidence of the limited usefulness and technical fragility of their equipment, instead of developing cheaper, tougher and more reliable equipment, are playing the planned obsolescence game. Moreover, demand in the market is not from community activists or video freaks, but from institutional users whether public or private. Thus the next generation of video equipment is being up-dated to ¾-inch and colour capability, a system whose increased sophistication and cost can only be fully realized with sophisticated and expensive facilities. In order to widen the market for this new equipment, the fashionable trend now being pushed is video art which, of course, requires colour capability and sophisticated equipment for its effects. Even with this equipment the video art so far created appears trivial in the extreme. But as disillusionment with community video spreads, untestable claims for video art appear to open the door to State sources of art-funding as a source of investment in this new generation of technological toys.

The claim for community video still, however, retains a lingering and dangerous propaganda force in the field of cable television. The major economic interests behind the manufacturer of electronic hardware are also involved in a concerted, long-term push to develop cable as a means of breaking the public control of broadcasting. The aim is to gain access to certain specialized and profitable segments of the audience to the detriment of that European tradition whereby broadcasting has a duty to serve the whole community. But in order to achieve their end it is necessary to sell cable as a vital contribution to community development; as 'your local broadcasting' as opposed to 'their national broadcasting'. To this end portable video is offered as the production tool by means of which the local community can create its own television. The case against this is fully and convincingly argued in a Council of Europe paper, 'New media and socio-cultural community development'. As it shows, not only because of the inadequacies of portable video as a production tool, but more importantly for systematic economic reasons, cable experience in the USA, Canada and Britain points to the conclusion that if you want to increase the contribution of TV to local community development the cheapest and most effective way of doing it is by limited expansion of over-air broadcasting using existing facilities and available frequencies and under public control. (They also argue, correctly in my view, that an obsession with video can lead to the unjustified neglect of radio.) However, the function of the video myths in this debate has been to persuade radical and libertarian groups at both local and national level, groups who would otherwise have been opposed to the development of these new forms of private economic control over communication, to support, naively and unwittingly, the plans of these major economic interests.

In Europe the economic depression gave time to expose the myth of video, to subject any plans for the expansion of cable distribution to the rigorous social, political and economic critique they require and to realize that we should not believe that we can hand over the solution of deep-seated political problems to the engineers and marketing men of Sony, Philips, RCS, Telefunken and all.

5

Pierre Bourdieu and the Sociology of Culture: An Introduction

The influence of Pierre Bourdieu upon Anglo-Saxon thought and research has been to date extremely fragmentary, restricted to the discipline of anthropology and to the subdiscipline of the sociology of education. These influences are marked by the publication in English of *Outline of a Theory of Practice* and *Reproduction*, respectively.

Other aspects, however, of what has been described as a theoretical system that may be the most elegant and comprehensive since Talcott Parsons's have been largely ignored. This is especially true of the work in the history and sociology of culture carried out by Bourdieu and his colleagues at the Centre de Sociologie Européenne in Paris and published in that Centre's journal *Actes de la Recherche en Science Sociale*. Neglect of this aspect of Bourdieu's work is not only damaging in its own right within cultural studies, but this fragmentary and partial absorption of what is a rich and unified body of theory and related empirical work across a range of fields from the ethnography of Algeria to art, science, religion, language, political science and education to the epistemology and methodology of the social sciences in general can lead to a danger of seriously misreading the theory. A notable example of this danger can be found in the recent attempt by Halsey and his colleagues to refute Bourdieu's theory of cultural capital (Halsey *et al.*, 1980).

Thus this introductory article takes the opportunity offered by the recent appearance in France of *La Distinction*, a book that sums up work, spanning over a decade and a half, in the sociology of French culture, to present a necessarily sketchy outline of the structure of Bourdieu's thought. Such an outline is intended to indicate what in particular Bourdieu's work has to offer the field of British media and cultural studies. For as his own theory would predict, the entry of this particular symbolic production into a different field from that in which it was produced will necessarily give it a specifically different function.

The development of British media and cultural studies over the past decade or so has been characterized by two successive stages of

---

This chapter was written jointly with Raymond Williams.

development, stages that Bourdieu's own theory helps us to explain. The first saw the rise out of literary studies of a culturalist Marxism in opposition to both the subjectivism of Leavisite literary criticism and to that empirical, ahistorical sociology of mass communication and popular culture whose intellectual and ideological roots lay in American sociology. The early work of the Birmingham Centre for Contemporary Cultural Studies marks that development. The second stage saw the development (and here the work of *Screen* is exemplary) under the influence first of Althusser and then of Lacan of a theoreticist Marxism which directed consideration of the problem of ideology away from economic and class determinants, seen as vulgarly economistic or sociologistic, and towards the 'text' as the privileged site for a relatively autonomous signifying practice and for the deciphering by means of symptomatic readings of the ideological effectivity of those practices. More recently this Althusserian current has been challenged by those reasserting from within an older Marxist tradition the value of empirical work in both sociology and history as against theoreticism and the need to restress the social efficacy and explanatory power of economic and class determinants.[1]

The potential value of Bourdieu's work at this moment within British media and cultural studies is that, in a movement of critique in the classic Marxist sense, he confronts and dialectically supersedes these partial and opposed positions. Thus he develops a theory of ideology (or rather of symbolic power since in general he reserves the term ideology for more explicit and coherent bodies of thought) based upon both concrete historical research and upon the use of the classical techniques of empirical sociology such as the statistical analysis of survey data. At the same time he develops his critique of theoreticism, in particular structuralist Marxism and its associated formalist tendencies, by specifying with accompanying empirical evidence the historical roots and economic and class determinants of the relative autonomy of intellectual practice, a relative autonomy that is in its turn the condition for the efficacy of intellectual practice as, in general, the practice of ideological domination.

'Ideologies owe their structure and their most specific functions to the social conditions of their production and circulation i.e. to the functions they fulfil, first for the specialists competing for the monopoly of the competences in question (religious, artistic, etc.) and secondarily and incidentally for the non-specialists. When we insist that ideologies are always *doubly determined*, that they owe their most specific characteristics not only to the interests of the classes and class fractions which they express (the sociodicy function) but also to the specific interests of those who produce them and to the specific logic of the field of production (usually transfigured into the ideology of 'creation' and the 'creator'), we obtain the means of escaping crude reduction of ideological products to the interests of the classes they serve (a short-circuit effect common in 'Marxist' critique), without falling into the idealist illusion of treating ideological productions as self-sufficient and self-generating totalities amenable to pure, purely internal analysis (semiology)' (Bourdieu, 1977b).

The work of which *La Distinction* is a summation is thus a frontal assault upon all essentialist theories of cultural appropriation (taste) and cultural production (creativity), upon all notions of absolute, universal cultural values and especially upon the intelligentsia and the ideologies of intellectual and cultural autonomy from economic and political determinants which that intelligentsia has constructed in defence of its material and symbolic interests as 'the dominated fraction of the dominant class'.

It can be argued that the central, indeed defining, problem of historical materialism is that of reproduction. This is a problem at both a material and symbolic level. That is to say it involves explaining not only how in social formations characterized by spatial extension and division of labour the actions of human agents are coordinated so as to ensure the intergenerational reproduction of the material conditions of existence (the problem of the mode of production) but also how the set of unequal class relations produced by that coordination is itself legitimized such that reproduction takes place relatively free from social conflict (the problem of the mode of domination). This of course also implies its converse, namely the problem of specifying the conditions under which reproduction does not take place leading to the more or less rapid transformation of the social formation (the problem of crisis and revolution).

It is to this general problem that Bourdieu's Theory of Practice is addressed. While Bourdieu has concentrated his attention upon the mode of domination, upon what he calls the exercise of Symbolic Power, his theory is cast in resolutely materialist terms and it is not just the terms borrowed from economics such as capital, profit, market and investment, which he uses to describe and analyse cultural practice, that link his theory to a properly economic analysis in the narrow sense of that term: the mode of production of material life.

The second important link between Bourdieu's work and the central tradition of historical materialism is that it is cast in the form of a 'critique' in the classical sense. One must not make the mistake of appropriating Bourdieu's theoretical and empirical analysis of symbolic power to some marginal subdiscipline such as cultural studies or the sociology of culture and knowledge. This analysis lies at the very heart of his wider general theory, just as theories of fetishization and ideology do in Marx's work, because it provides the conditions of its own potential scientificity. Bourdieu sees sociology as the science of the social conditions determining human practices. Thus the sociology of symbolic power is the science of the social conditions determining intellectual practice, conditions that are always concretely and specifically historical and the exposure of which are, in the movement of critique, the conditions for achieving an always partial because always socially conditioned escape from ideology into scientific practice and in that movement revealing the historically defined limits of available truth. This is, further, always a political act because it is the misrecognition of these conditions and limits that is the condition for the exercise of symbolic power to reinforce the tendency to reproduce the existing structure of class relations (Bourdieu, 1975a, 1980). 'The theory of knowledge is a dimension of political theory because the specifically symbolic power to impose the principles of the construction of reality – in particular, social reality – is a major dimension of political power' (Bourdieu 1977a: 166).

Bourdieu describes clearly in the preface to *Distinction* how his own thought has grown out of and in reaction to those successively dominant influences in French thought, Sartre and Levi-Strauss. (In particular he conducts a continual, ambiguous dance of intellectual repulsion and attraction with Sartre. Hence his choice of Flaubert as an exemplary case in his study of French cultural production.)

> It is by no means easy to recall the social effects produced in the French intellectual field by the work of Claude Levi-Strauss and the concrete mediations through which a new conception of intellectual activity imposed itself upon a whole generation, a conception which was opposed in an entirely dialectical fashion to that figure of the 'total' intellectual, decisively turned towards the political, of which Jean Paul Sartre was the incarnation. This exemplary confrontation undoubtedly contributed not a little to encouraging in many of those who were at that time turning to the social sciences, an ambition to reconcile theoretical and practical aims, scientific and ethical or political vocations, which are so often split, to fulfil their task as researchers, a sort of militant craft, as far from pure science as it is from the prophetic, in a humbler and more responsible way. (1980: 7–8)

Within Bourdieu's theoretical discourse the terms subjectivism and objectivism point to these two poles of post-war French intellectual life. His work in sociology has developed as a specific critique of these two schools of thought which he sees as two successive dialectical moments in the development of a truly scientific theory of practice which in its turn is the condition for an escape from the unconscious cycle of reproduction. Subjectivism, or as he calls it, 'the phenomenal form of knowledge' (including such tendencies as social psychology, ethnomethodology as well as existentialism and phenomenology) focuses upon the individual actor and upon the experiential reality of social action. It is, according to Bourdieu, a characteristic tendency of sociology which studies its own society and within which the observer is himself or herself also a participant.

Objectivism on the other hand, by which Bourdieu refers to all types of structuralism and functionalism, but especially to Levi-Strauss and Althusser, goes beyond the immediate experience of the individual actor to identify the 'social facts', the observable regularities of social action, but in so doing has a tendency to fetishize the structures, making the agents mere performers of preordained scores or bearers of the structure. This Bourdieu sees as a tendency to which anthropologists are especially prone as observers of societies of which they are not a part. While subjectivism cannot recognize the social determinants of human action, the objectivists have a tendency to succumb to that blindness to which intellectuals are particularly prone, indeed it is the ideology specific to wielders of symbolic power, namely the failure to recognize in the idealization of the structure and its logic an expression of their failure to recognize the social conditions of their own practice by failing to recognize the socially and historically specific conditions determining all human practice.

Inextricably intertwined in Bourdieu's work are the discourses of sociology and history. In developing his Theory of Practice or 'science of the economy of human practices', he sets himself the task of overcoming the opposition between subjectivism and objectivism by explaining the relationship between on the one hand the observed regularities of social action, the structure, and on the other the experiential reality of free, purposeful, reasoning human actors. In addition, his theory requires that any solution to this sociological problem must at the same time provide a properly historical explanation by specifying the social conditions under which the structure will be reproduced or conversely will be more or less rapidly transformed. Nor are these seen as two separate problems. One of Bourdieu's main criticisms of traditional sociology, whether subjectivist or objectivist, is what he calls its 'Genesis Amnesia' (1977a: 79). As Keynes in economics, so Bourdieu is concerned to stress that any satisfactory explanation of human action must take full account of the fact that all human action, unlike its reconstruction in science, takes place irreversibly in time (1977a: 5–6). Thus for Bourdieu all human actors are involved in situations of which the outcome is uncertain because their strategies are opposed by the strategies of other actors. The problem therefore is to specify the mechanism by which unbeknownst to the actors (if they knew they would alter their strategy to take account of this knowledge) these strategies of improvisation are objectively coordinated (1977a: 1–30).

The regulating mechanism Bourdieu proposes is the habitus (1977a: 72–95). This he describes as

> the strategy-generating principle enabling agents to cope with unforeseen and ever-changing situations . . . a system of lasting, transposable dispositions which, integrating past experiences, functions at every moment as a matrix of perceptions, apperceptions and actions and makes possible the achievement of infinitely diversified tasks, thanks to the analogical transfer of schemes permitting the solution of similarly shaped problems.

The habitus is not just a random series of dispositions but operates according to a relatively coherent logic, what Bourdieu calls the logic of practice.

This logic is shaped primarily in early childhood within the family by the internalization of a given set of determinate objective conditions both directly material and material as mediated through the habitus and thus the practices of surrounding adults (especially the parents). While later experience will alter the structure of the habitus's logic of practice, these alterations from school or work will be appropriated according to the logic of the existing habitus.[2]

Since it must be operated unconsciously and since it cannot be explicitly inculcated, this logic of practice must be both a reductive logic in the sense of working with simple categorical distinctions, and also flexible enough to be applied as the structuring principle of practice across a wide range of situations. Thus it operates with such simple dichotomous distinctions as high/low, inside/outside, near/far, male/female, good/bad, black/white, rare/common, distinguished/vulgar, etc., principles of categorization that develop in the immediate environment of the young child but can be subsequently applied across a wide range of fields and situations as unconscious regulating principles (Bourdieu, 1977a: 96–158).

The habitus is a unified phenomenon. It produces an ethos that relates all the practices produced by a habitus to a unifying set of principles. The habitus is also by definition not an individual phenomenon. That is to say it is internalized and operationalized by individuals not to regulate solitary acts but *interaction*. Thus the habitus is a family, group and especially class phenomenon, a logic derived from a common set of material conditions of existence to regulate the practice of a set of individuals in common response to those conditions. Indeed Bourdieu's definition of class is based on the habitus (1977a: 81–7).

Thus individual practice as regulated by the logic of practice is always a structural variant of group and especially class practice. However since the habitus regulates practice according to what Bourdieu calls a probabilistic logic – practice in a given situation is conditioned by expectation of the outcome – practice is also determined by trajectory. By this Bourdieu refers to upward or downward social mobility of either the family, the class fraction or the class, in a hierarchy of determinations from class to family. Upward mobility will give an optimistic view of possible outcomes and downward mobility a pessimistic view, each of which will determine a different set of practical orientations towards the various fields of social struggle. Bourdieu's classic example of the effect of expectations on practice is that of working-class attitudes to involvement in formal education. The point about these expectations is that like other aspects of the logic of practice they reflect not just random individual reactions to the social environment but on the contrary are realistic assessments, in terms of the habitus, of the objective probabilities offered by a given state of the social field to an actor in a given class position (Bourdieu 1974, 1980: ch. 2).

So when Bourdieu turns to the specific field of cultural consumption, or rather appropriation, the regularities his survey data reveal in taste patterns across a wide range of fields from food, clothing, interior decor and make-up to sport and popular and high art serve as markers of the habitus of classes and class fractions. What Bourdieu is concerned to reveal is not a particular pattern of consumption or appropriation, since in a different state of the field other markers could be used for the same relational positions, but the logic which explains this particular relationship between a range of cultural goods and practices and the operation of class habitus. Bourdieu's analyses of the concrete specificities of contemporary French cultural practice are thus part of his wider theory of symbolic power, its empirical validation and refinement, as well as a political intervention in symbolic class struggle.

> Art is the site par excellence of the denial of the social world. But the same unconscious intention of denial is the underlying principle of a number of discourses whose overt purpose is to talk of the social world and which as a consequence can be written and read with a double meaning. (How many philosophers, sociologists, philologists came to philosophy, sociology or philology as places which because they are not properly fitted into social space allow one to escape definition? All those in effect utopians who do not wish to know where they are, are not the best placed to know about the social space in which they are placed. Would we have otherwise so many readings and 'lectores', materialists without material, thoughts without instruments of thought, thus without an object, and so few observations and as a consequence 'auctores'). We cannot advance and expand the science of the social world unless we force a turn of the tide by neutralizing this neutralization and by denying denial in all its forms of which the denial of reality inherent in the exaggerated radicalism of certain revolutionary discourses is by no means the least significant. Against a discourse that is neither true nor false, neither verifiable nor falsifiable, neither theoretical nor empirical which like Racine speaks not of cows but of lowing, cannot speak of Daz or of the singlets of the working class but only of mode of production and of proletariat or of the rôles and attitudes of the 'lower middle class', it is not enough to criticize it is necessary to show, objects and even people, to touch things with one's fingers – which does not mean pointing a finger at them – and to make people who are used to speaking what they think they think and so no longer think about what they say to make such people enter a popular bistro or a rugby ground, a golf course or a private club. (Bourdieu, 1980: 596–7)

Bourdieu, in the Durkheimian tradition, sees symbolic systems, as such, as arbitrary, undetermined taxonomies, structuring structures in the sense that they do not reflect or represent a reality, but themselves structure that reality. Moreover, as in the Saussurean model of language, such systems are based upon 'difference' or 'distinction'. However he criticizes the idealism of the Durkheimian/Saussurean tradition by stressing that these systems, although arbitrary in themselves, are not arbitrary in their social function. That function is to represent in a misrecognized form the structure of class relations. The symbolic systems at once represent class relations and in the same movement disguise that representation because their logic is that of 'distinction'. In English as in French the double meaning of that word, both a categorical and a social term, precisely mirrors the function of symbolic power.

Thus symbolic systems serve to reinforce class relations as internalized in the habitus since in the internalizing movement of appropriation their specific logic confirms the general logic of class-determined practice. The internalization of the specific logic of symbolic systems or rather, since it is unified, *the* symbolic system, confirms a hierarchically organized range of distinctions such as rare/common, distinguished/vulgar, disinterested/interested, freedom from necessity/necessity, etc.

For Bourdieu all societies are characterized by a struggle between groups and/or classes and class fractions to maximize their interests in order to ensure their reproduction. The social formation is seen as a hierarchically organized series of fields within which human agents are engaged in struggles to maximize their control over the social resources specific to that field – the intellectual field, the educational field, the economic field – within which the position of a social agent is determined by the totality of the lines of force in that field. The fields are hierarchically organized in a structure determined by class struggle over the production and distribution of material resources. Each subordinate field hence reproduces within its own structural logic, the logic of the field of class struggle.

> the field which cannot be reduced to a single aggregate of isolated agents or to the sum of elements merely juxtaposed is, like a magnetic field, made up of a system of power lines. In other words the constituting agents or system of agents may be described as so many forces which, by their existence, opposition or combination, determine its specific structure at a given moment of time. In return each of these is defined by its particular position within this field from which it derives positional properties which cannot be assimilated to intrinsic properties. (Bourdieu, 1971: 161)

Social groups and classes in each generation develop and deploy their strategies of struggle on the basis of a historically given level of material, social and cultural endowment which may be transformed into capital. Although the symbolic field is a field of class struggle and what is at stake is legitimizing or delegitimizing power, there is a tendency for the symbolic field to legitimize a given state of class relations by means of the mechanism of misrecognition by which symbolic systems represent in a 'euphemized', 'disinterested' form its balance of forces and hierarchical structure (Bourdieu, 1977a: 159–97, and 1980).

Bourdieu is also working with a model of historical development. He argues, starting from his anthropological field work with the Kabyle in Algeria, that in pre-industrial, social formations characterized by limited spatial extension, limited division of labour and simple reproduction, the material and the symbolic, the mode of production and the mode of domination, cannot be separated. In such societies, with a low level of material resources, symbolic power has a direct economic function and symbolic violence is the preferred mode for the exercise of power because overt differences in wealth could not be tolerated. Moreover, lacking the objectification of power in institutions such as a market or a church, and associated instruments of objectification such as writing, power relations have constantly to be reasserted in direct human interaction. The overt exercise of force would be too expensive in material resources to allow for simple reproduction. Such societies exist in a state of Doxa, where the symbolic system is both common to all and taken-for-granted because existing as an implicit logic of practice rather than as an explicit discourse (Bourdieu, 1977a: 171–83).

In the next stage of historical development, Bourdieu argues, economic development leads to the growth of an autonomous sphere related to the development of exchange relations and in the same movement breaks the thrall of the Doxa and creates a relatively autonomous symbolic sphere which, by making the symbolic system more explicit, creates class struggle in the symbolic sphere between orthodoxy and its necessary corollary heterodoxy. At the same time there is created both a specialized group of symbolic producers with an interest in securing a monopoly of the objectified instruments of symbolic struggle, especially written language, an interest that pits them against the dominant economic class in a struggle over what Bourdieu describes as 'the hierarchization of the principles of hierarchization'. At the same time this specialized group shares a mutual interest with the dominant economic class in maintaining the overall set of material class relations both because cultural capital must ultimately be transformable into economic capital and because the dominant economic class now require the services of the producers of symbolic goods in the imposition and maintenance of orthodoxy. Because of this mutual interest the symbolic system tends to reproduce the given state of class relations. However once heterodoxy has been created, both political consciousness and science become possible and class struggle and its relation to science can never be exorcised from the symbolic field.

However in a transitional stage, Bourdieu argues, the creation of a market economy and of competitive capitalism did lead to the more open exercise of material class power. This in its turn led to more overt revolutionary and reformist opposition such that the dominant class was forced progressively to shift back to the use of symbolic power as the preferred mode of domination.[3] It is with the specific modalities of this third contemporary phase and with its roots in the nineteenth century that Bourdieu is now principally concerned. Human agents enter the field of struggle that is the social formation with historically given endowments, either in an incorporated state within the habitus as dispositions and competences, or in an objectified state, as material goods. It is these endowments that Bourdieu refers to as capital, for the purposes of this exposition divided into *economic* and *cultural* capital. Each agent enters the struggle with the aim of reproducing the capital of his or her group and if possible augmenting it. To this end he or she pursues strategies of investment which involve choosing the subfields and the modes of intervention in those subfields likely to yield the highest profit on a given investment, one of the objects of struggle being the relative returns to an investment in a given field vis-à-vis investments in other fields (Bourdieu, 1977a: 171–97, 1975b, 1977d). As Bourdieu puts it, he treats 'all practices, including those purporting to be disinterested or gratuitous, and hence non-economic, as economic practices directed towards the maximizing of material or symbolic profit' (1977a: 183).

This general struggle is ultimately determined by economic struggle in the field of class relations because while there is convertibility between economic and cultural capital in both directions (at differing rates of exchange) it is the convertibility of cultural into economic capital that ultimately defines it as capital and determines the overall structure of the social field, because economic capital is more easily transferable from generation to generation and therefore is a more efficient reproductive mechanism. This is why the educational system plays such an important role within Bourdieu's theory, because the development of such a system, as a system of certification, created a market in cultural capital within which certificates acted as money. They did so both in terms of a common, abstract, socially guaranteed medium of exchange between cultural capitals and, crucially, between cultural capital and the labour market and its access to economic capital (Bourdieu, 1977a: 183–97).

Cultural practice involves appropriation rather than mere consumption. If one can use the analogy of food, the act of ingestion is merely the necessary condition for the process of digestion which enables the organism to extract those ingredients it requires for physical reproduction and reject the rest. In certain conditions digestion will not take place at all. Thus while it remains important that cultural stratification is in part determined directly by the unequal distribution of economic capital and thus of cultural goods (that is, the working class cannot afford picture collections, large personal libraries, frequent visits to the theatre and opera, etc.) in terms of the legitimation of cultural practice, the ways in which these objective class distinctions are internalized within the habitus as differing dispositions, differing attitudes towards culture and differing abilities to utilize cultural objects and practices are more important. This is why Bourdieu has been particularly concerned to analyse the class determinants of the use of and attitudes towards widely available cultural practices such as museums and photography.[4]

The cultural field serves as a marker and thus a reinforcer of class relations for two reasons. First because a field occupied by objects and practices with minimal use-value, is a field in which *par excellence* the struggle is governed by a pure logic of difference or distinction, a pure logic of positionality. Secondly, because the creation of art as a special social object and practice, defined by its difference and distance from everyday material reality and indeed its superiority to it, objectively depends upon the distance from economic necessity provided by the bourgeois possession of economic capital. Works of arts, Bourdieu argues, require for their appropriation first an aesthetic disposition, that is to say an internalized willingness to play the game of art, to see the world from a distance, to bracket off a range of objects and practices from the immediate urgency of the struggle for social reproduction. This disposition is the determinate expression in an incorporated form in the habitus of the conditions of existence of the dominant class, the bourgeoisie (1980: 11–96).

In addition, specific competences are required, that is to say a knowledge of the codes specific to a given art form, competences that are not innate but can only be acquired either through informal inculcation in the setting of the family or through formal inculcation in school. Bourdieu argues that distinct patterns of cultural consumption are associated with these different modes of acquisition of cultural competence. These modes of acquisition oppose one another culturally but also in a social hierarchy related to the age of the family's economic capital. The old bourgeoisie acquires its cultural competence in the family so that it appears to be second nature. Theirs is a natural gift for discrimination. The new bourgeoisie acquire their cultural competence through school and are exposed to all the cultural scorn and insecurity directed at the autodidact, an insecurity that leads them to stick closely to the hierarchies of cultural legitimacy while the children of the old bourgeoisie can express the assurance of their natural taste in a contempt for such hierarchies and by legitimizing new forms of cultural practice such as cinema and jazz.

One of the main ways in which the convertibility of economic and cultural capital is assured is via control over that scarce resource, time. This control takes two forms. First the ability to invest economically in educational time. It is this relation between economic and cultural capital that is reflected in differential class access to different levels of education and to the certification that accompanies it, which in its turn legitimates the stratification of cultural practice linked to achieved level of education (for instance newspaper readership). But secondly and more originally, Bourdieu argues that it has been characteristic of the development of cultural practice in the narrowly artistic sense to maximize the complexity of coding (expressed in common parlance as the level of 'difficulty') both textually and inter-textually (thus requiring a wider and wider range of cultural reference, art being increasingly about other works of art). This development has meant that art necessarily requires for its appropriation high levels of consumption time (for instance in order to see films from the point of view of *auteur* theory one has to see all the films by that *auteur*). Since cultural consumption time is differentially available between classes and between fractions of the dominant class, this development steadily reinforces class divisions while legitimizing these divisions by labelling those excluded from the cultural discourse as stupid, philistine, etc.

But the investment of consumption time is not an absolute governed simply by its availability. Since time is always a scarce resource the decision to invest time in a given mode of cultural appropriation will depend upon the relations of force within a given field which in their turn will determine the returns that can be expected from a given investment. Those expectations will, in their turn, as in all fields of practice, be determined by the habitus. Thus for instance whether a given agent chooses to cultivate literary, musical or artistic competences in general as opposed to sporting or technical competences will depend upon the market objectively open for the investment of his capital and the relative valuation within these markets of these competences. Whether someone chooses to acquire and mobilize in social intercourse knowledge of the field of football or of western European art, of train spotting or avant-garde cinema, competences between which it is crucial to restress no hierarchical valuations are being or can be made, will depend upon the cultural and economic endowments with which he or she enters the social field, the fields objectively and realistically open for investment given the position of class origin from which he or she starts, and (finally) the relative weight of various fields (Bourdieu, 1975a,b, 1980).

It may be possible to acquire rapidly and mobilize against weak opposition a competence in film criticism whereas if one entered the field of fine art scholarship with weak cultural capital one would be doomed to marginality and failure. In this context, for example, the recent much discussed differences between Britain and some of her industrial competitors in terms of the differential social and therefore economic profit resulting from investment by an individual and by a class in cultural rather than technical competences is very relevant (Bourdieu, 1980: 68–101).

Thus the logic of the cultural field operates in such a way as to create, reproduce and legitimate (reproduce because legitimate) a set of class relations structured around two great divides, those between the dominant and dominated classes and within the dominant class between the dominant and dominated fractions. The dominant class, roughly equivalent to what the Oxford Social Mobility study calls the service class (Halsey *et al.*, 1979), is composed of those possessing high amounts of economic and cultural capital and the dominated class those possessing exiguous amounts of both (Bourdieu sometimes refers to them as working-class (*classe ouvrière*) and sometimes as *les classes populaires* (i.e. including the peasantry as a distinct class). The primary distinction operated by the dominant culture and the cultural practices it legitimates is of culture as all that which is different from, distanced from the experiences and practices of the dominated class, from all that is 'common', 'vulgar', 'popular'. In response, at the deepest level of the class ethos the dominated class reject the dominant culture in a movement of pure negation. However in opposition they construct, at an implicit level, as what Bourdieu calls the aesthetic of the culture of necessity, an aesthetic that relegates form at the expense of subject and function, that refuses to judge works of art or cultural practices on their own terms but judges them according to the social and ethical values of the class ethos, that values participation and immediate (sensual) gratification at the expense of disinterested and distanced contemplation (1980: 11–96). Bourdieu sees his work as part of an essentially political effort to legitimize this implicit aesthetic against all current formalisms whether of the right or left, against both what he calls the racism of class which dismisses working-class taste as beyond redemption by culture and against a naive populism that tries to assimilate that taste to the norms of legitimate culture, seeing miners' banners as works of art. He is particularly severe upon the left 'deconstructionists' whose theories and practices he sees as the latest and most effective of the ideologies of those monopolizers of cultural capital, the dominated fraction of the dominant class, ideologies that always serve to reinforce through misrecognition the dominance of the dominant class (Bourdieu, 1980: 543–64).

> Brechtian 'distanciation' can be seen as the movement of withdrawal by which the intellectual affirms, at the very heart of popular art, his distance from popular art, a distance that renders popular art intellectually acceptable, that is to say acceptable to intellectuals and, more profoundly, his distance from the people, a distance that this bracketing of the people by intellectuals presupposes. (1980: 568)

The two fractions into which the dominant class is divided are defined in terms of the relative weight in their patrimony of economic and cultural capital. Bourdieu sees a historical development whereby the dominant class has divided into two specialized groups, the dominant one concerned with material reproduction in the sphere of production, the dominated concerned with the legitimation of material reproduction through the exercise of symbolic power. While for reasons already given the specialized producers of symbolic goods will ultimately always remain subordinate to economic capital, they nonetheless are involved in a struggle with the dominant fraction over the relative legitimacy and therefore value of cultural as opposed to economic capital. Thus intellectuals in the widest sense of that term will always struggle to maximize the autonomy of the cultural field and to raise the social value of the specific competences involved by constantly trying to raise the scarcity of those competences. It is for this reason that while intellectuals may mobilize wider concepts of political democracy or economic equality in their struggle against economic capital they will always resist as a body moves towards cultural democracy.

It is precisely by stressing their 'disinterestedness' in the sense of their distance from crude material values that they maximize their interest in terms of the value at which they can ultimately convert their cultural capital into economic capital or alternatively ensure the reproduction of their cultural capital, in particular through their control of the education system and, increasingly, of the state bureaucracy in general. For the problem that Bourdieu is concerned with is not merely that of establishing a determinate relationship between class and cultural appropriation in a given state of the field of cultural consumption or between cultural production and class in a given state of the field of cultural production. The problem is more difficult and complex than that. What his general theory of practice as well as his specific theory of symbolic power require him to explain is how the free, apparently autonomous practices of the agents involved in the two different fields so interact as not only to produce but to reproduce the class patterns of cultural practice, and by so doing, to reproduce the given set of class relations in general.

Bourdieu argues on the basis of detailed studies of the class origins, cultural practices and associated ideologies (that is critical theories) of French intellectuals in the nineteenth and twentieth centuries and of the corresponding consumption patterns among the dominant class as a whole that the struggle between the fractions takes the form of a struggle between intellectuals for dominance within their specific subfield, for example painting, literature, social science, the academic world, etc., and for the dominance of their subfield within the intellectual field as a whole. It is this constant struggle that explains sociologically and historically that process of constant renewal, or at least change, that the Russian Formalists identified as the dynamic principle of art itself. The notion of 'making new' (Bourdieu, 1975a, b).

Thus a new entrant, especially a new generation of potential symbolic producers, faces a field in which the dominant positions are already occupied. This hierarchy of dominance is ultimately determined by the economic market for symbolic goods provided by the dominant fraction and thus by the rate at which different forms of cultural capital can be transferred into economic capital. The field is thus arranged along two axes. One axis relates to the direct transfer of cultural capital into economic capital via an immediate transfer in the cultural market, that is by painting pictures for rich buyers, writing novels or plays which appeal to the dominant fraction, or by entering sub-disciplines which the dominant fraction values highly and to which it thus gives high salaries, research grants, consultancies, etc. (that is, medicine and the natural sciences rather than the social sciences or humanities; within medicine, heart surgery rather than geriatrics). However too obvious a success in the market, or what is worse, too obvious a desire for such success leads to cultural delegitimization because of the overall struggle between cultural and economic capital. Thus the other axis relates to the maximization of cultural capital which translates the principle which structures the economic class field, namely wealth and the distance from necessity that wealth allows and represents, into rarity and cultural purity. Along this axis the avant-garde is more highly valued than mainstream, so-called 'bourgeois' art, pure science than applied science, fine art than graphic art, until recently at least left-wing rather than right-wing politics and so on (Bourdieu, 1971, 1975a, b, 1980: 68–101).

Facing this specifically structured field, which presents a variety of investment possibilities, are a cohort of potential producers themselves structured according to the laws of the formation of the habitus by the same class relations that structure the field of symbolic production. Firstly entry to the field at all is structured on class lines by the range of dispositions resulting from the objective assessment of the likelihood of success from any given class starting point. Thus a working-class agent is simply less likely to see him or herself as a painter or novelist (or at least as a professional painter or novelist) than a member of the bourgeoisie because such a career requires a high investment of cultural capital which implies for a member of the working class a high investment of time in education to acquire the necessary competences. However since economic success also requires the ability to fit the disposition for cultural appropriation of the bourgeoisie (for instance, surgeons or conductors or successful novelists and playwrights require objectively bourgeois social attributes) a working-class entrant will be forced in the direction of attempting to maximize the return on acquired cultural capital, which is indeed the point of entry into the dominant class for members of the dominated class, by choosing to enter fields which maximize the possible return while minimizing the possible risks.

However the strategy of maximizing cultural capital is both economically risky and expensive since it requires in the early years of practice an ostentatious refusal of direct economic interest and is directed against those who are occupying the culturally most powerful positions within the symbolic field. Thus, Bourdieu argues, particularly in relation to Flaubert and the art-for-art's sake movement, that the strategy of maximizing cultural capital although it often takes on the lineaments of political radicalism, of opposition to the bourgeoisie, requires existing membership of the dominant fraction of the dominant class to be a viable strategy. He argues specifically against Sartre's psychological analysis of Flaubert's artistic development, contending that this cannot explain the properly sociological fact that all the leading practitioners and theorists of 'art for art's sake' came from the provincial bourgeoisie, thus disposing them to challenge the dominant cultural forms of the Parisian bourgeoisie, while at the same time they all had private means to sustain an uneconomic cultural strategy. He also argues that Flaubert's position as a younger son was typical, and that there is a consistent class strategy of using the symbolic field much as the church and the army were used by the aristocracy to ensure a comfortable, high status career for younger sons and daughters without dissipating the family's economic capital (Bourdieu, 1975b). As a new twist to this strategy he sees the growth of new media-related professions and marginal service industries such as restaurants, craft shops, health clinics, etc., as related to the need (created by the relative democratization of education) to make new jobs for members of the old bourgeoisie where inherited as opposed to acquired cultural capital can be put to the most profitable use (Bourdieu, 1980: 415).

Thus both direct economic pressures and the cultural investment required for successful competition for cultural dominance ensure a tendency for the class structure of the dominant class to reproduce itself and its control over symbolic production. This is because those entering the field will possess a habitus which either predisposes them to support the dominant ideology (for example, members of the dominant fraction directly entering dominant positions or upwardly mobile members of the petty bourgeoisie forced to invest their small amount of hard-earned cultural capital in the lower echelons of economically favoured positions ensuring a relatively risk-free but low return on their investment). On the other hand, what opposition there is, is transmuted into the terms of the practical logic of cultural struggle which values rarity and cultural distinction with its associated modes of cultural appropriation, requiring high levels of cultural competence and capital, and thus excluding objectively the dominated class from consumption while legitimizing class distinction as cultural distinction.

Bourdieu's work raises a number of questions for us. First and most obvious is the need, within the terms of the theory, for comparative work to analyse the similarities and differences inscribed in different histories of the strategies of domination and resistance employed by the dominant and dominated classes and between fractions of the dominant class in Britain as opposed to France.

Another research problem is the effect on the operation of symbolic power of the increased intervention of economic capital directly into the field of the production of symbolic goods via the so-called culture industries, and the ways this might affect the field of force in the struggle between the fractions of the dominant class, and this in a situation in which the economic interests of the dominant fraction directly threaten the cultural interests of the dominated fraction.

Then there is the question of Bourdieu's politics. Di Maggio described his position as that of a Durkheimian anthropologist rather than a Marxist revolutionary and the French Marxists, who are so often the target of his attacks, have in return accused him of a relativistic pessimism. If to be as objective as possible about the possibilities of a major and immediate transformation of the social formation of advanced capitalism is to be pessimistic, then Bourdieu is, rightly, pessimistic. However it has to be stated that unlike many who would criticize this position he is resolutely committed to a materialist theory of class struggle and of the position of symbolic struggle within that wider struggle. Furthermore, and especially in *La Distinction*, he exhibits a very rare attribute on the left, namely a positive and unpatronizing valuation of the cultural values and aspirations of the working class which at the same time never lapses into naive populism or workerism. Lastly, his theory, while focused on the problem of symbolic power, allows fully for the concrete analysis of the contradictions between the objective social conditions determined by the mode of production and the consciousness and practices of classes and class fractions, contradictions that might offer the concrete possibility of revolutionary mobilization and action. However, it has to be said that there seems (and this is very much a question of tone, nuance and attitude) to be a functionalist and determinist residue in Bourdieu's concept of reproduction which leads him to place less emphasis on the possibilities of real change and innovation than either his theory or his empirical research make necessary. In my view it is necessary to distinguish within the process of reproduction between 'replication' and 'reformation'. (Williams, 1980). Reformation points us towards the spaces that are opened up in conjunctural situations in which the dominant class is objectively weakened and which thus offer opportunities for real innovation in the social structure, for shifts in the structure of power in the field of class relations. These, while falling short of 'revolution' in the classical sense, are nonetheless of real and substantial historical importance and are objectively 'revolutionary' within a longer historical rhythm. For instance it seems that Bourdieu points to just such a potential for 'reformation' in his analysis of the contradictions produced by the current state of class relations in the field of education and employment in France. Here he argues that the dominant class, as part of the wider historical movement towards the use of symbolic power as the preferred mode of domination, has increasingly shifted from economic to cultural capital as its preferred mode of accumulation (for instance gaining privileged access to economic power via control of the higher reaches of the state and state-economic bureaucracy which in its turn is controlled by means of privileged access to the dominant institutions of higher education – the so-called *Grandes Ecoles*). This shift, because of the relative inefficiency of cultural capital for reproduction purposes unless it can be translated back into economic capital, presents the dominant class with a major problem. As a result of the increased 'democratization' of education in response to reformist pressures, pressures which had in part to be met in order to retain the legitimizing power of schooling as a reproduction mechanism, the working class's educational expectations have been raised and at the same time because of the necessary linkage between school and the job market its expectations of the better job associated with that attained educational level. These expectations are not being and cannot be met because in order to retain schooling as a operation of hierarchization through which they retain control of the new centres of economic power and thus legitimate that control, the dominant class are forced objectively to devalue educational qualifications, while at the same time the objective development in the field of material production is yielding to massive de-skilling and the proletarianization of sectors of traditional mental labour. This is a problem, some would argue, that is already calling forth a strategy of domination increasingly reliant on direct rather than symbolic violence. What is not clear is the extent to which Bourdieu himself would draw these conclusions from his own concrete analysis (Bourdieu, 1980: 145–85).

Finally, there is the epistemological problem of the social conditions of Bourdieu's own intellectual practice. This of course relates to the problem of social change, of 'reformation'. If Bourdieu's is a progressive political intervention, as he clearly believes, let us ask him whether the structure of the symbolic field according to his own theory dooms the intervention to recuperation and futility, or whether on the other hand there are conditions under which the logic proper to the symbolic field can produce contradictions at the symbolic level such that they no longer reproduce given class relations?

Notes

1 See for instance Williams, 1977; Thompson, 1978; Golding and Murdock, and Johnson in Barret *et al.* (eds), 1979; Garnham, 1979.
2 See Bourdieu, 1977a; 77–8. The primacy and relative inertia of early-childhood influence on the habitus leads to what Bourdieu calls the hysteresis effect and explains his concern with inter-generational as well as inter-class differences and struggles (1977d). In particular he uses it to explain the conservative and nostalgic tendencies in much progressive politics as well as its reactionary alternatives.
3 For this model of historical development see Bourdieu, 1977a: 183–9.
4 See Bourdieu, 1968, 1980: 301–21. For the relationship between the notion of cultural competence and the political role of opinion polls see Bourdieu 1979 and 1980: 436–42.

References

Barret, M., Corrigan, P., Kuhn, A., Wolff, J. (eds) (1979) *Ideology and Cultural Production*. London: Croom Helm.
Boltanski, L., Bourdieu, P., Castel, R. and Chamboredon, J. C. (1965) *Un Art Moyen: Essai sur les Usages Sociaux de la Photographie*. Paris: Editions de Minuit.
Bourdieu, P. (1968) 'Outline of a sociological theory of art perception', *International Journal of Social Science Research*, 20 (Winter): 589–612.
Bourdieu, P. (1971) 'Champs de pouvoir, champ intellectuel et habitus de class', *Scolies*, 1.
Bourdieu, P. (1974) 'The school as a conservative force: scholastic and natural inequalities', in J. Eggleston (ed.), *Contemporary Research in the Sociology of Education*. London: Methuen, pp. 32–46. (Also in Dale, R. *et al.* (eds), (1976) *Schooling and Capitalism*. London: Routledge, pp. 192–200.)
Bourdieu, P. (1975a) 'The specificity of the scientific field and the social conditions of the progress of reason', *Social Science Information*, 14 (Dec.): 19–47.
Bourdieu, P. (1975b) 'L'invention de la vie artistique', *Actes de la Recherche en Science Sociale (ARSS)*, 2 (Mar.).
Bourdieu, P. (1977a) *Outline of a Theory of Practice*. Trans. R. Nice. Cambridge: Cambridge University Press. (Original edn, 1972, *Esquisse d'une Théorie de la Pratique*. Geneva: Droz.)
Bourdieu, P. (1977b) 'Symbolic power', in D. Gleeson (ed.), *Identity and Structure*. Driffield: Nafferton Books, pp. 112–19. (Also in *Critique of Anthropology*, 4(13/14) 1979.)
Bourdieu, P. (1977c) *Reproduction in Education, Society and Culture* (with J.-C. Passeron). Trans. R. Nice. London: Sage.
Bourdieu, P. (1977d) 'La production de la croyance', *Actes de la Recherche en Science Sociales*, 13: 3–43.
Bourdieu, P. (1979) 'Public opinion does not exist', in A. Mattelart and S. Siegelaub (eds),

Communication and Class Struggle. International Mass Media Research Centre, vol. 1. Paris: Bagnolet.

Bourdieu, P. (1980) *Distinction*. Trans. R. Nice. Harvard, MA: Harvard University Press. (Original edn, 1979, *La Distinction*. Paris: Editions de Minuit.)

Bourdieu, P., Darbel, A. and Schapper, D. (1966) *L'Amour et l'Art: Les Musées d'Art Européens et leur Public*. Paris: Editions de Minuit.

Garnham, N. (1979) 'Subjectivity, ideology, class and historical materialism', *Screen*, 20(1).

Halsey, A. H., Heath, A. F. and Ridge, J. M. (1980) *Origins and Destinations*. 2 vols. Oxford: Clarendon Press.

Thompson., E. P. (1978) *The Poverty of Theory*. London: Merlin.

Williams, R. (1977) *Marxism and Literature*. London: Oxford University Press.

Williams, R. (1980) *Culture*. London: Fontana.

6

Politics and the Mass Media in the United Kingdom

The occasion of this essay was the appearance of *The Challenge of Election Broadcasting* (hereinafter cited as CEB) by Blumler, Gurevitch and Ives (1978). This was a report of an inquiry commissioned by nominees of the Conservative, Labour and Liberal Parties, the BBC and the IBA. This study merits close attention for a number of reasons, firstly because of the importance of its specific subject matter.

In the words of the authors, it 'raises for public discussion a number of fundamental issues about the role of television in British election campaigns'. There was a time when to be concerned with such issues was itself considered to be a sign that one was tarred with the empiricist and liberal-pluralist brush. But given the increased attention being given within historical materialism to Gramscian theories of hegemony and given the developments covered by the term Eurocommunism, it now seems that Marxist or Marxian mass media researchers can no longer afford to take such a dismissive attitude, whether they regard the mechanisms of bourgeois democracy as a repressive ideological and political mechanism or whether they regard them as important democratic gains won by popular political struggle and to be developed and extended rather than overthrown.

All students of the subject now agree that the role of TV, in what Anthony Smith (1978) has dubbed 'a maturing telocracy', is central to our political process. Was there too much coverage or too little? Did the coverage influence the result? Was there bias as between the political parties? In that debate the proposals for changing the modes of election broadcasting contained in CEB are likely to be influential, both because of the nature of its sponsorship and because of Dr Blumler's unique status in this field. Since in my view these recommendations for change are fundamentally misguided, I believe that there is a political duty to explain why with some care. And in order to do so it will be necessary to examine Dr Blumler's other recent work in this general field.

This work raises two general questions. One is methodological, namely the status of empirical investigation within the study of mass communication and the relation of that empirical investigation to what Blumler calls 'grand theory', a term referring in the context of current debates within British media studies to a range of Marxist or Marxist-influenced positions. The other question concerns the relationship between research and researchers on the one hand and communications policy on the other.

I do not raise these questions at random in connection with CEB, for they are explicitly foregrounded in the text itself:

> In assembling its results first priority was given to the production of this report, to be focused centrally on *policy* concerns. (p. 7, italics in original)

> We hoped to produce a report that would be enjoyable to read and could engage interest in its ideas. It was composed as a policy document for public action and not as a learned treatise. (p. 12)

> We have no wish to become known as the Don Quixotes of election broadcasting policy – as visionaries 'inspired by lofty and chivalrous but unrealisable ideals'. (p. 9)

These explicit policy aims are linked to the methodological question, because Blumler *et al.* put forward as one of their means of overcoming possible resistance to their proposals, the placing of their 'diagnosis within the context of a realistic analysis of recent political trends affecting the audience reception of election messages' (p. 12). That is to say they are involved not only in an ideological operation, namely the use of the prestige or the supposed scientificity of empirical research to gain acceptance for normative policy proposals, but they are also guilty in the report of a sneaking positivism in believing that their proposals in some way naturally flow from this empirical evidence. The use here of the word 'realistic' is revealing.

Dr Blumler has been consistent in condemning radical critics of the media for mere negativism, for failing to couple their criticisms with alternative concrete policy proposals. He has made this critique even when these critics, as in the case of *Bad News* (Glasgow University Media Group, 1976), use empirical methods. In general I share this position and applaud the resolutely practical and relevant tone of CEB. I support Blumler's desire to relate research to the actual hurly-burly of policy, against either those who would see their science as a value-free positivistic activity which merely accurately describes a world progressing independently beyond the confines of their ivory towers or, on the other hand, those Marxists who are so arrogantly secure within their self-justifying sociopolitical theories that the workings of the actual society in which they live is reduced to triviality by the march of history. It is important to stress this because I wish to argue that Blumler's own view of what policy research amounts to is narrowly circumscribed with potentially dangerous ideological and policy results and because I also wish to argue that the specific policies he advocates do not follow from his own empirical data. That is, I would wish to question the 'realism' of his analysis.

A critique of the Blumler position is important because it illuminates the nature of the dispute in which Blumler has been engaged with the 'grand theorists'. Blumler's most complete statement of his position appears in a course unit on *The Political Effects of the Mass Media* which he wrote for the Open University course 'Mass Communication and Society'. There he writes:

> Some sociologists of mass-communication are not all that enamoured of mass-media effects research; they have given the systematic attempt, empirically and quantitatively, to measure the impact on audience members' ideas of the flow of mass-communicated messages what can only be termed a 'bad name'. In fact, effects research is virtually treated in some quarters as the brothel of media studies: the 'madam' rather than the 'queen' of our science. The critics, then, have variously portrayed such research as arid and trivial in outcome: tarnished with the discredited promises of atomistic mass-society theory; obsessively preoccupied with issues of technique and method; wedded to naïve and atheoretical versions of positivism and empiricism; and (most damning indictment of all) as essentially supportive of the *status quo* . . . one reason for doubting the validity of more extreme lines of criticism arises from the very fact that political communication effects research is still being actively pursued today and is even enjoying a vigorous renaissance. Indeed it is difficult to see how this field could dispense entirely with some kind of effects research – unless, that is, its devotees really do want all their observations about the relationship between mass-media systems and social and political orders to remain in the realm of high-pitched polemic and high-flown (and, unsubstantiated) speculation. (Open University, 1977: 6)

It is tempting when reading CEB to respond that Blumler himself is involved in low-pitched polemic and low-flying and equally unsubstantiated speculation. What Blumler is engaged in is a dual enterprise. He is presenting political effects studies in general, and his work in particular, as a testing ground for the validity of the 'effects research' tradition. And he is at the same time claiming extra validity for his policy proposals, because they are based upon effects research. What I will attempt to show is that Blumler's own work is susceptible to the criticisms levelled against effects research in general and that the empirical evidence, when interpreted from a different theoretical position, leads to quite other policy conclusions to those arrived at by Blumler and his colleagues.

He argues that the 'methodological individualism' of effects research must be distinguished from 'social atomism':

> In media effects research, 'the main object of attention is the individual and his relationship to the mass media', but the adoption of such a form of investigation does not entail any particular view of how the individual is related to other members of society – and certainly not an atomistic one. (Open University, 1977: 6)

However, Blumler does in fact adopt an essentially atomistic political theory in which individual voters make political decisions issue by issue and he is led to this position by data which do indeed reflect a society in which people are being driven into a position of social atomism and into a politics that results from that atomism. This general line of thought starts with Blumler and McQuail in *TV in Politics* (1967), in which they argue on the basis of their audience research for a shift away from broadcasting as a platform for party rhetoric and more towards its use as a window through which the voter can get a true view of the political arena. This position was then further developed by Katz in his famous essay 'Platforms and windows', where he argued that 'Again and again, one is led to the conclusion that election campaigns are better designed to serve the political parties, particularly the dominant ones, than to serve society or the voter – if the liberal desiderata of optimizing rationality and participation are accepted' (Katz, 1972: 369–70).

While in CEB Katz's extreme anti-party, pro-broadcaster position is explicitly rejected, perhaps, as the authors half admit out of a pragmatic need to win party support for their proposals, there is little question that a consistent theme in the Blumler position is a negative valuation of the political party, and a corresponding positive valuation of the non-partisan individual voter who, in Katz's words, 'wants, in return for his investment of time, the feeling that he has fulfilled his duty as a citizen by orienting and updating himself to the political situation. He wants to be able to identify the candidates and the issues; he wants the issues clearly and interestingly explained; he wants to know where parties stand with respect to the issues and how these stands are likely to affect him' (Katz, 1972: 363).

Paralleling this positive vision of the rational individual voter, supposedly constructed from empirical research in the Uses and Gratifications tradition, is placed an equally consistent negative valuation of politicians and the political party.

> Realism dictates, and experience demonstrates, that at campaign time the top priority of the parties is to conquer power not to disseminate enlightenment. Left to their own devices, they may side-step awkward issues, fail to give an ordered picture of the issue agenda, slant facts and figures in their favour, declaim in high generalities, and try to deflect attention away from their own policies to their opponents' short-comings. (CEB, p. 68)

Since large-scale industrial societies have found no substitute for representation as the mechanism of democratic participation; since, that is to say, political action cannot be carried out by direct citizen participation and since also coherent political action in a world of interconnections cannot be carried out either on the basis of single issues and isolated yes/no decisions, any withdrawal of the political party as the organizing instrument requires the substitution of an alternative mechanism of representation. In the Katz/Blumler model this is to be found in public service broadcasting. As CEB puts it, 'Broadcasters should act as trustees of the voters' campaign information needs' (p. 68).

Blumler and Gurevitch explicitly contrast the broadcaster to the political party in a way which, within their liberal theory, clearly endorses the broadcaster's role as opposed to the politician's: 'The centrality of the service function in the behaviour of media professionals is reflected in the claim commonly made by them to be concerned primarily to serve the audience members' "right to know", as distinct from the primary concern of the politician to persuade them in the course of political and partisan goals' (Blumler and Gurevitch, 1977).

There is no inkling here that politicians and political parties exercise a representative function and that they are not primarily persuaders but spokesmen for and articulators of group or class interests, while broadcasters, as the empirical evidence shows, represent none but themselves. Although Blumler recognizes this problem, he ultimately endorses the Katz view of the broadcaster's role on the grounds that it is consonant with available evidence as to what voters want.

> But how should the attempt of the BBC current affairs producers to contribute to election broadcasting policy in 1966 be evaluated? This observer found it acceptable, for the overriding aim was to use television to achieve a more revealing campaign than the political parties were likely to provide through their unaided efforts. And that is consistent with a function which viewers themselves wish television to discharge in its coverage of an election campaign. (Blumler, 1970)

Before reviewing the general empirical evidence in this field, and Blumler's interpretation of this evidence, let us first examine the claim made above. It and similar claims in CEB are based upon work within a Uses and Gratifications framework carried out by Blumler and McQuail in the UK and McLeod and Becker in the USA. This research was concerned to find out not what effect political broadcasting had on viewers but, on the contrary, why viewers watched political broadcasting. Viewers' responses to this line of enquiry were then gathered into four audience role clusters: *the monitor, the spectator, the partisan and the liberal citizen* (for a review of this research, see Blumler, 1977). In brief, the monitor wants to see what politicians are, or are likely to be, up to. In Katz's words 'they want to know "what will happen" to them and their country' (Katz, 1972: 360). The spectator wants to watch a good fight, the partisan 'to use the information as ammunition in arguments with others' and the liberal citizen (a phase of significant valuation) wants help in making up his mind how to vote. The evidence showed that monitors and liberal citizens, that is to say those in search of neutral information, were in a clear majority and that partisans 'comprised a distinctive and possibly declining minority' (Blumler, 1977: 15). On the assumption that viewers are rational in these role choices, Blumler then consistently argues that broadcast political communication must be designed to appeal to this vast majority of monitors and liberal citizens who want information, a new version of 'giving the people what they want'.

The first question Blumler's evidence raises is what kind of rationality does this viewer-wish for what Blumler has dubbed 'surveillance' express? In my view it can best be explained as the rational response to perceived powerlessness. It is essentially defensive and protective and is closely allied to the increased disenchantment with politics reflected in the decline of voter turn-out and surveys of viewers' attitudes to political communication. As we shall see this measured viewer-response is a crucial symptom of the kind of coverage given to politics in particular and to views of the world in general by TV. That is to say it is a distant, strange and threatening world out there which one confronts as an isolated and powerless individual. It is, in fact, an expression of an internalized rational response to the reality of TV agenda setting. Blumler never asks why people use TV in this way. He accepts it as a *fait accompli*. But the failure to ask this question leads to an acceptance of the surface evidence as a validation of a process that then becomes self-justifying and self-reinforcing.

In answer to an even more central question, What is politics about?, one can reasonably claim that the responses of individual viewers as expressed to the Users and Gratification researchers are irrational, an expression precisely of false consciousness. In a revealing phrase Blumler describes politics as 'the competition-through-communication that is waged in a democratic pluralist society (Blumler, 1977: 18). But nowhere in his work is there any hint of what this competition might be about. This lack is most clearly expressed in his essay with Gurevitch, 'Linkages between mass media and politics', in which they enunciate a so-called systems approach to political communication research which is totally devoid of any political content. Given Blumler's career, with its long, close and honourable connection with the British Labour movement, this remains to me a surprising and inexplicable lacuna, perhaps related to the value-free biases of the effects research tradition. Be that as it may, if one undertakes work on political communication from the assumption that politics is a process concerned with the preservation or elimination of systematic and structured inequalities, in short, that it is about class conflict, one is then led to interpret Blumler's data as the perfectly explicable expression of a familiar ideological formation, namely that social atomism and its related 'possessive individualism', which is objectively against the class interests of those expressing it and which is also one of the principal methodological biases of which effects research has been accused. When we now come to examine other available evidence we will see the crucial role that TV appears to play in the development and maintenance of that very ideological formation, a formation that is undoubtedly there and that therefore is measured by Blumler's effects research.

In Blumler's presentation of the argument, not only in CEB but also in Appendix E of the Annan Report, it is very difficult to tell in a characteristically positivist operation, where presentation of the evidence ends and theoretical and normative interpretation comes into play. In his defence of empiricism and attack on 'grand theory' Blumler states:

> Although effects investigators are still committed to the task of finding out how people actually react to mass communication . . . such investigators now fully accept that (a) the media constitute but one factor in society among a host of other influential variables, (b) the exertion of their influence may depend upon the presence of other facilitating circumstances and (c) the extent and direction of media influence may vary across different groups and individuals.

They are not innocent of theory, though they do tend to assign it a more modest role than the rather ambitious task given it by more wide ranging thinkers. . . . In their eyes the accumulation of knowledge is more like a step-by-step venture than the attainment of some comprehensive illuminating weltanschauung all at once . . . secure gains are more likely to be won by working within the bounds of some carefully delineated territory. . . . It may even be suspected that those who protest so vociferously about the limitations of empiricism only manifest thereby their own determination to keep out of the way of awkward facts. (Open University, 1977: 6–8)

But, as I hope to demonstrate, Blumler is himself guilty, in his interpretation of the available data, of neglecting the wider context that he claims effects investigators now take into account; as a result he too neglects 'awkward facts'. This neglect stems precisely from a too-careful delineation of his territory and the granting of too modest a role to theory. Whether this neglect stems from intellectual conviction or from the tactical necessities of his version of policy research it is difficult to say. But the result is that in CEB he overlooks or suppresses interpretations that he shows elsewhere he knows exist and so ends up involved in a self-fulfilling prophecy of profound political significance. By positivistically interpreting his effects data, he may in fact be contributing to the creation of those very effects. That is to say that many of the voter characteristics upon which he calls as support for his position that the broadcasters should play a greater role in the electoral process and the political parties a lesser role, while no doubt flattering to the broadcasters who commission his research, may be reinforcing the very trends he is measuring.

Let us then look at the available evidence and how it can be interpreted. The earlier tradition of empirical political effects studies came to the conclusion that party loyalties stemmed from family and class, that they were relatively stable, that the mass media during election campaigns served to activate voters, i.e. it affected turn-out rather than attitudes and reinforced existing political loyalties through the phenomenon of selective perception. As Blumler himself puts it, 'a key lynch pin of this edifice of interpretation . . . concerned the role of party loyalty in mass electoral psychology' (Blumler, 1977: 3). The 'new look in political communication research' thus stems from the growing evidence across a range of established bourgeois democracies of electoral volatility. This volatility not only makes election campaigns more crucial, since there are more 'floating voters' to be won, but evidence also shows that in those election campaigns the influence of the media, especially television, is independently important. In the past, evidence showed that floating voters, because they also possessed low political motivation, were those least likely to be reached by political communication via the mass media, whereas evidence now shows that floating voters may also be high consumers of political communication, especially on TV. Indeed, TV seems to have played a key role in this, because 'large numbers of people are watching election broadcasts not because they are interested

in politics, but because they like viewing television' (Katz, 1972: 359). However there has also developed over recent elections, a clear trend of declining turn-out and a growing antipathy to all political communication and indeed to the politics about which that communication attempts to talk. (See Blumler (1977), CEB, and Open University (1977) for details of this evidence.)

Blumler's response to this evidence is not just to recognize it, but to give it normative endorsement, as we have seen. That is to say, since the evidence points to an increasingly non-partisan, issue-oriented public, and since the public says that, in general, it wishes to use television to gather political information and to monitor the political process, then policy proposals must aim to give them what they want and this will be good for democracy. Since party loyalty is on the wane, the role of the parties in political communication must be diminished and in their place must be put the broadcasters who, working with their inherited traditions of neutrality, impartiality and fairness, will hold the political ring, and make sure the issues are presented and clarified so that individual voters can reach a rational decision on the issues.

That this is not a necessary interpretation of the available data, even from within a shared liberal-pluralist perspective, can be seen if we turn to the work of Seymour-Ure, who advocates a diametrically opposed solution to the problem of election broadcasting, and one with the general purpose of which I agree. He argues that the decline of direct party access to TV should be massively reversed and that in order to balance any increased freedom for the broadcasters in their watchdog role, regular current affairs time throughout the year with matching resources should be handed over to the political parties (Seymour-Ure, 1974: chs 6, 7 and 8).

Seymour-Ure arrives at this diametrically opposed conclusions for three crucially important reasons: (a) he regards the political party and not the individual voter as central to the political system, (b) he also considers the relationship between broadcasting and newspapers and (c) because he approaches the problem historically. In brief, Seymour-Ure argues that historically there is a close and important relationship between political parties and the press; that what evidence there is shows both that parties of change have a greater need for what he calls a parallel press, i.e. a press with which the party has some degree of ideological convergence, and that in advanced industrial democracies left-wing parties have less than their fair share of press parallelism: that there is a tendency towards conflict politics where you find press parallelism and towards consensus politics where you don't: that there has been a steady decline in press partisanship in Britain ever since the so-called Northcliffe revolution, a shift in the nature of the press the consequences of which he describes as 'overwhelmingly conservative': that possibly with a cause and effect relationship the press and statutorily non-partisan broadcasting have converged in this respect. He foresees further convergence

and, so far as broadcasting is concerned, the symptoms of such a convergence are remarkably close to what Blumler actively advocates, namely 'broadcast programmes increasingly free of rules imposed from outside about party balance at election time: and an orientation in current affairs broadcasting that was similar to what has been called positive criticism in the press'. But his judgement on the effects of such a convergence are harsh:

> Such convergence could cause serious dislocation in the political system. It is debatable whether political parties can effectively sustain mass support without the opportunity for their leaders to project themselves and their policies as they themselves wish, and whether general elections can operate as an instrument of effective representation in the absence of well organised and coherent parties. (Seymour-Ure, 1974: 237)

This is part of the answer to a challenge that Blumler has made to the 'grand theorists'. After reviewing (Open University, 1977: 37–41) the evidence presented by Lang and Lang (1966), by Robinson (1976) and by Miller *et al*. (1976), that the domination of television has contributed to the citizens' general distrust of politics, Blumler asks:

> How do these conclusions contrast with the views of Murdoch and Golding that the mass media are essentially agents of legitimation, that is, forces that maintain 'the central assumptions and values of the ruling or core ideology, which in turn sustain the prevailing social and political order.' (Open University, 1977: 41)

Blumler assumes that the answer to his question is that the empirical evidence conflicts with this more Marxist view, when he goes on to answer himself:

> Perhaps this provides an illustration of the confrontation between 'grand theory' untested by effects research designs and empirical work, which strives so to operationalize speculative hypotheses that their validity can be independently checked against a set of relevant facts. (Open University, 1977: 41)

But Murdoch and Golding and those who think like them cannot so easily be driven from the field. In the first place, as Seymour-Ure shows, the effect of this delegitimation has a differential effect on rival political forces and parties. It is a delegitimation that acts precisely to reinforce consensus. It is the parties of change that are worst affected. Moreover, it can be plausibly hypothesized that this general distrust of politics stems, at least in part, from the way in which television sets, not only the content agenda, but also the form agenda, the way in which it approaches politics in general. It breaks politics down issue by issue rather than on a basis of coherent ideologies; it reaches people individually or in small groups in their homes rather than at work. The inherent ideology of non-partisanship then reinforces the professional anti-government ideology of media practitioners based upon notions of

the Fourth Estate. If then one looks at the growing evidence that it is the control of these practitioners over the long-term issue agenda which is politically crucial, it can be plausibly argued that TV in both its form and its content reinforces a general political theory or ideology that sees the State as separate from and inferior to civil society and so both reinforces the existing power structure of economic inequality in civil society and at the political level supports those parties or those elements within parties who favour less State intervention. And I think it is clear in contemporary British politics which side that favours.

It is within an analytical context of this sort that one needs to look at the tension between the Labour Party and the BBC. As both Grace Wyndham-Goldie (1977) from within, and Butler and King (1966) from without, together recognize the Labour Party looked upon party access to broadcasting as a means of counteracting the general bias against them in the press. As the evidence marshalled by Seymour-Ure shows, they were not wrong so to do. Indeed one of the key results of Blumler's own study of a group of Leeds first-time voters was to show the crucial effect of press partisanship upon voter turn-out. In that study it was the partisanship of those papers that supported Labour which helped to stop potential Conservative voters actually voting (Blumler and McLeod, 1974). But since that study was done the crucial partisanship change has been that of the *Sun*, which on Blumler's evidence should act as a potent motivator of abstention among potential working-class Labour voters. So not only were the Labour Party right, their need for this counterweight has grown stronger as their effective access to TV has declined. Where they were wrong, however, was in believing that public service broadcasting as at present structured could fulfil this function, for it is the very non-partisan nature of broadcasting that works against the Labour Party's necessary ideological commitment to social change. Blumler is himself honest and perceptive enough to recognize this, when he is not writing specifically for broadcaster consumption, as he avowedly is in CEB. Elsewhere he writes:

> Since broadcasting may not support individual parties, it is obliged to adhere to such non-partisan – perhaps even anti-partisan – standards as fairness, impartiality, neutrality and measured choice – at the expense, then, of such alternative values as commitment, consistent loyalty and a forthright readiness to take sides. Thus television may tend to put staunch partisans on the defensive and help to legitimate the less certain attitudes of those who feel that a conditional and wary commitment is the outlook most appropriate to a model citizen. (Blumler, 1977: 13)

Blumler's avoidance in CEB of his own 'awkward question' is symptomatic both of his general attitude to broadcasters and of the limitations of his version of policy research. He has for a long time largely endorsed the broadcasters' own view of their role, both out of a personal sympathy and because it chimes in with his liberal-pluralist political theory and with his resulting interpretation of the empirical evidence.

This is clear in his 1966 study of 'Producers' Attitudes towards Television Coverage of an Election Campaign', in Appendix E to the Annan Report, and even more clearly in CEB. But in the latter it is in part tactical and his adoption of it does, I think, well illustrate the dangers of attempting to narrow policy research to those areas of policy and those policy recommendations the broadcasters can accept. This is an issue of wide importance in the political struggle to make broadcasting more accountable. Blumler himself recommended, in his evidence to the Annan Commission, the setting up of a Broadcasting Centre to carry out independent research as part of the accountability structure of British Broadcasting. Annan rejected this and similar proposals on the extraordinary grounds that they were 'sceptical whether research which is not commissioned by those responsible for decision taking is likely to be of direct use in making policy decisions' (*Report of the Committee on the Future of Broadcasting*, 1977: para 6.25, p. 63).

There seems little doubt that the kind of policy research exemplified by CEB reinforces this entrenchment of broadcaster autonomy and of the persistence of closed government in our broadcasting system. This point relates to the criticism levelled at Katz's report on broadcasting research by Professor Halloran, among others (*Journal of Communication*, 1978). And it is perhaps not without significance that Blumler was the only British researcher to be favoured with a commission among those projects set up by the BBC following the publication of the Katz report. Perhaps the core of Blumler's position on this matter is expressed in his Annan Appendix, where having reviewed research evidence that, as he puts it, 'casts fundamental doubts on the viability of a philosophy that pins its faith on the development of a sense of responsibility among mass media executives and staff communicators themselves to ensure that higher expectations of public service are met', he then goes on to argue that 'the attitudes of television and radio journalists matter, . . . because no proposal for change could possibly succeed in the teeth of professional resistance' (Blumler, 1977: 22).

What I would wish to argue is that the Blumler strategy and the reading of the empirical evidence that stems from it is excessively concerned to avoid such resistance. This is particularly damaging in the policy context under discussion where, as we have seen, much of the evidence points precisely to broadcasters, or the present structure and behaviour of broadcasting institutions, as being a central part of the problem. Now of course neither Blumler or the broadcasters would deny this. But they define the problem, as a result of their position, in a way which leads Blumler in his role as policy researcher to ignore important evidence which, from other contexts, one knows he recognizes to be important.

Thus, in his Annan Appendix, he recognizes the need to see broadcasting in relation to the press, but fails, when advising the broadcasters, to pursue the logic of that recognition. Above all, he also recognizes the increasing importance within 'new look' political communication research of the 'cognitive approach', an approach which clearly leads to conclusions opposed to those advocated in CEB. In brief, this 'cognitive approach' has shifted the attention of effects researchers away from persuasion and attitude change and towards information perception. This new trend demonstrates not the opposition between empirical effects research and 'grand theory', but its increasing convergence for it is, within a different intellectual tradition, really just another version of the general study of ideology.

As Becker, McCombs and McLeod have pointed out, 'Most of the resources of newspapers and news-staffs of television and radio stations are devoted to information transmittal, not persuasion' (quoted in Blumler, 1977: 7). That is to say, the media help, by providing the informational building blocks, to structure views of the world, views towards which people may doubtless have a variety of attitudes and from which may stem a range of actions. Nonetheless, these structured views of the world, or ideologies, set limits upon the range of attitudes that people can adopt.

Within this tradition emphasis has been placed upon the agenda-setting function of the mass media: 'Thus more emphasis is now being placed on how the media project definitions of the situation that political actors must cope with than on attitudes towards those actors themselves' (Becker, McCombs and McLeod, 1975). As Blumler himself puts it:

> Newsmen in the several mass media are engaged in propagating images of political reality that few people can challenge for lack of first-hand experience. And in so far as reporting of news topics achieves a consonance that excludes alternative perspectives, to that extent is the chance increased that an influence will be exerted on how audience members think about them. (Blumler, 1977: 8)

So we have a situation in which current empirical research seems to be consonant with the study of ideology within the 'grand theory' tradition in putting forward the following explanation of how political communication in Britain is actually working.

1 Because of increased electoral volatility, itself in part created by the dominance of TV, the mass media possess an increased potential for political influence.
2 This influence is exerted, as much between as during elections by the media setting their own issue agenda.
3 This agenda is in part mediated via 'news values' that are a highly artificial social construct and are in general supportive of the *status quo*.
4 The agenda is *also* set by the non-partisan nature of TV itself, which not only projects a consensual, socially atomized view of the world, but also leads to a sense of trust that reinforces this influence. As Blumler puts it, 'Where overt persuasion is recognized, its [the audience's] guard may tend to be raised. But mass media content may

be received in a less sceptical spirit if it purports to shed an informative light on political events and how these could impinge on voters 'personal circumstances' (Blumler, 1977: 13).

5 Broadcasters have little real idea of the needs and values of their audience, but construct their agenda under the influence of institutional, peer-group and class pressures (Blumler, 1977: 7). (See especially Tracy (1977), McQuail (1969), Elliott (1972) and Burns (1977).)

All this evidence would seem to point to the conclusion that since the role of the agenda set by TV is crucial, the setting of that agenda must be brought more squarely into the political arena. And yet Blumler proposes the opposite, an even more autonomous role for the broadcasters during election campaigns. They would, for instance, if his reforms were carried out, immediately be allowed to challenge the parties' own statement of their case. 'Normal' news values will operate in campaign reporting rather than the present strict 'balance'. I imagine that there are no other serious mass communication researchers, with the possible exception of Katz, who would at this time and on the available evidence join Blumler, Gurevitch and Ives in their call for greater broadcaster autonomy in this field. Interestingly, Grace Wyndham-Goldie, the doyen of BBC political coverage, who might have been expected to share Blumler's views, in fact argues consistently and cogently against them and warns broadcasters that they will take over more power from the politicians at their peril. But then she has a proper respect for the calling of politics and is clear that broadcasting is there at its sufferance to serve it, not vice-versa. Unfortunately, her solution to the dilemmas of political communication, the television coverage of Parliament, seems inadequate to the problem.

To criticize Blumler is not to deny that there is a serious problem. Anthony Smith has pointed out the extent to which TV is now a crucial institution within the political process; 'the broadcasting environment of a society is an element in the political environment and has responsibilities to it, not merely to reflect it but to sustain it' (Smith, 1978: 96) and this because it provides 'the basic structure by which politicians communicate with people' (Smith, 1978: 98). But a recognition of this leads to a major challenge to broadcasting institutions, to their present relationship to the political system and to the whole liberal-pluralist theory within which Blumler (and indeed Anthony Smith) works. That Blumler avoids the most reasonable approach to solution of the problem because of this theoretical disposition is clear from his Annan Appendix where he writes: 'It is extremely difficult to conceive a promising strategy for raising journalistic standards in the news media. We lack confidence in policies of authoritative intervention into mass-media affairs and in the likely consequences of supporting an unfettered exercise of media freedom. The former runs unacceptable political risks and is at odds with long-established liberal tradition' (Blumler, 1977: 22). He thus in effect puts his name to proposals that would lead us further down the road to unfettered media freedom.

In short, the lessons that I would like to draw from this examination of Dr Blumler's work are the following.

1 The conflict within British mass media research should not be defined, as one between empiricism and theory, but as one between different political and social theories and their differing interpretations of the empirical evidence. Judgement between those theories should be based both upon their normative presuppositions and upon their cogency.

2 Mass media researchers do indeed have policy responsibilities. Not only are they examining the workings of an important contemporary social institution with social consequences, but their findings will be used, often unscrupulously, in the battles over policy, whether they wish it or not. However, a commitment to the policy implications of their research must not lead them to define policy research in such a way as to allow the vested interests to define their questions or their area of inquiry or in such a way as to see 'realistic' policy proposals as those which will be acceptable to their vested interests in the short term and without a struggle. It is always dangerous in such an undertaking to try to guess what will be acceptable and it can act as a distraction from the very real difficulties of working out and then fighting for what you believe to be true.

As Morris Janowitz wrote in his introduction to a book, which ironically contains one of Blumler's most important recent studies:

Social policy-making is enriched by an admixture of the search for broad hypotheses and a recognition of the concrete and specific context. The assessment of the causal patterns and sequences in a particular social setting investigated by survey research, supplies no mechanical guidelines to other circumstances; each application must involve reasoned judgements beyond the findings of social research. In fact to isolate patterns of influence does not necessarily indicate the likeliest and most legitimate approach for social intervention and social policy, which requires political imagination, moral conviction and the ability to create new solutions and build institutions without being confined to the patterns of influence which have operated in the past. But the essential component of survey research findings, grounded in some elements of sociological theory, is that they offer alternative explanations as a basis for estimating the consequences of various social policies (see Blumler and McLeod, 1974: 12).

References

Becker, L. B., McCombs, M. E. and McLeod, J. M. (1975) 'The development of political cognition', in S. H. Chaffee (ed.), *The Development of Political Communication*. London: Sage.

Blumler, J. (1970) 'Producers' attitudes towards coverage of an election campaign', in J. Tunstall (ed.), *Media Sociology*. London: Constable.

Blumler, J. (1977) 'The intervention of TV in British politics', *Report of the Committee on Broadcasting*, Cmnd 6753–I, Appendix E.

Blumler, J. and Gurevitch, M. (1977) 'Linkages between mass media and politics', in J. Curran, M. Gurevitch, and J. Woollacott (eds), *Mass Communication and Society*. London: Arnold.

Blumler, J., Gurevitch, M. and Ives, J. (1978) *The Challenge of Election Broadcasting*. Leeds: Leeds University Press.

Blumler, J. and McLeod, J. M. (1974) 'Communication and voter turn-out in Britain', in T. Legatt (ed.), *Sociological Theory and Survey Research*. London: Sage.

Blumler, J. and McQuail, O. (1967) *TV in Politics*. London: Faber & Faber.

Burns, T. (1977) *The BBC: Public Institution and Private World*. London: Macmillan.

Butler, D. E. and King, A. (1966) *The British General Election of 1966*. London: Macmillan.

Elliott, P. (1972) *The Making of a TV Series*. London: Constable.

Glasgow University Media Group (1976) *Bad News*. London: Routledge & Kegan Paul.

Journal of Communication (1978) 28(2) Spring.

Katz, E. (1972) 'Platforms and windows', in D. McQuail (ed.), *Sociology of Mass-Communication*. Harmondsworth: Penguin.

Lang, K. and Lang, G. (1966) 'The mass media and voting', in B. Berelson and M. Janowitz (eds), *Reader in Public Opinion and Communication*. New York: Free Press.

McQuail, D. (1969) 'Uncertainty about the audience and the organisation of mass-communication', in P. Halmos (ed.), *The Sociology of Mass Media Communicators*. University of Keele Press.

Miller, A. H., Erbring, L. and Goldenburg, E. (1976) 'Type-set politics: impact of newspapers on issue salience and public confidence', paper presented to the Annual Meeting of the American Political Science Association.

Open University (1977) *Mass Communication and Society, Unit Eight.*

Report of the Committee on the Future of Broadcasting (1977) Cmnd 6753.

Robinson, M. J. (1976) 'American political legitimacy in an era of electronic journalism', in D. Cater and R. Adler (eds), *Television as a Social Force*. London: Martin Robertson.

Seymour-Ure, C. (1974) *The Impact of the Mass Media*. London: Constable.

Smith, A. (1978) *The Politics of Information*. London: Macmillan.

Tracy, M. (1977) 'The absent framework: the audience-communicator relationship', in *The Production of Political TV*. London: Routledge & Kegan Paul, ch. 7.

Wyndham-Goldie, G. (1977) *Facing the Nation. TV and Politics 1936–76*. London: Bodley Head.

PART II

POLICY AND POLITICS: PUBLIC SERVICE BROADCASTING AND THE INFORMATION MARKET

7

The Media and the Public Sphere

It is a commonplace to assert that public communication lies at the heart of the democratic process; that citizens require, if their equal access to the vote is to have any substantive meaning, equal access also to sources of information and equal opportunities to participate in the debates from which political decisions rightly flow. I want to argue that it follows that changes in media structure and media policy, whether these stem from economic developments or from public intervention, are properly political questions of as much importance as the question of whether or not to introduce proportional representation, of relations between local and national government, of subsidies to political parties; that the policy of western European governments towards cable TV and satellite broadcasting is as important as their attitude towards the development of a United Europe; that the FCC's policy towards broadcast regulation is as important as the question of States' rights and that politicians, political scientists and citizens concerned with the health and future of democracy neglect these issues at their peril.

However, political theory has largely neglected the implications of such a position and, in particular, has neglected the problem of how, materially, the institutions and processes of public communication are sustained. It has ignored the specific ways in which a given social formation may provide those resources.

II

I argue elsewhere, in Chapter 9, that our inherited structures of public communication, those institutions within which we construct, distribute and consume symbolic forms, are undergoing a profound change. This change is characterized by a reinforcement of the market and the progressive destruction of public service as the preferred mode for the allocation of cultural resources; by a focus upon the TV set as the locus for an increasingly privatized, domestic mode of consumption; by the creation of a two-tier market divided between the information rich, provided with high-cost specialized information and cultural services, and the information poor, provided with increasingly homogenized entertainment services on a mass scale; lastly, by a shift from largely national to largely international markets in the informational and cultural spheres. Symptoms of this shift are the expansion of new TV delivery services such as videocassette, cable and direct broadcasting satellite under market control and on an international basis; the progressive deregulation and privatization of national telecommunication monopolies; the shift of Reuters from a general news agency to being largely a provider of specialized commercial information services; the increased penetration of sponsorship into the financing of leisure and culture; the move, under the pressure of public spending cuts, of educational and research institutes (such as universities) towards the private sector; proposals to make profitability the criterion for the provision of public information through such bodies as the Stationery Office, the Ordnance Survey and the US Government Printing Office; the shift in the library service (in the US at least) away from the principle of free and open access to public libraries towards access to proprietary databases on a payment-by-use basis. All these are examples of a trend to what has been dubbed, usually by those in favour of these developments, the Information Society or Information Economy. This trend represents an unholy alliance between western governments desperate for growth and in deadly competition with one another for that growth, and multinational corporations in search of new world markets in electronic technology and information goods and services. The result of this trend will be to shift the balance in the cultural sector between the market and public service decisively in favour of the market, and to shift the dominant definition of public information from that of a public good to that of a privately appropriate commodity.

What are the implications of these developments if we accept the argument that channels and processes of public communication are integral to the democratic process?

III

The debate about the political function and effect of modes of public communication has traditionally been carried on within the terms of the dichotomy between Hegelian State and civil society. The dominant theory within that debate has been the liberal theory of the free press, which has either assumed that the market will provide appropriate institutions and processes of public communication to support a democratic policy or, in its stronger form, argues that only the market can ensure the necessary freedom from State control and coercion. The critique of this position has been able to collect impressive evidence of the way in which market forces produce results, in terms of oligopoly control and depoliticization of content, that are far from the liberal ideal of a free market-place of ideas. But the strength of the hold that liberal theory still exercises can be judged by the inadequacy of proposals for press reform generated by the Left and the weakness with which such proposals have been pursued. For the Left itself remains trapped within a free press model inherited from the nineteenth century. The hold of this model is also illustrated by the way in which no equally legitimate theory has been developed to handle the dominant form of public communication, broadcasting. The public service, State-regulated model, whether publicly or privately funded, has always been seen not as a positive good but as an unfortunate necessity imposed by the technical limitations of frequency-scarcity. Those on the Left who are opposed to market forces in the press nonetheless have given no more than mealy-mouthed support to public service broadcasting. They have concentrated their critique on the question of the coercive or hegemonic nature of State power. Seeing the public service form as either a smokescreen for such power or as occupied from within by commercial forces, they have concentrated on criticizing the inadequacy and repressive nature of the rules of balance and objectivity within which public service broadcasting is forced to operate. The Left has, therefore, tended to fall back either on idealist formulations of free communications given no organizational substance or material support, or on a technological utopianism which sees the expansion of channels of communication as inherently desirable because pluralistic. Both positions are linked to some version, both political and artistic, of free expression: thus the long debate and campaigns around Channel 4, the touching faith in cable access, Left support for 'free' or 'community' radio and so forth. Alternatively the problem has simply been postponed until after the take-over of State power.

In my view the implications of current developments are better understood, and an escape from the bind of the State/market dichotomy as well as from the hold of free press theory and the necessary accompanying re-evaluation of public service is better served, by looking at the problem from the perspective of the theory of the public sphere.

IV

The theory of the public sphere, as articulated in particular by Habermas, argues that, just as the participatory democracy of the Athenian agora depended upon the material base of slavery, so it was the development of competitive market capitalism that provided the conditions in eighteenth-century Britain for the development of both the theory and practice of liberal democracy. It did so by making available to a new political class, the bourgeoisie, both the time and material resources to create a network of institutions within civil society such as newspapers, learned and debating societies, publishing enterprises, libraries, universities and polytechnics and museums, within which a new political force, public opinion, could come into existence.

This public sphere possessed the following key characteristics. It was protected from the power of both Church and State by its access to the sustaining resources of a wide range of private individuals with an alternative source of economic power. It was in principle open to all in the same way that access to the market was open to all, because the cost of entry for each individual was dramatically lowered by the growth in scale of the market. The public sphere thus took on the universalistic aspects of the Hegelian State, membership of the public sphere being coterminous with citizenship. All participants within the public sphere were on terms of equal power because costs of participation were widely and evenly spread and because social wealth within the bourgeoisie was evenly distributed. It was distinct from the private interests that governed civil society on the other hand because, in the Enlightenment tradition, it obeyed the rules of rational discourse, political views and decisions being open not to the play of power, but to that of argument based upon evidence, and because its concern was not private interest but the public good. It thus also took over the rationalist aspects of the Hegelian State.

Habermas went on to argue that the public sphere – this space for a rational and universalistic politics distinct from both the economy and the State – was destroyed by the very forces that had brought it into existence. The development of the capitalist economy in the direction of monopoly capitalism led to an uneven distribution of wealth, to rising entry costs to the public sphere and thus to unequal access to and control over that sphere. In particular the rise of advertising and public relations has embodied these trends since they represent direct control by private or State interests of the flow of public information in the interest, not of rational discourse, but of manipulation. At the same time these developments in the economy led to related development by the State, which itself became an active and major participant in the economy, thus coming to share the private interests there pursued. At the same time the State was called in, by those class forces which wished to defend and expand the public sphere against the encroaching power of private capital, itself to provide material support, for instance through the provision of public education, public libraries, systems of public cultural subsidy and so forth. In addition the growth of the State's role as coordinator and infrastructural provider for monopoly capitalism led to the massive development of State power as an independently administrative and bureaucratic interest, distinct from the rationalist determination of social ends and of the means to those ends in that political realm guaranteed by the existence of the public sphere. Thus the space between civil society and the State which had been opened up by the creation of the public sphere was squeezed shut between these two increasingly collaborative behemoths. In Habermas's words:

> The liberal model of the public sphere . . . cannot be applied to the actual conditions of an industrially advanced mass democracy organized in the form of the welfare state. In part the liberal model had always included ideological components, but it is also in part true that the social pre-conditions, to which the ideological elements could at one time at least be linked, had been fundamentally transformed. (Habermas, 1979)

Habermas wishes to distinguish between the set of principles upon which the bourgeois sphere was based and which, in the fight against feudalism, it brought into existence on the one hand, and the set of institutions which embodied those principles on the other. For Habermas, while the forms in which they are embodied will vary, the principles are the indispensable basis of a free society. These principles are: general accessibility, especially to information, the elimination of privilege, and the search for general norms and their rational legitimation.

The set of concrete institutions within which public opinion is formed, which include the media of public communication, elections, publicly accessible courts, and so on, are distinguished from the State, although the legitimation of the democratic State lies in its role of guarantor of the public sphere through law.

Public opinion, in turn, is to be distinguished from *mere* opinion as presupposing the existence of a reasoning public.

The centrality of these principles for Habermas derives from his more general concern with 'undistorted communication'. Pursuing the tradition of critical theory Habermas has sought concrete grounds for the validation of critical social judgement and for the claims to human emancipation. He has attempted to ground truth claims in the social sciences upon what he has called the Ideal Speech Situation. He argues that human interaction, the field of meanings and values, presupposes language and exists in language. He goes on to argue that we can therefore discover within the structure of speech itself the essential grounding presuppositions of all human interaction and thus of all social organization. He argues that every time we speak we are making four validity claims, to comprehensibility, truth, appropriateness and sincerity, which in their turn imply the possibility of justifying those claims. Thus the claim to truth implies a social context within which factual claims about external nature can be validated by evidence and logical argument, while claims to appropriateness, that is, to the social right to make the statement, imply a social context in which social norms can be rationally debated and consensual agreement arrived at. In actual societies characterized by differential power relations and resource distribution such conditions do not hold, and we are thus in the presence of 'distorted communication'. But for Habermas the essential human attribute of speech provides the ground for an ideal society against which existing societies can be judged and found wanting and to which we can aspire (Held, 1980; Habermas, 1982).

Thus the concept of the public sphere and the principles it embodies represent an Ideal Type against which we can judge existing social arrangements, and which we can attempt to embody in concrete institutions in the light of the reigning historical circumstances.

The strengths of this concept (to which we need to hang on tightly) are that it identifies and stresses the importance for democratic politics of a sphere distinct from the economy and the State, and thus helps us to escape from the elision of the two to which I pointed earlier, as being one of the major blocks to the formulation of a democratic response to current developments in the media.

Another strength is that the concept identifies the importance of rationality and universality as key moments in any democratic political practice and holds out a proper resistance to the reduction of politics either to the clash of power, in particular class interests, or to questions of State administration. It forces us to remember that in politics universal ends are always at issue, as are choices between incompatible public goods, which cannot be reduced to differences of material interest. Thus on the one hand the concept of the public sphere challenges the liberal free press tradition from the grounds of its materiality, and on the other it challenges the Marxist critique of that tradition from the grounds of the specificity of politics.

V

I want now to return to my starting point and look at the implications of the concept of the public sphere for the debate on the structure and function of the mass media. In doing so I shall focus upon broadcasting and upon the public service model of broadcasting as an embodiment of the principles of the public sphere. Such a focus is a conscious corrective to the more normal focus in debates about the media and politics upon the press, and upon a free press model derived from the history of print communication.

The great strengths of the public service model, to which we need to remain loyal through all the twists of the argument that has raged around it, are twofold. First it presupposes and then develops in its practice a set of social relations which are distinctly political rather than economic. Second, it attempts to insulate itself from control by the State (which, as is often forgotten, is not synonymous with political control). Reith's original vision was undoubtedly drawn from the tradition of the Scottish Enlightenment and, within the very narrow limits within which the economic and political forces of the time allowed him to operate, the early practice of the BBC (as Scannell and Cardiff's recent research shows) made a noble effort to address their listeners as rational political beings rather than as consumers (Scannell, 1980; Cardiff, 1980). It is easy to argue that the agenda for debate and the range of information considered important were hopelessly linked to a class-based definition of the public good. It has been further contended that the BBC's venture into class education was doomed to failure because public aspirations were already so moulded by the consumerist ideology secreted by the dominant set of social relations in society, that this alternative set (as the experience of Radio Luxembourg demonstrated) could be imposed on listeners only by the brute force of monopoly. But this is to miss the point of the enterprise and its continuing importance as both historical example and potential alternative. After all, one could use the same argument (indeed people are already using this argument in relation to the power of local government) that because of declining voter turn-out one should simply abolish elections.

For the problem with liberal free press theory is not just that the market has produced conditions of oligopoly which undercut the liberal ideal, or that private ownership leads to direct manipulation of political communication (although it does). The site of the problem is the fundamental contradiction between the economic and the political at the level of their value systems and of the social relations which those value systems require and support. Within the political realm the individual is defined as a citizen exercising public rights of debate, voting, etc., within a communally agreed structure of rules and towards communally defined ends. The value system is essentially social and the legitimate end of social action is the public good. Within the economic realm on the other hand the individual is defined as producer and consumer exercising private rights through purchasing power on the market in the pursuit of private interests, his or her actions being coordinated by the invisible hand of the market.

Once we recognize this irresolvable contradiction then the analytical task becomes one of mapping the interactions between the two spheres, and the political task one of working out the historically appropriate balance between recognizing, on the one hand, that pursuit of political freedom may override the search for economic efficiency, while on the other, that the extent of possible political freedom is constrained by the level of material productivity.

The field of the mass media is a key focus for this contradiction because they operate simultaneously across the two realms. A newspaper or a TV channel is at one and the same time a commercial operation and a political institution. The nature of the largely undiscussed problems this creates can be illustrated if one points to the elaborate structure of law and convention which attempts to insulate politicians, public servants and the political process from economic control – rules against bribery, laws controlling election expenditure, the socially validated objection (however often venality occurs) against the use of public office for private gain. And yet at the same time we allow what we recognize as central political institutions such as the press and broadcasting, to be privately operated. We would find it strange now if we made voting rights dependent upon purchasing power or property rights; yet access to the mass media, as both channels of information and forums of debate, is largely controlled by just such power and rights.

But the incompatibility between the commercial and political functions of the media is not just a question of ownership and control, important as such questions are. It is even more a question of the value system and set of social relations within which commercial media must operate and which they serve to reinforce. For it is these that are inimical, not just to one political interest group or another, but to the very process of democratic politics itself. Political communication is forced to channel itself via commercial media. By this I mean not just the press but also public service broadcasting so far as it competes for audiences with commercial broadcasting and on its dominant terms. Public communication is transformed into the politics of consumerism. Politicians appeal to potential voters not as rational beings concerned for the public good, but in the mode of advertising, as creatures of passing and largely irrational appetite, whose self-interest they must purchase. Such a politics is forced to take on the terms of address of the media it uses and to address its readers, viewers and listeners within the set of social relations that those media have created for other purposes. Thus the citizen is addressed as a private individual rather than as a member of a public, within a privatized domestic sphere rather than within public life. Think, for instance, of the profound political difference between reading a newspaper in one's place of work or in a café and discussing it with those who share that set of social relations on the one hand, and watching TV within the family circle or listening to radio or watching a videocassette on an individual domestic basis on the other. Think of the Sony Walkman as a concrete embodiment of social isolation, as opposed to participation at a rock concert.

VI

However, while I want to argue that the public service model of the media has at its heart a set of properly political values, and that its operation both requires and fosters a set of social relations, distinct from and opposed to economic values and relations essential to an operating democracy, at the same time in its actual historical operation it has so far shared with the Habermasian concept of the public sphere a crucial failure to recognize the problem of mediation within the public sphere and thus the role of knowledge-brokers within the system. In particular the public service model has failed to come to terms with the proper and necessary function of both journalists and politicians. In relation to both groups there is a failure sufficiently to distinguish between two communicative functions within the public sphere: the collection and dissemination of *information*, and the provision of a forum for *debate*.

Journalists within public service broadcasting, under the banner of balance and objectivity, claim to carry out both functions and to do so in the name of the public. However, this produces a contradiction. Obviously, the function of information search and exposition as carried out at its best, by teachers, cannot simply be equated with political advocacy. Here Jay Blumler is right (Blumler *et al.*, 1978). But journalists are not in any way accountable to the public they claim to serve and themselves constitute a distinct interest. How then are we to ensure that this expository function is carried out responsibly? It needs to be accompanied by legislation for freedom of information and so forth. It also needs much better-trained journalists. Finally, its sheer expensiveness depends upon public provision, since otherwise high-quality information will become not a public good but an expensive private asset. All this complex institution needs a public accountability structure of its own, together with a code of professional values distinct from the political debate. Within such a structure, much greater direct access must be given to independent fields of social expertise. It is a perennial and justified criticism of journalists by experts that journalists themselves decide the agenda of what is relevant, and at the same time too often garble the information for presentational purposes. Perhaps bodies such as the Medical Research Council, the Economic and Social Research Council, Greenpeace, Social Audit (one could list many others) should have regular access to broadcasting and print channels and employ their own journalists to clarify current issues for the general public as a background to more informed political debate.

At the same time, the conduct of debate in the mass media needs to be *more* highly politicized with political parties and other major organized social movements having access to the screen on their own terms. One might indeed envisage a situation where any group that could obtain a membership of over a certain size would be eligible for regular access to airtime and national newspaper space. Habermas himself seems to envisage some such arrangement when he argues that the public sphere today requires 'a public body of organized private individuals'. Such organizations would themselves, he argues, have to have democratic internal structures. The public sphere, he writes, 'could only be realized today on an altered basis as a rational reorganization of social and political power under the mutual control of rival organizations committed to the public sphere in their internal structure as well as in their relations with the State and each other' (Habermas, 1979: 201).

VII

One of the strengths of the public sphere concept which I stress, and which I want to link to any revitalized notion of public service broadcasting, is that of universalism. I mean by this the notion that the scope of a political decision structure must be coterminous with the scope of the powers it aims to control. In recent tradition this has meant within the boundaries of the nation-state, so that citizenship of such states is defined in terms of certain nationally universal rights and obligations. The principle of tying voting to property rights was an important expression of this because it recognized the importance of the relationship between the right to participate in decision-making and a not easily avoidable involvement in the consequences of those decisions. It is precisely for this reason that capital, so long as it can flow internationally with ease, should not be accorded such rights. Within this envelope of rights and obligations all citizens, whether they are on the winning or losing side of a political debate, are forced to live with its consequences. Thus proper democratic participation cannot be irresponsible by definition. In some countries this important truth is embodied in laws requiring all citizens to vote. Now, while it would clearly be both impossible and undesirable to require all citizens to participate in a minimum amount of political information consumption and debate, or to make electoral participation dependent upon such participation, in principle it is a mere corollary of a requirement to vote. Indeed this is the principle which trade unions have correctly if unsuccessfully mobilized against the institution of mandatory postal ballots. Public policy should, if democracy is to be taken seriously, favour citizen participation in such debate. If that is the case debate must include as many of the existing views in a society on the relevant issues as possible. This cannot, by definition, be provided by sectionalized, ghettoized media talking only to a particular interest group or the party faithful. In terms of national issues it must take place at a national level and is undercut by a multiplication of simultaneous viewing and listening options. It is this that is the rational core of the argument mobilized in favour of the existing public service broadcasting duopoly in Britain. Namely, that the existence of a national focus for political debate and information is important to the national political process. The problem of the relations of scale needed between communication channels and political power then takes on a different dimension when we consider the transnational aspect of current media developments.

If we see media structures as central to the democratic polity, and if the universalism of the media must match that of the polity, then the current process by which national media control is being eroded is part of that process by which power is being transferred in the economy to the international level without the parallel development of adequate political or communication structures. This is already apparent from the problem facing European governments in the face of satellite broadcasting of trying to match their different systems of advertising control. So too with their systems of political access.

Let us be clear. It is in the interest of the controllers of multinational capital to keep nation-states and their citizens in a state of disunity and dysfunctional ignorance unified only by market structures within which such capital can freely flow, while at the same time they develop their own private communication networks. The development of the *Financial Times* and the *Wall Street Journal*, and of private, high-cost, proprietary data networks and services on an international scale to serve the corporate community and its agents is a clear sign of this trend. Not only do we face the challenge of sustaining and developing the public sphere at a national level. Such a development will simply be bypassed if we do not at the same time and perhaps with greater urgency begin to develop a public sphere where at present one hardly exists at the international level. It is here that current threats to UNESCO and the ITU, led by the US government, but supported and abetted by the UK, need to be seen for what they are, attempts to destroy what small public sphere actually exists at an international level. It is significant that the crime of which these institutions stand accused is 'politicization'.

I have tried to argue here that the necessary defence and expansion of the public sphere as an integral part of a democratic society requires us to revalue the public service model of public communication and, while being necessarily critical of its concrete historical actualization, defend it and build upon the potential of its rational core in the face of the existing and growing threats to its continued existence.

References

Blumler, J., Gurevitch, M. and Ives, J. (1978) *The Challenge of Election Broadcasting.* Leeds: Leeds University Press.

Cardiff, D. (1980) 'The serious and the popular: aspects of the evolution of style in the radio talk 1928–1939', *Media, Culture and Society*, 2(1).

Habermas, J. (1979) 'The public sphere', in A. Mattelart and S. Siegelaub (eds), *Communication and Class Struggle*, Vol. 1. New York: International General.

Habermas, J. (1982) 'A reply to my critics', in John B. Thompson *et al.* (eds), *Habermas: Critical Debates.* London: Macmillan.

Held, D. (1980) *Introduction to Critical Theory.* London: Hutchinson.

Scannell, P. (1980) 'Broadcasting and the politics of unemployment 1930–1935', *Media, Culture and Society*, 2(1).

8

Public Service versus the Market

Even the most cursory study of the history of mass-communication development should make one chary of accepting any forecasts of rapid change. Indeed such forecasts, as now those associated with the so-called information or post-industrial society, are usually part of the propaganda for a particular form of social change. Nonetheless it is clear, I think, that in March 1982 British broadcasting entered a period of crucial historical transition which may in retrospect be as significant as the founding of the BBC itself. On 4 March the Home Secretary announced that the government was granting a licence to the BBC for the provision of two direct satellite broadcasting services with a planned start in 1986. One of these services is to be a pay-TV service, the other a best of British or best of Europe service financed out of an additional licence fee. The government did not rule out the possibility of granting further licences at a later date, but these will depend upon decisions as to the type of satellite system to be launched. In its earlier (1981) report on Direct Broadcasting by Satellite (DBS) the Home Office envisaged 'a modest but early start with a two-channel satellite system by 1986'. However, we now know that provision of the satellite will be left to a private consortium involving the Rothschild Bank, British Aerospace, GEC–Marconi and British Telecom, which will lease transponders to service providers. Since British Aerospace already have a contract to construct Europe's experimental L Sat, and since British Telecom in its commercially aggressive and deregulated mood will itself have a considerable demand for satellite capacity, there is a real possibility that a satellite with the capacity for the full five television channels allocated to the United Kingdom may be launched. It is, however, already four years late. In such an eventuality the government might well authorize additional satellite TV services perhaps from the Independent Broadcasting Authority (IBA), perhaps from private companies such as Satellite TV Ltd, who are at present broadcasting an experimental advertising-financed service to Europe.

[In the event these early UK satellite projects foundered because British Aerospace technology proved too expensive. Neither the BBC, nor a later consortium of the BBC with the ITV companies, felt confident that it could make the project pay on this basis. As a result the IBA was eventually allowed to license a consortium, British Satellite Broadcasting, to provide initially three, and later five, channels of DBS service using off-the-shelf US technology. This service, after long delays due in part to the difficulties of developing new receiving aerials and decoder chips, is due to start transmissions in April 1990. Satellite TV became Sky Channel when it was bought by Rupert Murdoch and started broadcasting four channels directed at the UK in April 1989, using the Luxembourg-based Astra satellite and on transponders leased from British Telecom. At the time of writing (February 1990) we still do not know whether anyone can make money out of direct broadcasting satellite services.]

On 22 March 1982 the Cabinet's Information Technology Advisory Panel (ITAP) issued a report on Cable Systems which advocated an immediate start on a massive £2.5 billion programme to cable urban Britain with a system capable of delivering at least thirty television channels.[1] They argued that this project should be undertaken by the private sector and that the necessary funds would only be made available in sufficient quantities and at sufficient speed if the entrepreneurs were allowed to offer deregulated pay-TV. Following this report the Home Office set up the Hunt Committee and gave it until September 1982 to consider, not whether this development of cable TV should take place, but given that it was to take place, whether and if so how existing broadcasting services should be protected.

The Hunt Committee then recommended that cable expansion be allowed to go ahead as soon as possible under a system of national regulation, 'so liberal as to be invisible'. It was proposed that a national cable authority should franchise cable operators for eight years; that all controls on programming and advertising content should be retrospective and in response to complaints; that although operators will have a monopoly in each area there should be no controls on pricing, as much advertising as they can sell, no quota of British material, no requirement to provide a balanced service or impartial coverage and merely 'a presumption that all systems should provide children's programmes, education and a community service'. Doubts about the effects of unrestricted competition on broadcasting schedules, of the fragmentation of audiences on the legitimacy of the licence fee, about the siphoning off of programmes and of advertising revenue were waved airily aside without serious argument. The only concessions made to the protection of public service broadcasting were the proposal to disallow pay-per-view, to extend to cable the provisions of section 30 of the Broadcasting Act 1981 which prevents anyone obtaining exclusive rights to specified national sporting events and to make the cable operators continue to carry the broadcasting services.

This last provision was in fact watered down by a suggestion that existing operators be allowed a five-year period during which they can drop the delivery of existing broadcasting services, so long as they provide their subscribers with alternative means of reception. This may yet have turned out to be the most significant recommendation in the whole report. Given the high capital cost of new high-capacity cable systems and the pessimistic projections of the potential profitability of cable services, the most likely immediate development will be an attempt by the existing operators to make a fast buck out of their existing, obsolescent systems rather than, as the government fondly hoped for several years, using revenues from entertainment cable TV to fund investment in new wide-band cable systems.

Nevertheless there has been a massive increase in the pace and scale of broadcasting developments, with scarcely any public debate. In 1946 the BBC TV service came back on the air after its wartime break. In 1956 the public service monopoly was broken and Independent Television (ITV) introduced commercial broadcasting into the UK. In 1964 BBC2 was launched and finally in November 1982 Channel 4 went on the air. Each of these stages of expansion involved a lengthy process of public enquiry and associated debate. Since 1981 there has been this rush to develop new television services. What are its implications?

II

What has happened in Britain has been part of a much wider international pattern. In the United States there has been the move to deregulate the broadcasting and telecommunications industries, in Europe a continuing campaign, most successful so far in Italy, to break the public broadcasting monopoly and introduce private, advertising-financed stations and networks. These developments are in their turn determined by underlying economic trends and the efforts of transnationals, often backed by the economic planning instruments of nation-states such as Japan and France, to develop the market for so-called information goods and services as a new growth sector. Since the late 1960s electronics has been one of the key sectors of the world economy from several points of view. As productivity levelled off and profits dropped in more traditional manufacturing sectors and product lines the transnationals moved into the electronics sector in search of new products, new markets and renewed growth. In many cases this was also a chance to capitalize on US government research and development expenditure in the defence and space industries. Furthermore, as competition in general sharpened in consumer markets, advertising and marketing expenditure rose and with it the pressure to find new media outlets for it. In addition, as the transnationals moved much of their labour-intensive manufacturing activity to the Third World in search of lower labour costs, they required ever more sophisticated communications systems in order to manage what had become 'dispersed' corporations. At the same time the member states of the Organization for Economic Cooperation and Development, in order to protect their economies, were forced at least to attempt to restructure those economies in the direction of high technology. But as the world recession deepened competition in this sector, both between firms and between nations, became ever fiercer.

Thus the drive to launch a British satellite and create, as rapidly as possible, a British cable industry was fuelled, as was openly admitted, by the needs of the corporate sector for enhanced communications facilities and the increasingly desperate national search for a share of the international market in high-technology products. In this situation not much sensitivity is likely to be shown to the possible domestic, social and cultural effects of such expansion. The irony is that in each individual European country the same story is being repeated. No-one really wants cable TV or a direct broadcasting satellite, they will say, but we must have it before the British or before the Germans or before the French, as a shop-window for foreign buyers of technology.

At the same time, white goods (washing machines, refrigerators, etc.) and TV set markets are saturated, so that manufacturers in the consumer electronics sector are in search of new products and new markets. Central to this search is an attempt to turn the domestic TV set into a multipurpose visual display unit, the core of a home entertainment and information processing centre, by offering a range of plug-in peripherals or enhanced facilities such as videocassette recorders, videodisc players, teletext and viewdata decoders, home computers, etc. Efforts are concentrated upon the TV set in part because it now occupies between 30 and 40 per cent of most people's available free time, is their major source of information and entertainment and absorbs about 25 per cent of household leisure expenditure. It also provides people's main point of entry into other sections of the entertainment industry and the arts. The introduction of so-called information technology into the cultural sphere is an attempt not only to sell new hardware products, but also an attempt by a range of cultural producers, by means of satellite, cable, cassette and disc, to find new means of delivering audiovisual products for viewing on the domestic TV sets, which circumvent the control of that supply at present exercised by the publicly regulated broadcasting institutions. this is particularly clear in the case of advertising, and one of the main commercial interests in European direct satellite broadcasting is the opportunity it offers to break the very tight control on advertising time and content maintained on most European national TV systems. Britain, unfortunately, with its comparatively high level of both TV advertising time and advertising expenditure, appears to be the base for such operations, much to the disquiet of some of our European neighbours.

While there are quite explicit elements of national economic planning in the current situation I do not want to foster an impression of a huge capitalist conspiracy. The corporations, and indeed nations, involved are driven by an increasing sense of desperation, and many of the initiatives in this area have failed and will continue to do so. The various videodisc systems, for instance, appear so far to have been a very expensive flop. There are many in the industry who regard the BBC's satellite pay-TV plans as foolhardy. And the figures put forward by the ITAP to support their argument that cable expansion will be financed out of pay-TV profits no longer make sense.

The capital cost of the system seems to have been seriously under-estimated. The figure quoted of £2.5 billion to cable half UK households was based upon the £200–300 per house yardstick for 'green-field' sites. A more realistic industry estimate is £500–600 per household, giving a total of £5–6 billion. British Telecom's 1982 estimate is £5–6 billion. These figures are important because they indicate the likely measure of profitability of any investment in cable systems and therefore the scale of the resources that the industry is likely to be able to devote to programming. If we extrapolate revenue figures for Britain from existing US figures by scaling down for the smaller British market, we arrive at a total system revenue of £340 million per annum and pay cable revenue of £80 million per annum at 1982 prices, which does not provide an adequate return on the capital investment, let alone cover administration and programme costs. Moreover the revenue would be roughly equivalent to that of an admittedly underfinanced Channel 4, and is supposedly to be spread across a multiple channel provision.

Yet these figures must be regarded as optimistic in the extreme, since several factors favour cable in the United States as compared with the United Kingdom. The dispersed suburban style of urban development there puts a greater stress on home entertainment. Bad over-air reception means that 48 per cent of those receiving just the basic cable service say they do so primarily for enhanced reception of network TV. The level of advertising on US network TV puts a real competitive premium on ad-free services. Perhaps most important of all there is a market on a continental scale within which satellite distribution of pay cable has made a crucial economic difference by enabling entrepreneurs to put together small, scattered market segments into one serveable market. Notoriously, figures demonstrate the danger of extrapolating consumption growth curves. The de-connection rate is now as high as the connection rate in the US.

The figures also look unrealistic if compared with actual UK consumer expenditure patterns. The ITAP suggest a likely expenditure, based upon US expenditure of $23 per month (in 1982) per average pay cable subscriber, of £13 per month, £5 for the basic service and £8 for addi-tional pay services, in addition to the purchase or rental of a decoder. Such a figure should be set against Family Expenditure Survey figures showing an average monthly household expenditure on all media enter-tainment and associated hardware of £21.60 per month (1982 prices). Of this £5.40 is spent on the reception of existing over-air broadcasting, that is licence and rental or purchase of the set. We must assume that this proportion will be sustained. The other major item of expenditure is books, magazines and newspapers at £6.80 per month. This is potentially vulnerable to an expansion of cable with perhaps serious social and industrial consequences. But it is hard to imagine a shift of consumption patterns sufficient to match the assumption of £13 per month on cable. Alternatively, if such a shift were to take place, the consequences across the whole range of our social and cultural life would be serious.

III

The advocates of the benefits of information technology in the cultural sphere argue that it will usher in a new era of cultural freedom, diversity and abundance. One argues that it will mark 'a great shift from producer to consumer sovereignty in Western European societies', creating 'an Alexandria without walls' (Smith, 1980). Another claims that cultural freedom will be secured 'by making information in every form cheaply and conveniently available' (Hyman, 1980). In particular the argument is couched in terms of deregulation, the need and opportunity to sweep away what they present as the stuffy, bureaucratic, confining censored old world of public service broadcasting in favour of the exciting new world of market provision. As another advocate recently put it:

> Once the technical pretext for electronic publishing has gone the whole inverted pyramid of regulation and control must be dismantled. Those who are passionately for freedom in communication and publishing, whether print, electronic or simply oral, need now to gird themselves for a prolonged struggle against old habits and vested interests to ensure that the new freedoms which new technology will make possible, are translated into real freedoms for both producers and consumers. (Jay, 1981)

There are two different and equally unjustified assumptions lying behind such arguments. First, that the public service is based upon scarcity of frequencies. Second, that once technology gives us the means, the market is superior to a regulated public service as a mode of cultural production and distribution. The first argument is simply untrue. The available frequencies could have been engineered to provide thirteen channels in the major population areas and, within the public service tradition, even with the priority given to equal coverage for all, the fourth channel has been available for allocation since Pilkington reported in 1962. Channels have been limited, whether rightly or wrongly, for social and economic, not technical reasons. The second argument cannot be sustained against the weight of evidence of how media provision governed by market forces actually operates. For the truth is that while the public regulation of broadcasting has been *legitimized* in terms of frequency-scarcity, its *justification* lies in its superiority to the market as a means of providing all citizens, whatever their wealth or geographical location, equal access to a wide range of high-quality entertainment, information and education, and as a means of ensuring that the aim of the programme producer is the satisfaction of a range of audience tastes rather than only those tastes that show the largest profit.

I wish to challenge the view that the market is superior to public service as a mode of cultural production and consumption, and to show that we are here in the presence of ideology in its pure, classical form; that is to say a social analysis that not only misrepresents its object of analysis by focusing on its surface rather than its underlying structure and by denying its real history, but also misrepresents it in such a way as to favour the interests of the dominant class. In this case the trick is played by concentrating upon the technical potentialities rather than upon the social relations that will determine the form in which those potentialities are realized and by denying history by exaggerating the novelty of the process in question. Now I would not want to deny either the manifold failings of public service broadcasting or the marginal increase in individual freedom offered by a video-recorder in terms of the ability to watch the offerings of the broadcaster at times of your rather than the scheduler's choice. But what we are in fact being offered is not a more socially responsive, politically accountable, diverse mode of cultural interchange in the electronic sphere, but on the contrary the expansion of price and profit, of commodity exchange, as the dominating mode of organization in yet another area of cultural production and consumption, as though this were a new phenomenon. We are witnessing merely the latest phase in a process integral to the capitalist mode of production.

This is a process referred to variously as 'the industrialization of culture' (Briggs, 1960) and 'the colonization of leisure' (Sahin and Robins, 1981) by which 'massive market interests have come to dominate an area of life which, until recently, was dominated by individuals themselves' (Briggs, 1960). It is a development that goes back at least 150 years in Britain, part of a wider process by which commodity exchange invades wider and wider areas of social life and the private sphere expands at the expense of the public sphere, driven by capital's restless and relentless search for new areas in which to realize surplus value, thus introducing the 'dull compulsion of economic relations' to more and more spheres of social life. In assessing the likely impact of the new information technologies on broadcasting, and – because of the central position it occupies in the cultural field – on our whole cultural life, we are not entering entirely uncharted waters. We have a lot of accumulated historical experience of the dynamics of the culture sphere in a capitalist mode of production. When we hear the Peter Jays of this world arguing that the new technology gives us the opportunity to fight for 'freedom of the press' in the field of electronic publishing, we need to remember that the actual history of the press is not one of developing freedoms, but on the contrary that the growth of an advertising-financed, commercial mass circulation press destroyed the independent working-class and radical press (as was the intention), steadily reduced the range of available views and information, incorporated nascent oppositional movements, helped to depoliticize our society and placed control of the channels of information in fewer and fewer hands (Curran, 1977). We need to remember that we live in a class society and that not all producers and consumers are equal, and that in deciding the characteristics of the future 'information society' the preferences of the members of the board of AT&T and IBM and their corporate clients weigh somewhat heavier than those of any member of the European working class. Indeed it may at present be regrettably true that their preferences weigh more heavily than even those of the whole of the organized European working class.

Let us then turn to look in more detail at the structural dynamics of the cultural sphere within the capitalist mode of production. The first point to stress, against the grain of the ideological discourse that dominates cultural analysis, a discourse of individual taste, creativity, etc., inherited from a pre-industrial era, is that cultural relations are in general dominated by normal capitalist market mechanisms and most culture is produced and distributed, by what have come to be known as cultural industries, under conditions similar to those reigning in other economic sectors.

However, the sphere of cultural commodity production does have certain specific tendential characteristics that need stressing. First, because there is a sense in which each cultural product is a prototype, the cost of production, what are known in the newspaper industry as first copy costs, tend to be high relative to the cost of reproduction and distribution. This means that there are exceptionally high returns to economies of scale leading to a constant push towards audience maximization, since the marginal profit from each additional consumer is high relative to marginal cost. Second, because demand is highly elastic (in the sense that for any one cultural commodity it is impossible to predict whether it will be a hit or a flop) profitability depends upon being able to offer a repertoire, so that the very high profits from the few hits can subsidize the need to write off most of the rest of the product. In the record industry for instance only one single in nine and one LP in sixteen makes a profit, and in a typical company 3 per cent of the output can account for 50 per cent of the turn-over (Huet *et al.*, 1978). Similarly in the film industry in a typical year the top ten films out of 119 in the US market took 22 per cent of the box office receipts and the top 40 took 80 per cent (see Chapter 11 below). This has had two consequences:

1 The risks of cultural production can only be lowered to an acceptable level by a high and sustained level of investment in a whole production programme. The small independent producer in general and in the long run has no chance.
2 Reinforcing the high returns to economies of scale, this pattern of profitability makes control of distribution rather than of production crucial.

As the history of the US film industry amply demonstrates, a small group of companies has been able to retain tight control over both the US and world markets for over half a century without retaining control of exhibition and while actually reducing their direct involvement in production. Control of distribution, however, enables a wide range of 'independent' productions to be assembled into a programme and then offered to the widest possible range of audiences. Or rather, as the history of broadcasting shows, control of distribution allows the very construction of an audience out of disparate groups and individuals. Indeed there is a growing tendency in the cultural industries, legitimized by an ideology of creative freedom, for the profit centres founded upon control of distribution to maintain a network of dependent and exploited production satellites, often themselves partially sustained out of public funds through cultural and educational budgets, whose shoulders are those which carry the costs and risks of research and development. The result of these tendencies has been to produce culture industries characterized by a high level of oligopolistic control not only in national markets but across the world market (in the record industry five firms control 67 per cent of the world market; in the film industry seven firms control 90 per cent of the US domestic market, and 70 per cent of the world market; in Britain three groups control 74 per cent of daily newspaper circulation), and by a high level of horizontal integration, such as the development of conglomerates like Thorn-EMI in Britain and Warner Communications in the US with an important market share across a wide range of different media. This enables the principle of the repertoire to operate not just in one media market but across markets so that a firm can typically offer a package involving film, TV series, book, record and merchandizing such that each advertises the other and the risks can be spread.

These characteristics of the international culture industry are further reinforced by the specific structure of the consumer market in which the cultural distributors must compete to realize surplus value and maximize profit. This market is constrained by two factors: availability of time and availability of money. The free time available to the average working person has only marginally increased in recent years. US figures show an increase for men from 34.1 hours per week to 39.3 hours per week between 1965 and 1975, virtually the whole of the extra time being taken up by TV viewing. Intense competition for this limited time market has two consequences:

1 A tendency for one medium to partially supplant another, that is cinema to replace music-hall and TV to replace the cinema, newspaper circulation declining in the face of TV.
2 A tendency, as a Swedish study has shown (Ivre, 1981), for the cost to the consumer of each unit of consumption time to rise in real terms because each new media service, especially the ones that depend upon domestic investment in the technological delivery system, involves an increased investment which cannot be matched by an increase in consumption time. These tendencies will, of course, be heavily reinforced by an expansion of TV channels.

At the same time the discretionary expenditure available for cultural consumption is also strictly limited, having grown in the UK since 1968 from 5 to 7 per cent of total consumer expenditure. If real diversity is to become a reality it can only be produced either by a concomitant growth in that expenditure or by redistribution of expenditure by fiscal means. Present figures show in particular how, over the past decade, increases in consumer expenditure on electronic hardware, especially TV, have exceeded the increase in available discretionary expenditure, leading to a marked fall in real terms in expenditure on printed matter. Furthermore because, owing to what is known as Baumol's disease, the real costs of cultural production have been rising, markets have had to be expanded to support a given level of production, reinforcing the oligopolistic and internationalizing tendencies in the sphere of production itself (Baumol and Bowen, 1976).

This is particularly clear in both TV and book publishing. Rising production costs and the intense competition for this narrow consumption market has also led to a rapid acceleration in the rate of obsolescence of cultural products. In the film industry, for instance, a high proportion of a film's total box-office receipts are earned in the first few weeks of release in nine major US metropolitan areas during twenty key weeks of the year (see Chapter 11 below). It is now estimated that the shelf-life of the average paperback in the US is five weeks. Barriers to entry to these markets are being continually raised by rising promotion costs. The promotion of a feature film can now cost as much as the initial production costs.

The lack of discretionary consumer spending power has also led to a tendency right across the cultural field to make up the short-fall from advertising expenditure. While this too is not a source of income that can be expanded endlessly (indeed it may in the UK already be reaching its limits as a proportion of GNP) it also has serious distorting effects on cultural provision (Curran, 1981). In particular it reinforces the class stratification of cultural consumption that is already present in the structure of the market.

IV

The class determination of cultural consumption takes place at two mutually reinforcing levels. It is first determined materially by the differential availability of both time and money. Members of lower-paid groups work longer hours in more tiring conditions than those higher up the social scale. In addition, consumption of cultural goods and participation in cultural practices increases in range and amount over virtually the whole spectrum of activities (except TV viewing) as income rises. This is hardly surprising. It is just normally ignored in discussions of cultural policy. The higher level of TV consumption among the poorer sections of the community is attributable to the higher proportion of their total discretionary expenditure tied up in the relatively fixed invest-ment in the TV set and licence. Once this investment is made, subsequent consumption is virtually free, making them a captive audience. This material hierarchization of cultural participation is matched at a second level by the distribution of what Bourdieu has called dispositions and competences (see Chapter 5 above). Dispositions refer to the internalized cultural norms acquired during childhood within the family and the immediate social environment which relate given modes of cultural participation to a given lifestyle and class position such that those modes which are objectively unavailable for material reasons or because of lack of competences are de-legitimized and rejected as 'not for the likes of us'. Competences refer to the skills necessarily required for the consump-tion of certain forms of cultural product, for instance literacy for reading, but also and more subtly to a range of interpretive and social codes for painting, music, live theatre and art galleries. Such competences are acquired both inside the family and at school, and thus reflect and pass on the differential endowment of cultural resources in families of different social classes and the class-based differential participation rates in education. It is to the existence and importance of dispositions and competences that the evidence of a growing information gap in western societies between the information-rich and the information-poor points.

Not only does the nature of cultural production and distribution under capitalist market conditions tend increasingly to limit diversity of provi-sion and to place control of that provision in fewer and fewer hands and further and further from the point of consumption, the structure of the market also distributes what choice there is available in a highly unequal way. There is a tendency towards a two-tier market structure in which choice, being increasingly expensive, is offered to upper-income groups, while an increasingly impoverished, homogenized service is offered to the rest. This tendency is reinforced by advertising which differentially subsidizes media going to the rich and the poor. We can see this tendency clearly in the British press where middle-market newspapers such as the *Express* are very slowly being squeezed out.

Many will at this point want to argue that the current experience with cable TV in the United States contradicts this view. Not at all. The significance of the cable TV explosion in the US is that the linkage of cable systems by satellite has made it possible to bring together scattered pockets of upper-income cultural consumers who were not viable as separate local markets into one national market which it is now economic to service. But even then Home Box Office, which controls about 40 per cent of the pay-TV market, is only delivering feature films to a market that for complex social reasons has been lost to the cinema. It in no way threatens the basic structure of the international film industry. The signs are that all we are seeing at present is one new company, Home Box Office, itself part of the multi-media conglomerate Time-Life, joining the majors thanks to its oligopolistic control of Pay Cable Film distribution. So far as the all news network is concerned two points need to be noted:

1 that the US has no truly national newspapers with which such a service would compete;
2 that even if there is an economically viable place for such a service in the US market with a 5–10 per cent audience share, there is almost certainly not room in the long term for more than one.

Thus there will be a monopoly of news on cable and only a small addition to the diversity of provision across the nation as a whole. So far as the recently announced cultural channels are concerned it has been concluded, I think on good grounds (Winston, 1981) that most of them are unlikely to last and have been launched by the networks to pre-empt satellite transponder space while they fight anti-trust prohibitions on entering the entertainment cable TV market. Indeed CBS has just announced the closure of its Culture channel after only 11 months of operation and at a loss of 40 million dollars. The real danger of the US situation is that the history of its film industry will repeat itself and the US cable industry will use its large home market as a base for the invasion of the European market now that the technology is there to create the networks.

Thus the impact of information technology will not, as its advocates claim, lead to consumer sovereignty and greater choice. Such a claim can only be made if one looks at the technical determinants in the audio-visual field rather than the economic ones. If information technology is introduced, as its advocates propose and as seems likely, as part of a move of broadcasting out of the public sphere and into the private sphere, then it will have different effects at different class levels. It will reinforce existing tendencies to create a two-tier market with increased choice for the rich and decreased choice for the poor, no longer protected by the need for licence-financed broadcasting to make so far as possible a range of provision available for all, and thus open to the full force of the international market. If one looks at British television over the past twenty years it has made available a far wider range of cultural experience to a far wider range of people than the cinema or the popular press during the same period. I believe the same is true throughout Europe. For all its failings, European public service broadcasting has represented a real step forward in the attempt to create a common culture. The introduction of information technology is likely to represent a massive retreat.

Similar tendencies can be illustrated in the sphere of information as well as entertainment. As Dordick (1981) and Schiller (1981) have shown, the introduction of 'on-line' computerized information systems in the United States has led to a shift of information out of the public sphere and into the private where price barriers to access are making that information less freely available than it was before; where decisions on what information to make available, and in what form, are made on the basis of market considerations or other corporate interests rather than on the grounds of public interest. This whole development is seriously threatening the public library movement with its commitment to make information freely available to the whole population. What we are witnessing is a struggle to turn all information into private property and therefore a source of private profit rather than the claimed development of a system to provide information widely and cheaply to all. The recent shift in Prestel's marketing policy towards serving the business user is a symptom of a similar development which is leading in many spheres to a division not only between the rich and the poor in the sphere of private consumption, but between the business and the domestic markets such that developments of new information services are privileging corporate rather than public use.

Interactive capacity may indeed be useful for financial and commercial transactions, but claims that it allows the consumer in some way to talk back or the voter to be more fully involved in political decision-making are highly misleading. Such systems still place control over the agenda and questions in the hands of the controller of the network. Moreover it reinforces other tendencies in our society to what Sartre famously called 'serialization', that is, a social structure within which isolated individuals only relate to each other statistically. It is the model of the consumer rather than the citizen which privileges privatized forms of knowledge and experience, as opposed to group participation. The privileging of the domestic TV set by all these developments is part of this wider and deeper social development.

V

While one can recognize that what is at stake in the struggle surrounding the new information technologies is a battle between the public service and market modes of cultural production and consumption, it is less easy to formulate an appropriate political strategy in response. At a simple level we can say that public service broadcasting must be defended and that similar principles must be defended or extended to other cultural spheres as, for instance, in resisting the growth of sponsorship as a form of cultural subvention. But in order to do so public service itself needs to be rethought.

The crisis facing public service broadcasting throughout Europe is part of a wider political crisis, namely a profound shift in people's attitudes to the State and to the State's proper role in social life. There was once a time when the political battle-lines were clearly drawn. On the one hand, private capital and its allies defended the free market system against state encroachment; on the other, the forces of the Left fought for state intervention as a means of redressing the social inequalities of the capitalist market and (perhaps) eventually abolishing the market mechanism altogether. What marks the current crisis is a blurring of these old battle-lines by a widespread loss of faith in the Statist solution.

Behind the concrete economic and political problems facing public service broadcasting lies a crisis of the imagination – an inability to conceive of an alternative to broadcasting controlled by profit-seeking private capital other than as centralized, bureaucratic, inefficient, arrogantly insensitive to the people's needs, politically subservient to the holders of State power and so on. This crisis has its real material roots in the actual conduct of so-called public service broadcasting. Because the practice of public service broadcasting has been the practice of actual institutions, the BBC, RAI, ORTF, the nature and potentialities of public service broadcasting have become identified in the public's mind with the actual historical practice of those institutions. One way of rekindling faith in a public service alternative is to examine the record of such institutions and to show how far their actual performance is from being the necessary shape of public service broadcasting. In this respect what lessons can we learn from the recent history of the BBC?

In 1962 the Pilkington Report on the Future of Broadcasting delivered its verdict on eight years of competition between a commercial and a public service system of broadcasting and came down decisively in favour of the latter. It granted the BBC a second TV channel and refused such a channel to ITV unless major changes were made in the ITV system to better insulate programme provision from what Pilkington saw as the harmful effects of dependence upon advertising revenue. This judgement on the relative merits of the two systems was at the time widely endorsed by politicians, not only on the left, but also within the Tory Party as well, by intellectuals and more importantly by a significant proportion of the audience. After hitting a low of 27 per cent of the audience in late 1957, the BBC had fought back against ITV to a situation of rough parity with shows ranging from comedy (*Steptoe and Son, Hancock*), police series (*Z Cars*), drama (*Play for Today*), to current affairs (*Tonight*), and late night satire (*That Was the Week that Was*). Such programming gained not only large audiences but also widespread critical acclaim. For a short period, which included the launching of BBC2 and the introduction of colour, the BBC seemed, under the leadership of Sir Hugh Greene, to be in touch with and able to express a new, widespread, relatively progressive and popular political and cultural current. At this period a whole generation of intellectuals and cultural workers wanted actively to work for the BBC, seeing public service television in particular as one of the key areas of endeavour in a struggle to transform Britain in a politically and culturally progressive direction.

Within less than twenty years all that has changed. In their current financial crisis the BBC can now call on no significant sectors of public support among either politicians or intellectuals. While ironically their programmes are more popular than ever (they now regularly and convincingly win the ratings war with ITV) this seems to be with an audience that no longer sees any meaningful distinction between the two systems. The Annan Committee report in 1977 was, in marked contrast to Pilkington, on balance more critical of the BBC than of ITV and the current government with no real opposition has expanded the commercial system by authorizing a second commercial TV channel and by allowing commercial local radio to expand while so starving the BBC of funds that their system of local radio, far from expanding, is being cut back.

Many factors have led to this dramatic shift in the position of public service broadcasting, but I want only to examine those that can be attributed to the BBC's own practices.

In my view the BBC through the 1960s and 1970s betrayed public service broadcasting by progressively alienating the potential supporters of the public service ideal both among the audience and among broadcasters.

Let us look at the audience first. If one examines the development of the BBC in the 1920s and 1930s one can see that the Reithian definition of public service upon which the BBC based its practice was one within which an enlightened political and cultural elite imposed its tastes and views of the world by means of the 'brute force of monopoly' upon a public whose views and tastes were not to be trusted. The structure of Board of Governors and Advisory Committees was one designed to protect and shield the BBC as an institution rather than to act as a conduit of popular views and pressures. It was this elitist practice, also significantly centralized in London, that led in part to the early success of ITV. From the start ITV consciously adopted a more populist and less condescending tone in news and political coverage as well as in entertainment and was structured by Sir Robert Fraser, the first Director-General of the Independent Television Authority, on a regional basis as an admitted reaction against the centralized London bias of the BBC's structure.

In the late 1950s and early 1960s under the leadership of Sir Hugh Greene a new generation of BBC producers, in reaction to ITV, began to break out of the old BBC mould. However, for whatever reason, these initiatives were not pursued. Those groups outside the BBC who, in the more democratic and participatory climate of the late 1960s and early 1970s, were arguing for a BBC that would open itself fully to the diverse political and cultural currents within the country, that would openly recognize the breakdown of consensus, were actively rebuffed by a bureaucracy that exhibited an extreme arrogance and secretiveness that amounted at times to paranoia. This response included a notable unwillingness to cooperate with academic researchers, however impeccable their credentials, such that the BBC tried to suppress Tom Burns's now classic study (Burns, 1977), which they themselves had originally commissioned. All this was often in marked contrast to an ITV system which, in part because of its diversified centres of power (a federal regional system controlled by a separate and relatively small public bureaucracy in the IBA) always appeared more open and flexible, however little it gave away in fact.

The attitude of the BBC's management to the public was classically expressed by the then Director-General, Sir Charles Curran, in an article in the *Listener* on 28 February 1974, entitled 'The technocratic dilemma: planning and consent'. This article discusses the BBC's problems in dealing with the introduction of a new pattern of national radio broadcasting, as proposed in a BBC policy document 'Broadcasting in the seventies', and the widespread public opposition that these proposals aroused. Curran defines the problem, not as one of responding to public demands or of trying to involve the public in policy formation, but as one of manipulating public opinion to accept a management policy already agreed upon. Another notable example of the BBC's failure to respond to new audience needs and pressures has been its foot-dragging over the introduction of access programming, which remains entirely marginal to its output. One example of their obstructionist attitude in this regard was a programme produced by the Campaign Against Racism in the Media. For their programme on the BBC's access slot *Open Door* CARM asked to use BBC archive footage to illustrate their arguments, permission for which was refused (Gardner and Henry, 1979). The result of this history is a situation where political progressives have increasingly come to see the BBC, partly because it still remains the dominant force within British broadcasting, as the major obstacle to reform and the main target for attack. This in its turn has caused the BBC's defensive paranoia to deepen.

In part the BBC's failure to make common cause with those who wished to preserve the Corporation's public service role by extending it stems from its competitive position vis-à-vis the commercial system. The pressures of this competition have led the BBC increasingly to copy the methods of international commercial broadcasting. They have also resulted in the rise to management control within the BBC of a generation of broadcasters for whom this competition is the central experience and who see an alternative practice of public service broadcasting which takes a different view of audience needs and the proper way to serve them, as at best unrealistic or at worst irrelevant.

BBC management have similarly failed in relation to their other potential source of support, broadcasters themselves and the penumbra of associated intellectuals and cultural workers. As an institution the BBC has a long and well-documented history of opposition to trade union organization among its employees. The Ullswater Committee criticized it on this score as early as 1935, a criticism that was repeated by the Beveridge Committee in 1949. As a result the majority of BBC employees were organized in a supine staff association. Over many years this staff association evolved into an independent trade union, the ABS. But the slowness of the development is shown by the fact that the ABS did not finally affiliate to the TUC until 1966. To this day the BBC still refuses to recognize the ACTT, the major union of film and TV technicians which represents workers in ITV and the film industry. Consistently through the 1960s and 1970s BBC management took the narrowest and most reactionary line in its relations both with its permanent staff and with freelance writers, directors, etc. Its contracts are highly restrictive and it exerts its dominant power in broadcasting to impose highly unfavourable copyright terms on those writing for it.

The BBC has always organized its staff on highly hierarchical lines influenced both by military thinking and by class distinction, such that there is a wide divide between gentlemen who produce and manage, and those of lower class such as technicians. That this style has become increasingly unacceptable was marked by the first strike in the history of the ABS in 1969, an experience from which BBC labour relations never recovered.

At the same time BBC management continually rebuffed moves among broadcasters for greater worker participation, both in the actual production process by breaking down distinctions within production teams and also in the formulation of general broadcasting policy. This internal opposition came to a head when a significant section of the TV production staff, feeling that their superiors no longer spoke for them in regard to the future shape of British broadcasting, gave independent evidence to the Annan Inquiry. Resistance on the part of management to this internal reform movement was exacerbated by the increasingly heavy-handed imposition of censorship by top programme management. Or perhaps one should rather say that in a general climate in favour of greater worker participation and autonomy the old styles of censorship and editorial control were no longer acceptable.

At the same time the BBC lost the opportunity, partly, it is true, through lack of resources, but in spite of the urgings of government, to respond fully to demands for greater regional devolution and diversification – a move that could have implanted the BBC more firmly in the life of the community. In marked contrast, some at least of the ITV companies undoubtedly are able to call upon local and regional loyalties unavailable to the BBC. Indeed there are those who would argue that the BBC went in the opposite direction and effectively destroyed what regional autonomy existed, turning the major regional centres into production factories for a London-controlled network with little if any independent programming autonomy. Similarly, BBC local radio has been tightly controlled from the centre.

In the battle for the hearts and minds of the public over the future of public service broadcasting it is important to stress that the historical practices of supposedly public service institutions such as the BBC do not necessarily correspond to the full potential of public service, and may indeed be actively in opposition to the development of those potentials. Over the past twenty years the BBC, while competing successfully with its commercial rival for ratings, has become essentially a multi-media conglomerate whose relations with the public and with its workers is no different from, and in some cases may actually be worse than, a commercial company. That it is non-profit-making and does not accept advertising revenue remain important differences. Indeed they remain the basis for its potential as a public service. But it has totally failed to respond to calls made to it by both the public and by broadcasting workers to forge a more participatory, collaborative and democratic relationship which might truly serve the public by expressing their political and cultural diversity rather than serve the State and associated power elites by transmitting an elitist, authoritarian and manipulative political and cultural message.

I have concentrated attention on the BBC because it is the chief symbol and mould of public service broadcasting in Britain. However, with powerful ideological and political forces now advocating total deregulation, we must not disregard the IBA as an alternative model for public service control of broadcasting. Unfortunately its history has demonstrated similar failures. In its early days it became too much the spokesman for the companies it was supposed to regulate and, as the early history of London Weekend Television demonstrated, was unwilling to use its powers to force companies to keep the programming promises on the basis of which their contracts had been awarded. Following the criticism of Pilkington, it became more interventionist in scheduling and and programming policy, but progressive programme makers have not looked to it as their defender against pressure from either commercial interests or the State. In the awarding of radio franchises it has demonstrated a marked lack of sympathy for alternative, more democratic and popular models of control and programming philosophy. But perhaps most important of all it has consistently dragged its feet over opening up either the awarding of franchises or the on-going assessment of the services to proper public scrutiny.

VI

Perhaps the most dramatic and concrete contemporary result of this history is Channel 4, and it demonstrates all the ambiguities and contradictions of the present situation. On the one hand much of the idealism and energy that went into the campaign that produced Channel 4 as opposed to an ITV2 was undoubtedly inspired by a genuine desire to extend and redefine the practice of public service broadcasting in the stated conviction that both the BBC and the IBA had in important respects failed. To this extent of course the granting of the fourth channel to the IBA, rather than to an Open Broadcasting Authority, was a defeat; but the fact that we didn't simply get ITV2 demonstrates that successful resistance to privatizing trends is possible.

On the other hand this idealism and energy led to a result which has weakened public service broadcasting because it was based upon a fundamentally flawed analysis of cultural production and distribution. It was based upon a notion of cultural freedom as expansion of provision without regard for how this expanded provision was to be funded. More damagingly still it was essentially a broadcasters' campaign for their own 'freedom' based upon a nineteenth-century artisanal model of cultural and intellectual work. The cries of pain from independent producers at the 'interference' and tough contractual terms imposed by Channel 4 already demonstrate that such a model is incompatible both with the regular flow of product a TV channel requires to hold its audience and with the power that control of a scarce national distribution system necessarily gives. At the same time these producers will discover that by escaping from the relatively protected environment of the BBC and the ITV companies they have obtained the freedom to be exploited on the international market. If it ended there it would be merely a story of individual tragedies, but once a group of producers has rejected the existing model of public service broadcasting in favour of an 'independent' market mode they become a pressure group for the expansion of that market in a desperate attempt to find a viable niche for themselves. They can thus be recruited in the name of 'creative freedom' to support the campaign for the rapid expansion of satellite and cable provision.

The refusal to face the reality of scarcity is at present the greatest general weakness of the socialist movement. Socialism has itself been infected by that ideology of ever-expanding choice secreted by the long capitalist boom of the post-war years. The field of media policy is but one sub-set of this more general problem. Thus any socialist response to cable and satellite must be, so far as possible, to oppose expansion and face openly and coherently the inevitable charges of Luddism. The first priority remains, within the bounds of our existing cultural resources, to defend and expand the public sphere. Political imagination and energy must be devoted to changing our existing system of public service broadcasting for the better and to persuading both audience and broadcasters that only within such a public service can a democratic culture be created and sustained. The difficulties facing such a political project should not be under-estimated. My experience on the Labour Party's Media Study Group has suggested that in the present climate broadcasting workers, or at least their union leaders, will tend to resist any suggestion of change. It is partly in order to enlist their support that priority must be given to defending existing broadcasting institutions against the threat from cable and satellite. This must, of course, include opposing the BBC's satellite plans.

However, the problem runs deeper than that. The non-accountable model of cultural production by a privileged elite enshrined in the institutional structures and practices of British broadcasting is deeply entrenched in the consciousness of both the medium's workers and of politicians. I never thought I would hear even MPs and activists on the left of the Labour Party arguing, when democratically elected bodies to control broadcasting were proposed, that this was very dangerous because 'the wrong kind of people might be elected'. One can find a parallel to such an attitude in the contempt and lack of sympathy for popular tastes still all too prevalent among supposedly progressive cultural workers in the film and video field.

On the other hand we have also to accept that the steadily increasing privatization of cultural consumption makes the public itself resistant to participatory models of cultural production and consumption. That the UK at a time of deep recession was the fastest-growing market in the world for video-recorders should give us pause for thought. It is clear therefore that much campaigning work needs to be done within the socialist movement to change deeply ingrained attitudes to cultural production and consumption before there is any hope of achieving concrete reforms.

Finally, a viable international cultural politics must be developed. This represents the most intractable problem in contemporary cultural politics precisely because culture has for a long time now been conceptualized and indeed experienced on the level of the nation-state. In this context the New World Information Order must not be thought of as just a North/ South issue. The threats and potentialities of satellite broadcasting can only be handled at a transnational level. The French government is active diplomatically to develop the concept and practice of a European public cultural space which would include the public service control of European satellite broadcasting. There are forces both in the European Parliament and Commission, and within the Council of Europe, who recognize the urgent need to create European institutions and regulations which would embody the principle of public service. The media unions are beginning to formulate joint policies. It is extremely important that cultural workers in Britain respond to these initiatives and help to build upon them, if only because Britain, whose media industries represent one of the few areas of economic growth and success on the international market, is sure to be the European launching pad for the assault on the public cultural sphere. Indeed the present government's satellite and cable plans are openly presented as such. Alongside this is ranged the risk capital of Messrs Murdoch, Maxwell, Berlusconi, and all. If this battle is lost the dispersed corporation will create a dispersed culture in its own image. Within it a certain local autonomy will perhaps be tolerated, but the centres of strategic intelligence and cultural power will be elsewhere.

Note

1 Throughout 'billion' means 1,000 million.

References

Baumol, W. J. and Bowen, W. G. (1976) 'On the performing arts: the anatomy of their economic problems', in M. Blaugh (ed.), *The Economics of the Arts*. Oxford: Martin Robertson.

Briggs, A. (1960) Fisher Memorial Lecture. University of Adelaide.

Burns, T. (1977) *The BBC: Public Institution and Private World*. London: Macmillan.

Curran, J. (1977) 'Capitalism and control of the press 1800–1975', in J. Curran, M. Gurevitch and J. Woollacott (eds), *Mass Communication and Society*. London: Edward Arnold.

Curran, J. (1981) 'The impact of advertising on the British mass media', *Media, Culture and Society* (Jan.).

Dordick, H. (1981) *The Emerging Network Marketplace*. New York: Ablex.

Gardner, C. and Henry, M. (1979) 'Racism, anti-racism and access television: the making of *Open Door*', *Screen Education*, 31 (Summer): 69–79.

Huet, A., Ion, J., Lefèbvre, A., Miège, B. and Peron, R. (eds) (1978) *Capitalisme et Industries Culturelles*. Grenoble: Presses Universitaires de Grenoble.

Hyman, A. (1980) *The Coming of the Chip*. London: New English Library.

Ivre, I. (1981) 'Mass media: costs, choices, freedom' *InterMedia* (Sept.).

Jay, P. (1981) 'Speech to the Edinburgh TV Festival', *The Times*, 27 August.

Sahin, H. and Robins, J. P. (1981) 'Beyond the realm of necessity', *Media, Culture and Society* (Jan.).

Schiller, H. (1981) *Who Knows: Information in the Age of the Fortune 500*. New York: Ablex.

Smith, A. (1980) *Goodbye Gutenberg: The Newspaper Revolution of the 1980s*. London: Oxford University Press.

Winston, B. (1981) 'Showdown at Culture Gulch', *Channels* (Aug./Sept.).

9

Telecommunications Policy in the United Kingdom

Two contrasting positions have dominated the debate on UK telecommunications policy. On the one hand, the government and its supporters have argued the benefits of competition in encouraging innovation and efficiency in the delivery of the telecommunication goods and services necessary for the UK to compete in the developing world information economy. On the other hand, the Post Office Engineering Union (POEU) and the Labour Party have argued for the maintenance or restoration of a national, state-owned monopoly on the grounds of efficiency, social equity, national security and industrial and economic strategy. In this chapter I will argue that neither alternative is an adequate response to the problems currently posed in the formulation of telecommunications policy. On the one hand, I will argue that government policy cannot deliver what it promises, both because competition is unrealizable and inefficient in the provision of public switched network services, and because there is an unresolved contradiction between a policy that favours telecommunication service users and one that supports the equipment industry. On the other hand, I will argue that for technical, economic and social reasons a monopoly is both unsustainable and undesirable.

II

How a nation's telecommunications network is organized and controlled is a matter of central and growing social importance. Even in its present form, as a deliverer in the main of what the Americans call Plain Old Telephone Service (POTS), British Telecom (BT) is a massive organization. Its 244,592 employees were only topped by the National Coal Board when it was among the nationalized industries, and now far outstrip most of its private sector rivals. Its annual turnover in 1985 was £6876 million and its assets £9198 million. Among *The Times* 1000 it is fifth rated in terms of capital employed and sixth rated in terms of profits. In addition its investment programme, running at an annual rate of £1700 million, is largely responsible for the economic health of the UK telecommunications equipment industry, a sector dominated by GEC, Plessey and STC, with annual sales of between £2123 and 2477 million, 50 per cent of which is accounted for by sales of main exchange equipment to BT.

Moreover BT and the associated UK telecommunications equipment and services industry are the indispensable foundation for the development of an indigenous information technology and information services industry, the development of which the UK government, along with its partner governments in the OECD, has, rightly or wrongly, identified as crucial to future national prosperity.

In addition the convergence of computing and telecommunications is tending to transform all social information flows into an electronic, digital form. This dissolves the traditional demarcations between, on the one hand, the media of mass communication and their associated institutional, legal and regulatory frameworks, based as these are on distinct technologies of reproduction and distribution (newspapers on paper and print, the cinema upon photographic processes, broadcasting on over-air analogue transmission) and, on the other hand, telecommunications services based upon the technology of twisted-pair copper wires. The end-point of this development, the installation of a world-wide Integrated Services Digital Network (ISDN), promises to create a single, intermingled bit-stream, even if for final consumption this information is translated back into printed words, images or sounds. Thus how that pathway is controlled, and with what implications for access to it, is as important as any political question we face.

III

Since Alexander Graham Bell filed his basic telephone patents in 1876 the telephone has been developed to its present level, in advanced industrialized societies, as a ubiquitous instrument of social and business communication, for the most part by national monopolies. In Europe these monopolies were arms of the state (PTTs). In the US the job was left to a regulated private company, American Telephone and Telegraph (AT&T).

This arrangement was defended and, as I will show, can still be defended, on the grounds that the provision of the basic switched public telecommunications network is a natural monopoly. Its natural monopoly status flows from large sunk costs associated with low marginal and average costs producing large scale economies. Moreover the opportunities for alternative routing over a complex network meant that only control of a unified network made feasible optimum system investment to cover peak loading and that the value of the network rose exponentially with each additional subscriber. In addition, and unrelated to the natural monopoly argument, monopoly control of all equipment attached to the network was defended on the grounds of protecting the technical integrity of the network and of the need for technical compatibility.

Although operating in the market sector, that is, selling goods and services to consumers, these monopolies were used to pursue essentially sociopolitical ends, namely the provision of low cost universal service to all citizens throughout the territory of the nation-state. The service was universal in terms both of geographical location and price, and its provision involved a process of cost-averaging so that areas and routes of high density notionally subsidized those of low density. I say notionally because, as I will argue, the notion of subsidy within the economics of a switched network is problematic.

These monopolies also developed a closely integrated relationship with the domestic telecommunications equipment industries of their respective countries (indeed in the US these needs were largely met by a wholly owned and vertically integrated subsidiary of AT&T, Western Electric). The monopsonic structure prevalent in Europe was defended on the grounds that the network controller alone can determine both the technical needs and pace of development of the network and thus inevitably dominates, and requires a close, stable long-term relationship with, the industry supplying its network equipment needs. As telecommunications bulked ever larger in national accounts this relationship also became a crucial cornerstone of governments' industrial policies.

IV

Since the Thatcher government came to power in the UK in 1979 this inherited structure has been pushed through a radical process of change. The UK experience is often compared with that in the US, indeed by many the US has even been taken as an example for highly uncritical emulation (see Beesley, 1981). But in five short years the UK telecommunications industry has been forced through a process that took the US twenty-five years to complete from the Above 890 and Hush-a-Phone decisions of the Federal Communication Commission (FCC) in 1959 up to the final break up of AT&T in 1984.

Thus BT has been transformed from a state-owned and controlled monopoly supplier of all telecommunications goods and services, except Private Automatic Branch Exchanges (PABXs) of over 100 lines, into a limited public company operating under licence in which the government will hold only a 49 per cent share stake. The terminal market has been completely liberalized. From 1 January 1985 BT lost its right to install the first telephone, and the approval of equipment for attachment to the network has been taken out of BT's hands and transferred to a British Approval Board for Telecommunications (BABT), a subcommittee of the British Standards Institute (BSI).

A competitive company, Mercury, a wholly owned subsidiary of Cable and Wireless, has been licensed to offer switched telecommunications services on its own network across the whole range from local loop through trunk to international with full interconnect rights with the BT network. While BT and Mercury retain duopoly of trunk voice telephony and data transmission, competition has been introduced at the level of the local loop by licensing two competitive cellular radio consortia, one jointly owned by BT and Securicor, the other by Racal and Millicom, and by allowing local cable operators to offer data services in all markets except those of Central London, Birmingham, Manchester and Glasgow. In addition a general licence has been offered to operators of Value Added Network Services (VANS), in US parlance 'enhanced services', of which to date 370 are being offered by eighty-four licensees.

This new structure is regulated by an Office of Telecommunications (Oftel) under a Director General of Telecommunications (DGT) who will advise the Secretary of State for Industry on the granting of licences within the terms of the Telecommunications Act, section 3 of which lays out the broad aims of UK telecommunications policy, including the provision of universal service, the promotion of competition, economy and innovation, the guarantee for consumers of a choice between alternative goods and services, and the development of the UK as a base for international companies and for the development of an internationally competitive telecommunications equipment and information services industry. Once a licence has been granted it will be the duty of DGT and Oftel to police its observance and in so doing they will have considerable independence from government. Admirable as many of the objectives laid down by the Act may be, the major problem facing Oftel is that they are in many instances either incompatible or unrealizable, and the necessary choices and compromises between these clashing objectives will be necessarily political. It is not clear that Oftel has either the resources, status or political legitimacy to take on that political role.

I want now to examine why this process is taking place, what are its implications and what are the specific policy problems it throws up.

V

The national monopoly PTT model for the provision of telecommunication services is under intense pressure to change for the following reasons:

1 Technical developments, in particular the convergence of telecommunications and computing, have broken up the simple homogeneity of the old switched-voice telephony service. As a result it has become increasingly difficult for telecommunications administrations to make choices between a bewildering range of possible service offerings and customer needs without using the mechanism of the market.
2 Technical developments of distribution systems rival to twisted-pair copper wires, such as satellites, broad-band cable, microwave and optical fibre, have both in part undercut the old natural monopoly argument and provided the opportunity for major new corporate

actors, often closely linked to defence funding such as satellite companies, to enter the message transmission market.

3 The close monopsonic relationship between a national monopoly network provider and the national monopoly equipment supply industry has come under intense pressure because of rising R and D costs, which mean that national markets are no longer large enough to amortize the necessary investment. As a result industry analysts have predicted that only perhaps three companies will survive world-wide as manufacturers of telecommunication switching equipment by the mid-nineties. Hence recent moves through the European Commission to create a unified European market; hence recent bilateral deals such as that between Germany and France on the provision of telephones and between Britain and France on digital switching apparatus; and hence AT&T's recent links with Philips and Olivetti.

4 Changes in business practice, in particular the development of trans-national, multi-plant operations and the development of the service sector, especially international financial services, have meant that telecommunications have become, for many corporations, a major business cost and therefore control of those costs has become a high management priority and the efficiency of the service provided a major ingredient in a firm's competitivity.

(For a fuller discussion of these issues see OECD, 1983.)

VI

How is the UK reacting to these pressures? In assessing UK telecommunications policy we need to distinguish two levels of debate. There is first the question of whether the government's policy works in its own terms and second the question of what alternative policies might be feasible or desirable.

The first question has dominated recent debate, such as it has been, largely because those opposed to government policy, most notably the POEU and the Labour Party, have reduced the second question to a demand for a return to the status quo ante, a position that I hope to show is both untenable and undesirable.

In judging the success of the government's policy in its own terms, the core question raised by its critics is whether in fact it has made good its claim to introduce sufficient competition to make the industry largely self-regulating, thus allowing Oftel to operate with a light touch, or whether, as its critics complain, it has merely unleashed BT as an uncontrollable private monopoly. Underlying this question is another that has received less attention. This is whether the industrial aims of government policy, which because of the scale of enterprise now needed for success in the international electronics and information technology (IT) market requires a dominant BT as the engine for the development of the UK IT industry, is compatible with the aim of promoting the interests of the users of telecommunication services by introducing competition in the supply of those services.

VII

In assessing government policy we first need to get out of the way the red herring of privatization. The decision to sell a majority shareholding in BT to the private sector has everything to do with the ideology of the Conservative government but nothing to do with its telecommunications policy. All its aims could have been pursued, and could in the future be pursued, for instance, by a Labour government, with BT remaining entirely in the public sector. The argument that it would have been starved of the necessary investment finance, as it has been in the past, is to raise the public sector borrowing requirement to the status of a fetish. However, the desire to privatize has had a major inhibiting effect on the development of a competitive telecommunications environment. In order that the maximum price could be raised for BT shares it could not be seen to be over-regulated. Similarly the option to split BT, on the lines of the AT&T break up, into separate long-line and local operating companies, an option actively canvassed by corporate lobbyists at the time of the 1983 General Election, had to be rejected by the government. But the decision to maintain BT as a massively dominant unified entity in the UK telecommunications market meant that Mercury had to be artificially sustained by guaranteeing no further competition in public switched network provision before 1990 and by forbidding the resale of private leased circuits, at least until 1989.

VIII

The British process of liberalization is often described, using the example of the US, as one of deregulation. It is, on the contrary, a move from a public monopoly to a regime of regulated competition. Because, unlike the US, the UK does not possess a culture of regulation with its penumbra of expert economists, lawyers and academics and its tradition of public interest debate and action around regulatory issues, the problems facing the UK's new regulatory regime are not fully or widely appreciated. What has in fact been constructed is a situation not dissimilar to the US situation prior to the break up of AT&T, but with BT also being able to operate, as AT&T was not, in unregulated markets. The process known as deregulation in the US has been undertaken, whether rightly or wrongly, precisely because the previous situation was seen to be unworkable. On the one hand, a small and relatively underfunded FCC (although the FCC makes Oftel look puny) was incapable of regulating AT&T, in particular because – and I shall return to this point – transparent accounts are impossible in switched network service provision. On the other hand, it was seen as necessary by US economic policy

makers to release AT&T into unregulated markets, particularly internationally, in order to compete more effectively against Japanese
competition and to discipline IBM.

The regulatory process, which Oftel will undertake, is based upon the
efficacy of competition. As Professor Littlechild put it (1983):

> Competition is indisputably the most effective means – perhaps ultimately the
> *only* effective means – of protecting the consumer against monopoly power.
> Regulation is essentially a means of preventing the worst excesses of
> monopoly; it is not a substitute for competition. It is a means of 'holding the
> fort' until competition arrives. Consequently the main focus of attention has
> to be on securing the most promising conditions for competition to emerge,
> and protecting competition from abuse.

In its turn this process depends upon the transparency of accounts. For
an interim period the *de facto* market dominance of BT is recognized by
using the RPI–3 formula for a transitional five-year period to control its
tariffs. Under this formula BT may not raise its bundle of inland tariffs
by more than the Retail Price Index minus 3 per cent. It has in addition
given a voluntary undertaking not to raise residential line rentals by more
than 2 per cent per annum. The RPI–3 formula has been preferred to
the more normal rate-of-return method used in the US because it encour-
ages productivity and avoids the gold-plating syndrome of which AT&T
has often stood accused. However, this formula is to be applied to a
bundle of tariffs sufficiently wide that, as an authoritative study by the
stockbrokers de Zoete and Bevan (1984) shows, ample room is left for
profitable tariff rebalancing manoeuvres. Moreover, many of the horses
have already bolted. BT has been busy in the past few years balancing
its tariffs with two ends in view. Firstly, it has raised inland rates at the
expense of the international so that BT has the lowest rates for private
circuits in Europe, the lowest international rates among major OECD
countries and the highest local call rates (see Tables 9.1 and 9.2). The
aim of this is to make the UK attractive to international business by the
provision of international services from which BT, as its accounts are
presently structured, reaps the highest profits. One result of this is that
BT, because of the way such services are accounted for between national
telecommunication entities, makes a loss on all outward international
calls and a profit on inward, resulting in a net balance-of-payments loss
to the UK. Secondly, in response to the threat of competition from
Mercury, BT has cut long-distance rates (mainly used by business) and
raised local charges. There is of course nothing in the RPI–3 formula
which allows DGT to redress these balances. Indeed international tariffs
do not come within the formula.

IX

But the core of the argument over telecommunications policy remains the
question of whether it is either possible or desirable to introduce

Table 9.1 *Comparative cost of private circuits from Europe to the USA, 1982 (£ sterling)*

UK	24,600
Belgium	29,793
Denmark	41,908
France	27,324
Italy	44,033
Ireland	37,917
Netherlands	40,049
Norway	54,845
Sweden	34,165
Switzerland	47,368
West Germany	48,677

At the exchange rate ruling during week beginning 24 January 1983
Source: British Telecom. Non-UK rates taken from 1982 edition of the *Eurodata Foundation Yearbook*.

Table 9.2 *National Utility Service: telecoms cost comparisons, 1983 (£s sterling based on prices ruling at 1 February 1983)*

Type of call	UK	Belgium	France	West Germany	Italy	Canada	USA
Local	0.086	0.06	0.05	0.06	0.04	0	0.05
Trunk *b*	0.516				0.47		
bi	0.387						
		0.30	0.77	0.92		0.95	0.87
b	0.645				0.76		
bi	0.516						
International	1.62	4.90	3.72	5.86	4.78	3.13	2.97

Notes: All calls of three-minute duration. Where charges vary according to time of business-day, the standard rate is shown first with peak rate below. Trunk calls are costed over a distance of 200 miles. International calls are between New York and Europe, except for Canada in which they are between Toronto and London. UK trunk calls are on a two-tier basis shown as *b* and *bi* (*bi* tariff is for 'low-cost routes'). Prices are given in £s sterling excluding VAT. Exchange rate as at 27 January 1983.

competition in the provision of public switched telecommunication services, or the Public Switched Telephone Network (PSTN) as it is often called. Much of the original push for liberalization came from the major corporate users organized in the Telecommunication Managers Association (TMA) and the International Telecommunication Users Group (INTUG). They argued, as they had done in the United States, that the price of their telecommunication circuits and services was unacceptably high, both because of what they saw as the inherent inefficiencies of monopoly, such as labour feather-bedding, and because major business users were being forced by cost-averaging to subsidize other subscribers, in particular residential subscribers. They argued that only the introduction of competition could rectify this situation and bring prices into line with costs. In addition, scared by a major POEU strike in the City of London, they argued that, given the increasingly vital role in many of their businesses of rapid, uninterrupted telecommunications flow, without an alternative service being available, they were extremely vulnerable, as Fleet Street had been in the past, to labour blackmail.

X

Before examining the core of the argument relating to the effects of competition on the PSTN, it is important to stress that BT as a nationalized monopoly was not inefficient by comparative international standards. Its labour productivity was in line with that of other telecommunication network operators, including AT&T, at similar levels of telephone penetration, which is the main determinant of labour productivity, according to a study of the Institute of Electrical Engineers (de Zoete and Bevan, 1984: 74). As we have seen, its rates for private circuits, long-distance and international calls are among the lowest in the world and its return on capital has been far superior to AT&T's (de Zoete and Bevan, 1984: 67–8). Many would argue of course that these comparisons are beside the point because the organizations with which BT is being compared are themselves monopolies and because, in the case of AT&T, it is rate-of-return regulation that explains the low return on capital.

However, the point is that there was and is no prima facie case that BT was inefficient. The case in favour of competition has to be demonstrated and that this case is as much a matter of faith and ideology as of economic analysis is demonstrated by the testimony of Dr Alfred Kahn, Professor of Economics at Cornell University and one of the gurus of the deregulation movement in the US, before the Senate Committee on Commerce, Science and Transportation:

> We will never resolve all of these issues to our satisfaction in advance. The essential job is to get on with the job, to make the decision to deregulate where we feel confident that that is the thing to do. The presence or absence of economies of scale in long distance or interexchange communications, and its relevance for the feasibility of competition, is a much more complicated question than, say, in the distribution of electricity, and it is one that I have not been able to resolve to my own satisfaction. . . . I certainly don't feel confident to decide in what sectors of communication the case for regulated monopoly remains compelling. . . . I warn you that whatever solution you devise will be imperfect because it will inevitably represent a compromise between competing values. (US Senate, 1982)

In order to understand how Kahn come to that conclusion we need to look at the structure of a PSTN, in this case BT's, and at the economics of its operation. The network can be split into three distinct sections for operational purposes. The local loop, run by BT's Local Communications Services division, links every individual subscriber to the local exchange and through that exchange to each other. This division accounts for the vast mass of BT's assets and operating revenue, 70 per cent of capital, 83 per cent of employees and 67 per cent of gross revenue. These local exchanges are then interconnected by the trunk network under the National Network division with 10 per cent of capital, 26 per cent of revenues and 4 per cent of employees. This division handles all trunk calls. Finally the trunk network is linked through international gateway exchanges to the international submarine cable and satellite networks and through them to the networks of other national telecommunication administrations. The handling of international calls through this network comes under BT International with 17.8 per cent of revenues, 6.5 per cent of capital and 5.2 per cent of employees.

XI

The essence of a public switched network is that it is an integrated network that carries inevitably a high level of shared facilities and costs. The value of the network to each subscriber is represented, not just by the number of connections that subscriber makes, but by the number of potential connections in which he or she could be involved as either initiator or receiver. Thus the value of the network increases exponentially with each additional subscriber, since such an addition represents one, plus all existing subscribers', additional potential connections. The problem, common in information economics, is how one gets subscribers actually to pay for these advantages when on a call-tariff-based system users only pay for the actual calls they initiate and not for the calls they receive or the advantages that the total system represents. Thus although a high proportion of the sunk capital cost of the network is in the local loop, where each subscriber line has a low average level of usage and thus apparently a low return on capital, users of the trunk and international services require the whole of the local loop to make their connections. In fact they are utilizing not just the actual switching and circuit capacity they use as a proportion of total traffic on the local loop, but also the potential made available by the local loop. The optimum economic solution to this problem in theory is to recoup the costs of network operation by a flat-rate rental charge on all subscribers and then to provide all calls free of charge, the system in fact used in many areas of the US for local calls. However, because to date, for economic and social reasons, the aim has been to expand the subscriber base and thus network usage and by so doing lower average costs, connection and rental have in fact been offered at a cost that produces an inadequate return on the capital directly employed. None of this matters so long as the network and the services offered over that network are under unified control. The fact remains that the arguments about cross-subsidy in which BT management, government, industry and the POEU have indulged are entirely fatuous and the figures presented in any set of BT accounts now available or in the future are, to a considerable extent, artificial and represent arbitrary allocations of costs and revenues designed for whatever accounting, management control or propaganda purposes such allocations are made.

XII

In this situation one can introduce four levels of competition: in the local loop, in the trunk network, in international circuits and in private leased circuits. At present in the UK Mercury has been licensed to compete with BT at all these levels. In addition there is potential competition at the level of the local loop from cable TV franchises and cellular radio. Full competition on the local loop is unlikely because of the high costs of entry and the low returns available. De Zoete and Bevan, for instance, consider the possibility of competition from cable TV. At present such franchises are only able to carry voice telephony as sub-licensees of either BT or Mercury. In reality, since BT already has a local loop, this means Mercury. If a local cable system were to set up, in association with Mercury, the necessary switching and billing mechanisms and assuming the unlikely total penetration of their 100,000 house franchise area, the total revenue from local calls between those 100,000 homes would be only £1 million per annum and BT would continue to take most of that. The bulk of long-distance calls would continue to be delivered by BT, which would charge commercial rates for so doing, so the cable operator would only be able to undercut BT on the local portion of the call where BT's economies of scale are much greater. It is therefore not surprising that there has not been a rush, so far as one knows, by potential cable operators to link up with Mercury.

XIII

Thus the main threat at the local level is bypass, especially since cable operators can carry data. The implications of bypass and its closely associated concept, cream-skimming, also apply in the areas where Mercury's main competitive thrust will come – long-distance and private circuits. Here it is important to realize that one-third of BT's revenues and one-half of its profits are derived from just 300 major user companies. This is the attractive market. These are the interests that pressed for liberalization. Mercury's figure-of-eight network is carefully designed to capture that traffic.

Bypass refers to the phenomenon whereby major bulk users of tele-communications capacity, whether voice or data, use a private (or in the case of Mercury) alternative circuit to bypass sections of the PSTN. If such users are allowed to switch in and out of the PSTN at will then, because these circuits do not bear the general network costs of switching, network control and especially investment in capacity to cover peak loads and breakdowns (the user of a bypass circuit can rely on the PSTN to supply this capacity when needed), these circuits can be offered at a significantly lower cost than usage of the equivalent sections of the PSTN. Moreover the user of a bypass does not pay for the externalities of that usage, namely the higher costs for remaining users caused by the withdrawal of the business of a major user, when those other low-volume users do not themselves have the economic option of withdrawal. We have here a phenomenon similar to the effect of the rise in private car ownership on public transport and with similarly damaging social results. In short, bypass enables its users to free-ride on the network and to transfer the cost of that ride to other less privileged users. As a result of the rapid development of bypass the US is having to consider seriously taxing bypass users to subsidize remaining users of the PSTN. The potential effect of bypass can at least be mitigated if interconnection with the PSTN is strictly forbidden and policed, but leakage of such circuits through digital PABXs into the PSTN, even where such interconnection is formally banned, will become increasingly prevalent. The effects of bypass can also be mitigated if the resale of private leased capacity is forbidden, as is the case in the UK at least until 1989. This stops major users clubbing together to set up private bypass networks or entrepreneurs doing the same for major users. The ban in the UK was motivated firstly by the need to protect the fledgling Mercury, which is in effect nothing but a major bypass network. But in addition it was probably motivated by pressure from European PTTs and major international users of private circuits. Certainly European PTTs have threatened to retaliate against the US, if it introduces resale into international circuits, by simply withdrawing all private circuits and charging major users of the PSTN on a straight usage basis as with other network users. This would be so disastrous for major multinational users of private circuits, such as the banks, that they have put considerable pressure on the FCC and the US government not to allow resale internationally. No doubt the UK government was subject to similar pressures.

XIV

So Mercury's major competitive thrust will come in the areas of private circuits, long-distance and international. So far as private circuits are concerned, BT's circuits are highly competitive both in terms of price and, with the introduction of the digital overlay stream family of services, technically as well. At present Mercury does not appear to have made much impact on the market and, although no doubt they can establish a small market niche providing really massive users with alternative capacity to protect them against what they see as the potential for union blackmail and to act as a bargaining counter with BT, this activity will remain largely irrelevant to the operation of the PSTN.

So far as long-distance is concerned, their ability to compete depends upon two factors – their ability as a new concern to use state-of-the-art technology with a better cost-performance ratio than BT's existing technology, and the interconnect terms with BT. The technology question is a major concern when considering the impact of competition upon an established network. Traditionally network operators have kept the cost of service down by using long capital depreciation schedules. Investment in BT's network has already been largely paid for by BT's subscribers. A new competitive entrant, using new technology with superior cost-performance ratios to the sunk capital investment of BT, devalues BT's and thus its subscribers' existing investment by reducing traffic on that network against which long-term investments had been made, and thus, in the case where competition is successful, locks BT into a higher cost network and by its very entry pushes up BT's average costs. At the same time it devalues BT's existing capital by forcing it to depreciate over a much shorter time-scale. This is one of the prices the system pays for the high rate of innovation demanded by sophisticated major corporate users and the apparatus supply industry. It has tended in the US and will tend here to put telecommunications network operators ever deeper in hock to the banks and will distort the distribution of national investment in ways which may be desirable, but which should be the result of political debate rather than of supposed market pressure. It is questionable whether the improving cost-performance ratios of new equipment outweigh the accelerated write-off time and therefore whether the end result is a more or less cost-effective systems.

In the end the viability of competition in the long-distance and international markets will depend upon the terms of interconnect between BT and any competitor, for the present, Mercury. For the reasons spelt out above the task of Oftel in policing this interconnect agreement is impossible, since Mercury should clearly pay a premium for interconnect that takes into account not just the direct costs incurred by BT, but also BT's provision of peak capacity, the value of the total network and the reduction in that value that would ensue were Mercury to be successful. The dilemma for Oftel is illustrated by condition 13 in BT's licence which enjoins DGT, in drawing up any interconnect agreement, to both ensure 'that the requirements of fair competition are satisfied' and 'that charging arrangements take account of the overall pattern of the Licensee's costs'. These aims are irreconcilable since if BT's overall pattern of costs is taken into account there is no price at which Mercury could undercut BT. The concept of predatory pricing in the provision of public switched telecommunication services is meaningless except within the narrow political terms of a predisposition to favour competition at all costs.

Finally there will be competition between BT and Mercury in the provision of international circuits. Here a different set of considerations arise because of the peculiar economics of international circuits. Both BT and Mercury's licences limit the extent to which the government will allow them to compete internationally, in particular preventing them from entering into arrangements with foreign carriers which are more favourable to the one than to the other. This is to stop a price war in international circuits which would not be to the advantage of the UK which at present benefits from the fact that 60 per cent of private circuits and 40 per cent of highly profitable switched traffic on the Europe/US routes goes through the UK. The danger of two freely competing UK operators stems from the way in which international tariffs are negotiated. Transfers between administrations for calls passing between them are based upon a negotiated accounting rate of so much per minute for handling incoming calls. This accounting rate bears no necessary relationship to the tariff actually charged to the consumer. Thus, for instance, it is at present considerably cheaper to call from London to New York than in the reverse direction. This means that BT can make a profit on its international call business while the UK suffers a balance-of-payments loss. As a result of this system, any competition between UK operators in negotiating an accounting rate with foreign operators would be likely to result not only in a loss to the UK balance of payments, but also in higher prices for UK consumers. There are stipulations therefore in the licences of both BT and Mercury that limit competition for international traffic. This problem may become more acute and more difficult for Oftel to police as pressures from the US to open up the international market in telecommunication services strengthen.

XV

The whole issue of the desirability or otherwise of introducing competition into the PSTN has, in part, been presented as a clash between business and residential subscribers. Business spokesmen claim that business is subsidizing residential subscribers and opponents of liberalization, such as the POEU, claim that it will result in a large hike in residential rental and local call charges, because existing cross-subsidies will have to be abolished as BT rebalances its tariffs to head off 'cream-skimming'. Cream-skimming refers to the practice already central to the strategy determining the design of Mercury's network, (covering as it does 60 per cent of the business population but only 20 per cent of BT's traffic) of only competing on high capacity routes and for high capacity customers. The potential economies of scale in these categories make it possible to undercut tariffs based on cost-averaging over a larger system. It should first be noted that frequent use of the US example by both sides in this debate is misleading, since the differences between local and long-distance rates in the US are much greater than in the UK, because local rates are regulated by State Public Utility Commissions and are highly susceptible to political pressure from local consumers against rate rises. Long-distance rates in turn are regulated by the FCC which is insulated from the same pressure (this is another example of the essentially arbitrary and political nature of telecommunications tariffs). Even in the US the idea that business has in fact been subsidizing local (and therefore residential, because it is business that is the major user of long-distance and international) has been cogently challenged in a number of studies (Melody, 1983). One of the main bases for this challenge, apart from the fundamental one of the difficulty of unbundling costs, is the fact that peak traffic on the local loop is business traffic, the residential subscriber only using the telephone on average for five minutes per day, largely in off-peak time. Thus a higher proportion of local loop investment is attributable to business traffic than its strictly proportional usage of the circuits and switches would imply. The real problem, however, does not lie here, for, as we have seen, to talk of cross-subsidy is problematic. The real problem is that after a period when growth in the subscriber base was residential-led we are entering a period of rapid business growth and this growth is taking place when demands for service are no longer homogeneous. That is to say, the average residential subscriber only requires POTS. Business subscribers, on the other hand, increasingly demand advanced digital network capacity and sophisticated terminal apparatus. The provision of these services and their cost is increasingly central to business operation because of the growth of multi-plant multinational corporations and because of a shift towards services that are more intensive users of telecommunication networks. Thus it is increasingly clear that the PSTN is taking on two distinct and diverging functions, providing a simple POTS for residential subscribers and a sophisticated ISDN for business. It is also clear that the proper balance between these diverging demands cannot be met by simply unleashing competition, as BT's licence recognizes by placing upon it a range of public service obligations. But nor can these conflicting demands be simply lost within the operation of the network, as in the days of a simple homogeneous service. However, nor can the networks and their related services simply be allowed to diverge, with business paying for what it wants and residential subscribers for what they want, not only because of the economics of network provision outlined above, but also because business requires access to and from residential subscribers for a growing range of marketing, such as tele-marketing, Freefone and so on, as well as for the range of new value-added services, such as home banking, electronic funds transfer, and remote booking and billing for a wide range of goods and services.

XVI

As customer demands for service diversify it becomes increasingly difficult without some market mechanism to respond efficiently to those demands. At the same time, as the fields of telecommunications and computing converge and become ever more strategic across wide areas of economic and social life, a development actualized and symbolized by the introduction of ISDN, the idea of one national monopoly controlling all of this development becomes both politically and managerially untenable. So the question remains: given the inefficacy of competition in network provision, how should the development and expansion of the network and its associated services be funded and controlled?

What is clear, I think, is that while the arguments on economic as well as social grounds for retaining a national publicly owned monopoly in the PSTN are strong, it is not possible simply to return to the status quo ante.

First, the liberalization of the terminal attachment market is, with one caveat, an irreversible improvement. The caveat relates to the supply and maintenance of telephones to residential subscribers. Experience in the US shows that, because it is impossible for the subscriber to know whether a fault is on the line or in the telephone, unless BT has an obligation to maintain all telephones including ones not supplied by itself, when the fault is in a non-BT telephone the customer is left paying a call-out charge to BT, while being left with an inoperable telephone. The only solution, as I see it, is to levy a fee on all telephones not sold by BT, to cover BT's maintenance obligation for all residential telephones. There remains the question of whether BT should be allowed to remain in the terminal market at all and whether that business can really be run at arm's length. In Germany the Monopolies Commission has argued that the economies of scope available to the PTT in the terminal supply and maintenance market are such that it should be allowed to compete and if necessary drive all others out of business, thus producing the happiest economic solution.

Similar questions are raised by BT's presence in other equipment manufacturing and marketing areas. Here we face one of the central contradictions of UK policy. On the one hand, there is an industrial policy that aims to use BT as the engine for the development of a UK electronic and IT industry capable of competing on a world scale and that therefore requires a powerful, fully integrated BT. On the other hand, there is a policy that favours competition in network provision and apparatus supply in the interests of users of telecommunication goods and services and of the development of an information services industry. These two aims are not easily compatible. This dilemma has also faced US policy-makers and the case can certainly be sustained that the terms on which AT&T was broken up were designed, not to enhance telecommunication services to US subscribers, but to release AT&T, through Bell Labs and Western Electric, to play a key role as a world market leader in competition with the Japanese and IBM.

One example of the clash between an industrial and service-based policy is the decision to license cellular radio as soon as possible, in order to bring a competitive service on stream, at the price of using US technology rather than waiting for an agreed alternative European standard. Another was the decision that recently faced the government on whether to grant a licence to the national value-added data network proposed jointly by BT and IBM. A decision in favour might have been best both for the rapid development of value-added service provision and for BT's international competitiveness. But such a decision would have been at the expense of the national computer industry, especially ICL, and of a competitive value-added service sector. It would have contradicted the government's present European strategy of supporting the development of Open Systems Integration (OSI) as a common European and international standard for system architecture and interconnection. Also it would have undercut the position of Oftel. In the end the government refused a joint licence, but indicated that it would welcome both IBM and BT as individual competitive licensees. This may well result in an IBM monopoly with its Systems Network Architecture (SNA) at the expense of both BT and OSI.

XVII

If the whole question of the proper relationship between BT as a developer, manufacturer and seller of equipment and BT as a network operator has to be resolved, there is also a continuing question concerning the relationship between network operation and the provision of value-added services. There is no common-carrier tradition in this country, no body of legislation or of economic and philosophical thought, such as exists in the US, focusing upon the important distinction between carriage and content. I have argued the need to maintain public monopoly control of the PSTN. But as an increasing range of social information flows transfer to this network as it develops ISDN capacity, the question of how access to that network is controlled and on what terms becomes crucial. At present BT is allowed to operate on equal terms with all other licensed providers of VANS on its own network. While for pragmatic reasons of industrial policy in the development of a UK information services industry it may be desirable to use BT's power, expertise and resources in this way, in the longer term it must be questionable whether the network operator should be itself allowed to operate in the value-added field. This may not be possible, however, because the development of the ISDN is likely to place considerable intelligence inside the network itself so that the basic network will be irreducibly a value-added service the price and efficiency of which depend upon the integral operation and the economies of scale and scope of that network. This becomes a particularly acute problem because with these services we enter the realm of the economics of information where there is an almost total decoupling of the costs of delivery from the value to the recipient. Thus not only does the attribution of costs within the network become arbitrary, but so does the relationship of prices to demand.

I have outlined some of the problems involved in the formulation and operation of UK telecommunications policy. These are common problems given a specific political and cultural colouring by the UK context. As I have indicated, the debate in the UK has been less than helpful, falling as it does into a sterile ideological dispute between pro-marketeers and defenders of an indefensible status quo. In addition the debate has been confused by the use, for propaganda purposes, of a trivialized and misleading version of the recent US experience. A way out of this situation will only be found by adopting a much more detailed and nuanced view of the role of telecommunications in our society and by escaping from a dichotomous view of the public sector versus the market into the complexities of their necessary conflicts and complementarities.

References

Beesley, M. F. (1981) *Liberalisation of the Use of the British Telecommunications Network: Report to the Secretary of State*. London: HMSO.

de Zoete and Bevan (1984) *British Telecom*. London: de Zoete and Bevan.

Littlechild, S. C. (1983) *Regulation of British Telecommunications' Profitability: Report to the Secretary of State*. London: HMSO.

Melody, W. H. (1983) *Telecommunications in Nova Scotia: A Cost of Service Study for Maritime Telegraph and Telephone Company Ltd, Canada*.

Organization for Economic Cooperation and Development (1983) *Telecommunications: Pressures and Policies for Change*. Paris: OECD.

United States Senate (1982) Hearings on S2469 before the Committee on Commerce, Science and Transportation, 97th Congress, 2nd Session. Washington: US Government Printing Officer.

PART III

THE POLITICAL ECONOMY AND THE PRODUCTION OF CULTURE

10

Public Policy and the Cultural Industries

This chapter was written in its first version for the Economic Policy Group of the Greater London Council in 1983. It was a contribution, presented at a GLC public debate, to the industrial strategy prepared for the capital by the GLC shortly before the council was forcibly dissolved by the hostile Tory government. Naturally such a strategy quickly discovered that the cultural industries dominated the city's economy: this chapter proposes ways of thinking about that remarkable fact.

II

To mobilize the concept of the cultural industries as central to an analysis of cultural activity and of public cultural policy is to take a stand against a whole tradition of idealist cultural analysis. This tradition, well delineated in the British form, for instance, by Raymond Williams in *Culture and Society*, defines culture as a realm separate from, and often actively opposed to, the realm of material production and economic activity.

This is important for our present purposes because, in general, public cultural policies have evolved from within that tradition. Public intervention, in the form of subsidy, is justified on the grounds (1) that culture possesses inherent values, of life enhancement or whatever, which are fundamentally opposed to and in danger of damage by commercial forces; (2) that the need for these values is universal, uncontaminated by questions of class, gender and ethnic origin; and (3) that the market cannot satisfy this need.

A further crucial component of this ideology is the special and central status attributed to the 'creative artist' whose aspiration and values, seen as stemming from some unfathomable and unquestionable source of genius, inspiration or talent, are the source of cultural value. The result of placing artists at the centre of the cultural universe has not been to shower them with gold, for artistic poverty is itself an ideologically potent element in this view of culture, but to define the policy problem

Table 10.1   *Public cultural expenditure in the UK, 1981–2 (£ million)*

	Central government	Local authorities	Total
Libraries	39.1	320.5	359.6
Museums and galleries	76.3	60.7	137.0
Other cultural facilities	97.6	79.6	177.2
Total	213.0	460.8	673.8

There is a high proportion devoted to libraries, particularly for local authority expenditure. It is worth noting that Greater London spent nearly five times as much per head of the population on cultural facilities other than museums and galleries as any other region in Britain. Of this figure of £469 per head in 1981–2, £336 was spent by the boroughs and £133 by the GLC.

as one of finding audiences for their work, rather than vice-versa. When audiences cannot be found, at least at a price and in a quantity which will support the creative activity, the market is blamed and the gap is filled by subsidy.

It is important to note that most of those on the left who have challenged this dominant view of culture as elitist have themselves tacitly if not explicitly accepted the remaining assumptions of the tradition they were rejecting. Indeed, in my view this in part accounts for their limited success in shifting the terms of the policy debate and the effortless ease with which they have been incorporated.

The result of this cultural policy-making tradition has been to marginalize public intervention in the cultural sphere and to make it purely reactive to processes which it cannot grasp or attempt to control. For, while this tradition has been rejecting the market, most people's cultural needs and aspirations are being, for better or worse, supplied by the market as goods and services. If one turns one's back on an analysis of that dominant cultural process, one cannot understand either the culture of our time or the challenges and opportunities which that dominant culture offers to public policy-makers.

We can get some idea of the relative orders of magnitude between public-sector expenditure on cultural activity and private, market expenditure if we compare the £673.8 million of public expenditure on libraries, museums and galleries and other cultural activities in the United Kingdom in 1981–2 (see Table 10.1) with the £15,538 million of 1982 consumer expenditure on recreation, entertainment and education (see Table 10.2) and with the total media advertising expenditure in 1982 of £3216 million (see Table 10.4).

An analysis of culture structured around the concept of the cultural industries, on the other hand, directs our attention precisely at the dominant private market sector. It sees culture, defined as the production and circulation of symbolic meaning, as a material process of production and exchange, part of, and in significant ways determined by, the wider economic processes of society with which it shares many common features.

Table 10.2 *Consumer expenditure on recreation, entertainment and education in the UK, 1982 (£ million)*

	1982	At 1980 prices		
		1980	1981	1982
Radio, TV and other durable goods	2,161	1,567	1,798	2,200
TV and video hire charges, licence fees and repairs	1,997	1,571	1,640	1,758
Sports goods, toys, games and camping equipment	1,304	1,211	1,153	1,163
Other recreational goods	2,700	2,288	2,328	2,504
Betting and gaming	1,832	1,572	1,496	1,462
Other recreational and entertainment services	1,608	1,396	1,294	1,198
Books, newspapers and magazines	2,396	1,856	1,805	1,729
Education	1,540	1,092	1,145	1,186
Total	15,538	12,553	12,659	13,200

This illustrates both the dramatic rise in the expenditure on domestic hardware and the high proportion that the buying, renting and servicing of such hardware, together with TV licence payments, occupies in total consumer leisure expenditure – approximately 25 per cent. These figures illustrate the trend for cultural consumption to withdraw into the home via a range of technological delivery systems focused especially around the TV set. This, of course, parallels TV viewing figures as a percentage of cultural consumption time.
Source: National Income and Expenditure

Table 10.3 *Average weekly household expenditure in GLC areas compared to the UK as a whole, 1981 (£)*

	GLC	UK
TV, radio, musical instruments and cine repair	2.87	1.82
Books, magazines, newspapers and periodicals	2.13	2.01
Cinema	0.31	0.14
Theatres, sporting events and other entertainment	1.19	1.05
TV licence and rental	1.20	1.44

There is higher spending on all categories except TV licence and rental, which is reflected in the marginally lower percentages of households with TV: 95.1 per cent in the GLC compared with 96.7 per cent for the UK in 1980–1. The higher levels of cultural expenditure in London in turn reflect higher average levels of household income, £193.47 for the GLC as opposed to £167.60 for the UK as a whole.

Thus, as a descriptive term, 'cultural industries' refers to those institutions in our society which employ the characteristic modes of production and organization of industrial corporations to produce and disseminate symbols in the form of cultural goods and services, generally, although not exclusively, as commodities. These include newspapers, periodical and book publishing, record companies, music publishers, commercial sports organizations, etc. In all these cultural processes, we characteristically find at some point the use of capital-intensive, technological means of mass production and distribution, highly developed divisions of labour and hierarchical modes of managerial organization, with the goal, if not

Table 10.4   *Total advertising expenditure and its relation to consumer*
expenditure and gross national product, 1952–82

	Total expenditure in 1975 prices[a] (£ million)	Total expenditure in current prices (£ million)	Total expenditure as a percentage of	
			Consumer expenditure[b]	Gross national product[b]
1952	NA	123	1.15	0.89
1956	NA	197	1.43	1.08
1960	NA	323	1.91	1.43
1961	897	338	1.90	1.40
1962	885	348	1.84	1.38
1963	925	371	1.84	1.38
1964	1,005	416	1.94	1.42
1965	1,002	435	1.90	1.39
1966	991	447	1.84	1.35
1967	976	451	1.77	1.29
1968	1,039	503	1.83	1.34
1969	1,067	544	1.86	1.37
1970	1,022	554	1.74	1.27
1971	997	591	1.66	1.20
1972	1,113	708	1.76	1.28
1973	1,259	874	1.91	1.36
1974	1,118	900	1.72	1.21
1975	967	967	1.50	1.03
1976	1,020	1,188	1.59	1.07
1977	1,110	1,499	1.75	1.19
1978	1,254	1,834	1.86	1.27
1979	1,285	2,131	1.82	1.27
1980	1,306	2,555	1.89	1.32
1981	1,287	2,818	1.88	1.34
1982	1,316	3,216	NA	NA

[a] Figures in this column are obtained by deflating the current price figures by the retail price index.
[b] Owing to revisions made by the Central Statistical Office to GNP and consumer expenditure data – often going back many years – the ratios given in this table may differ slightly from ratios given in previous years.

of profit maximization, at least of efficiency. I refer to this as a descriptive use of the term 'cultural industries' because it describes characteristics common to the cultural process in all industrial societies, whether capitalist or socialist. Within the descriptive usage we need to note a further distinction made by Adorno, who originally coined the term, between those cultural industries which employ industrial technology and modes of organization to produce and distribute cultural goods or services which are themselves produced by largely traditional or pre-industrial means (for example, books and records) and those where the cultural form itself is industrial (such as newspapers, films and TV programmes). We need to remember this distinction because the two forms tend to give rise to different relations of production and types of economic organization.

But the term 'cultural industries' can also be used analytically to focus upon the effects on the cultural process within the capitalist mode of production of cultural goods and services produced and distributed as commodities by labour, which is itself a commodity.

A key point here is that the cultural sector operates as an integrated economic whole because industries and companies within it compete:

1 for a limited pool of disposable consumer income;
2 for a limited pool of advertising revenue;
3 for a limited amount of consumption time;
4 for skilled labour.

III

Consumer expenditure on cultural goods and services has been rising slowly as a proportion of total expenditure, as consumption of basic essentials, such as food and clothing, reaches saturation point. However, this movement has been within limits, and studies have shown this expenditure to be inelastic not only in general but also in the sense that for individuals and families expenditure does not rise in line with income. This is probably linked to the question of limited consumption time.

IV

Table 10.4 shows the close relationship between total advertising expenditure and both consumer expenditure and GNP. Since 1952 it has varied between 1.94 and 1.15 per cent of consumer expenditure, and between 1.43 and 0.89 per cent of GNP. Moreover, in real terms, total advertising expenditure has remained remarkably stable, growing over the past twenty years by only £431 million and remaining virtually static from 1964 to 1976. Against a background of a high level of advertising in the UK in relation to GNP compared with other European economies, the limits of the advertising revenue pool are plain.

V

For most people, cultural consumption is confined to a so-called free time, the extension of which is limited by the material necessities of work and sleep. If we assume a working week including travel of 45 hours and sleep time of 48 hours per week, that leaves 75 hours per week in which all other activities have to be fitted. On average, 20 hours per week are taken up by TV viewing.

Cultural consumption is particularly time-consuming in the sense that the most common and popular form of culture, namely narrative and its musical equivalent, are based upon manipulation of time itself, and thus they offer deep resistances to attempts to raise the productivity of consumption time. This scarcity of consumption time explains:

1 the acute competition for audiences in the cultural sector;
2 the tendency to concentrate cultural consumption in the home, thus cutting out travel time;
3 as recent Swedish studies have shown, a sharp rise in the unit cost of each minute of consumption time, in particular as investment on domestic hardware increases while the time for using such hardware does not. Thus in Sweden between 1970 and 1979 time spent listening to music rose by 20 per cent while the cost rose by 86 per cent, with each hour of listening costing 55 per cent more.

VI

The various cultural industries compete in the same market for labour. Individual film-makers, writers, musicians or electricians may move in their work from film, to television, to live theatre. The electronic engineer may work in manufacturing or broadcasting. The journalist may work in newspapers, periodicals, radio or television.

This unified labour market is reflected in trade-union organizations. The Association of Cinematograph, Television and Allied Technicians (ACTT) organizes across film, television and radio, the National Union of Journalists (NUJ) across newspapers, books, magazines, radio and television. The Musicians' Union members work in film, radio, television and records as well as live performances, and so on.

As a result of these levels of integration within the cultural sector, a shift in one new television channel, such as Channel 4, restructures the broadcasting, film and advertising market in specific ways. Even more, of course, will this be the case with cable and satellite services. The introduction of a new colour supplement has repercussions upon the finances of other publications, but may well also have cross-effects on broadcasting revenue. The same holds true for public intervention. One needs to be aware that one may be playing a zero-sum game, and that all options are not simultaneously open.

A classic example of this interaction and of the ways in which the dynamics of the private sector impact on the public sector is the relation between ITV and BBC. Because ITV holds a monopoly of television advertising, and because there has in general been a high demand for this commodity, extra broadcasting hours means, for ITV, extra revenue, more efficient utilization of plant and thus higher profit. There has therefore been steady pressure from ITV, in common with commercial broadcasting systems throughout the world, to expand the hours of broadcasting – pressure which has been successful. For the BBC, on the other hand, expansion of hours leads to increases in costs with no increase in revenue. They have, however, been forced to respond to ITV because of the need to compete for audiences, thus increasing the pressure to spend more public money on broadcasting if the balance between public and private sectors is to be maintained.

VII

The particular economic nature of the cultural industries can be explained in terms of the general tendencies of commodity production within the capitalist mode of production as modified by the special characteristics of the cultural commodity. Thus we find competition driving the search for profits via increased productivity, but it takes specific forms.

There is a contradiction at the heart of the cultural commodity. On the one hand, there is a very marked drive towards expanding the market share or the form this takes in the cultural sector, audiences. This is explained by the fact that in general, because one of the use-values of culture is novelty or difference, there is a constant need to create new products which are all in a sense prototypes. That is to say, the cultural commodity resists that homogenization process which is one of the material results of the abstract equivalence of exchange to which the commodity form aspires. This drive for novelty within cultural production means that in general the costs of reproduction are marginal in relation to the costs of production (the cost of each record pressing is infinitesimal compared to the cost of recording, for instance). Thus the marginal returns from each extra sale tend to grow, leading in turn to a powerful thrust towards audience maximization as the preferred profit maximization strategy.

On the other hand, the cultural commodity is not destroyed in the process of consumption. My reading of a book or watching of a film does not make it any less available to you. Moreover, the products of the past live on and can be relatively easily and cheaply reproduced anew. Thus it has been difficult to establish the scarcity on which price is based. And thus cultural goods (and some services, such as broadcasting, for technical reasons) tend towards the condition of a public good. Indeed, one can observe a marked tendency, where they are not *de jure* so treated, for consumers to so treat them *de facto* through high levels of piracy, as is now the case with records, video cassettes and books. (It should be noted that this in its turn relates to another contradiction in the cultural sphere, on which I shall comment shortly, between the producers of cultural hardware and software. It is the development of a market in cheap reproduction technology that makes piracy so difficult to control.) In contradiction, then, to the drive to maximize audiences, a number of strategies have had to be developed for artificially limiting access in order to create scarcity.

The drive to audience maximization leads to the observed tendency towards a high level of concentration, internationalization and cross-media ownership in the cultural industries. The strategies to limit access have taken a variety of forms:

1 Monopoly or oligopolistic controls over distribution channels, sometimes, as in broadcasting, linked to the state. One often finds here a close relationship between commercial interests and those of state control.
2 An attempt to concentrate the accumulation process on the provision of cultural hardware – e.g. radio and television receivers, hi-fi, VCRs, etc. – with the programmes, as in the early days of British broadcasting, as necessary loss-leaders. The rationale for the introduction of cable in the UK is an example of this.
3 The creation of the audience as a commodity for sale to advertisers, where the cultural software merely acts as a free lunch. This has proved itself the most successful solution; both the increased proportion of advertising to sales revenue in the press and periodicals market, culminating in the growth of free newspapers and magazines, and the steady expansion of wholly advertising-financed broadcasting services, are indications of this.
4 The creation of commodities, of which news is the classic example, which require constant reconsumption.

VIII

The third key characteristic of the cultural commodity lies in the nature of its use-values. These have proved difficult if not impossible to pin down in any precise terms, and demand for them appears to be similarly volatile. As I have already remarked, culture is above all the sphere for the expression of difference. Indeed, some analysts would claim that cultural goods are pure positional goods, their use-value being as markers of social and individual difference. While this aspect of culture merits much deeper and more extended analysis, it is only necessary here to draw one key conclusion, namely that demand for any single cultural product is impossible to predict. Thus the cultural industries, if they are to establish a stable market, are forced to create a relationship with an audience or public to whom they offer not a single cultural good, but a cultural repertoire across which the risks can be spread. For instance, in the record industry only one in nine singles and one in sixteen LPs makes a profit, and 3 per cent of the output can account for up to 50 per cent of turnover. Similarly, in films the top ten films out of 119 in the UK market in 1979 took 32 per cent of the box-office receipts and the top forty took 80 per cent.

Thus the drive to audience maximization, the need to create artificial scarcity by controlling access and the need for a repertoire bring us to the central point in this analysis. *It is cultural distribution, not cultural production, that is the key locus of power and profit.* It is access to distribution which is the key to cultural plurality. The cultural process is as much, if not more, about creating audiences or publics as it is about producing cultural artefacts and performances. Indeed, that is why that stress upon the cultural producers that I noted earlier is so damaging.

We need to recognize the importance, within the cultural industries and within the cultural process in general, of the function which I shall call, for want of a better word, editorial: the function not just of creating a cultural repertoire matched to a given audience or audiences but at the same time of matching the cost of production of that repertoire to the spending powers of that audience. These functions may be filled by somebody or some institution referred to variously as a publisher, a television channel controller, a film distributor, etc. It is a vital function totally ignored by many cultural analysts, a function as creative as writing a novel or directing a film. It is a function, moreover, which will exist centrally within the cultural process of any geographically dispersed society with complex division of labour.

Taking these various factors into account, we are now in a position to understand why our dominant cultural processes and their modes of organization are the way they are. The newspaper and the television and radio schedule are montages of elements to appeal to as wide a range of readers, viewers and listeners as possible. The high levels of concentration in the international film, record and publishing industries are responses to the problem of repertoire. The dominance of broadcast television stems from its huge efficiency as a distribution medium, with its associated economies of scale.

For this reason, the notion that the new technologies of cable and VCR are fragmenting the market rather than shifting the locus of oligopolistic power needs to be treated with caution, since there are strict limits to how far such fragmentation can go economically.

IX

As I have noted, power in the cultural sector clusters around distribution, the channel of access to audiences. It is here that we typically find the highest levels of capital intensity, ownership concentration and multi-nationalization, the operation of classic industrial labour processes and relations of production with related forms of trade-union organization. These characteristics are exhibited to their highest degree in the manufacture of the hardware of cultural distribution, especially domestic hardware. This is a sub-sector increasingly dominated by a few Japanese corporations such as Matsushita, Sony, Sanyo, Toshiba and Hitachi, together with Eastman Kodak, Philips and RCA. The major UK firm of this type is the Maxwell empire.

Then there are the major controllers of channels of software distribution, often closely linked to specific modes of reproduction, such as record pressing or newspaper printing. In non-print media there is again a high level of concentration and internationalization, and US firms dominate, owing to the large size of the domestic US market. Here we find some of the same firms as in hardware, e.g. RCA, Thorn-EMI and Philips joined by firms such as Warner, CBS, Time-Life, Gulf-Western and MCA. The multinationalization of print media has been limited by barriers of language. None the less, apart from the high levels of concentration in the national UK market, with three groups controlling 74 per cent of daily newspaper circulation, two of these groups – News International and Reed International (now owned by Maxwell) – have extensive foreign interests.

The increasing tendency in this field, as an extension of the principle of repertoire, is the formation of multi-media conglomerates. Examples are Pearson-Longman and Robert Maxwell in the UK, who own interests across a number of media, thus enabling them both to exploit the same product, be it a film, a book or a piece of music, across several media, and also to expand the principles of risk-spreading not only across a range of consumer choice in one medium but also across consumers' entire range of cultural choice. The development of such centres of cultural powers also, of course, raises barriers to entry.

Around these centres of power cluster groups of satellites. These satellites can be either small companies, for instance independent production companies in relation to Channel 4, or individual cultural workers such as freelance journalists, writers, actors and film directors. In these satellite sectors we find high levels of insecurity, low levels of profitability, low levels of unionization and, where they exist, weak trade-union organizations. Often labour is not waged at all, but labour power is rented out for a royalty.

The existence of this dependent satellite sector fulfils a very important function for the cultural industries because it enables them to shift much of the cost and risk of cultural research and development off their own shoulders and on to this exploited sector, some of which is then indeed supported from the public purse. It also enables them to maintain a consistently high turnover of creative cultural labour without running the risk of labour unrest, or bearing the cost of redundancy or pension payments. Their cup brimmeth over when, as is often the case, the workers themselves willingly don this yoke in the name of freedom.

X

Before turning to the specific problems of London and of public intervention in the cultural sector, one last general analytical question must be raised: what should be our attitude to the relation between the market and the cultural process? There is that general tradition, to which I alluded at the beginning of this chapter, which regards culture and the market as inherently inimical. This view is powerfully reinforced within the socialist tradition by opposition to the capitalist mode of production.

I think it is crucial, however, to separate the concept of the market from the concept of the capitalist mode of production, that is to say from a given structure of ownership and from the special features derived from labour as a market commodity. In terms of this relationship between consumers, distributors and producers of cultural goods and services, the market has much to recommend it, provided that consumers enter that market with equal endowments and that concentration of ownership power is reduced, controlled or removed. However, we must be clear that removal of the power vested in private or unaccountable public ownership will not remove the need for the function I have described as editorial, whether such a function is exercised individually or collectively. It also has to be stressed that even within the capitalist mode of production the market has, at crucial historical junctures, acted as a liberating cultural force. One thinks of the creation of both the novel and the newspaper by the rising bourgeoisie in the eighteenth century and of working-men's clubs and the working-class seaside holiday in the late nineteenth century.

Indeed, the cultural market, as it has developed in the past 150 years in the UK as a substitute for patronage in all its forms, cannot be read either as a destruction of high culture by vulgar commercialism or as a suppression of authentic working-class culture, but should be read as a complex hegemonic dialectic of liberation and control – which makes an analysis, for instance, of the role of broadcasting and of the BBC public-service tradition so difficult.

What analysis of the cultural industries does bring home to us is the need to take the question of the scarcity and thus of the allocation of cultural resources seriously, together with the question of audiences – who they are, how they are formed and how they can best be served. For it needs to be said that the only alternative to the market which we have constructed, with the partial exception of broadcasting, has tended either simply to subsidize the existing tastes and habits of the better-off or to create a new form of public culture which has no popular audience; cultural workers create for the only audience they know, namely the cultural bureaucrats who pay the bill and upon whom they become psychologically dependent even while reviling them.

XI

As a result of the work for the public hearings on cable and the London Industrial Strategy, the Economic Policy Group (EPG) has identified the cultural sector as a prime site for possible GLC intervention, both because of its intrinsic importance to the London economy and because through the arts and recreation budget the GLC is already making a significant intervention which, if it is to produce the maximum long-term benefit in terms of access to cultural opportunities for Londoners, needs to be planned in the light of the economic dynamic of the cultural sector as a whole.

Because of London's historic role as not only a national but also an imperial capital city, the cultural industries are heavily concentrated in London as the hub of both a national and an international market. Printing and publishing is now London's largest manufacturing sector, employing in 1978 112,300, with book publishers exporting 34 per cent of their output. Electrical engineering, which provides the infrastructure of cultural transmission, is the second largest manufacturing sector, with 99,300. Between them these two sectors make up one-third of London's manufacturing employment.

A recent EPG study (EC 940) shows that about 50,000 people are employed in London in the broadcasting, film and video industry and that nearly 30 per cent of all UK cinema box-office receipts are taken in Greater London. A further 20,000 are employed in advertising, 59 per cent of the UK total.

The Institute of Employment Research at the University of Warwick estimated in their spring 1982 review of the economy and employment that for 1980–90 the category of literary, artistic and sports production would be the fastest-growing area of employment, increasing nationally by 30 per cent or 132,000.

XII

The implications for public cultural policy of the analysis I have outlined above are very much on the international agenda. In April 1980 the Council of Europe held a conference on the state's role vis-à-vis the cultural industries and is engaged in continuing work in this field. In 1978 UNESCO approved the implementation of a comparative research programme on cultural industries. As a result, a meeting of experts on 'The place and role of cultural industries in the cultural development of societies' was held in Montreal in June 1980, and this was followed by a World Conference on Cultural Policies in Mexico in July 1982.

The French government has recently set up an investment fund for the cultural industries, aimed both at helping those industries to compete against foreign, especially US, products in the domestic market, and at penetrating export markets.

The recent second report from the UK Government Information Technology Advisory Panel sees software in all its forms as a growing international market which the UK is in a good position to exploit, and it advocates government support, on grounds similar to the French initiative, for the development of what they describe as tradeable information, a category that includes entertainment.

These new approaches to public cultural policy are motivated in part by a realization of the growing economic importance of the cultural sector and in part by the perceived inadequacies of traditional approaches to cultural policy, which at best act as a temporary band-aid of almost total irrelevance to the health of the patient. They are in large part an attempt to prop up a largely nineteenth-century structure of cultural practice, to which the majority of citizens are wholly indifferent.

What, then, should our reaction be? What kind of policy questions do we now need to pose?

1 Debates, organizational energy and finance need to be directed towards broadcasting for two reasons:

   (a) Broadcasting is the heartland of contemporary cultural practice because of the high proportion of consumers' time and money devoted to it and because, as a result of that concentration of attention, it is itself both directly and indirectly the major cultural patron. For instance, the BBC spends more per annum supporting cultural workers in the narrow sense of that term, about £105 million more, than the Arts Council. In addition, the success of films, records and books is becoming increasingly dependent upon broadcasting exposure. Indeed, television and radio chat shows, those characteristic contemporary broadcasting forms, are now an integral part of the marketing apparatus of other media.

   (b) Broadcasting is now the major form of public intervention in the cultural process. The income of the BBC alone in 1982 was £563.6 million, nearly as large as all other public expenditure on culture, including public libraries and museums. However, if we include the ITV and ILR revenues, which were £820.2 million and £20 million respectively, on the grounds that their expenditure, through the Independent Broadcasting Authority (IBA) and the Channel 4 board, is under significant degrees of public control specifically designed to counteract market pressures, however inadequately, then we have some true measure of the weight of broadcasting as a public intervention in our culture. It is, therefore, a high priority both to defend this public sphere from the threats posed to it by current government cable initiatives and to work to make a reality of the possibilities of true public accountability which its existence makes possible.

2 Expenditure on public libraries represents over 50 per cent of all public expenditure on culture and a much higher proportion of local authority expenditure. A large and increasing proportion of that expenditure goes on staff and buildings. It must be sensible to see that maximum use is made of that asset. For instance, perhaps it is libraries that need to become both alternative film and video exhibition venues, distribution channels for cultural goods, marketing centres for cultural services.

3 We need to stop looking at the media in isolation. The public sector too needs to exploit economies of scale and the notion of repertoire.

Thus community bookshop initiatives have to be coordinated with policies to develop alternative, community-based venues for film and video exhibitions, for the performing arts and for the display of visual arts. Thus the distribution of books, records, periodicals, films and video needs to be analysed as one problem.

4 We need to concentrate our interventions not on production but on distribution in the widest sense. That is, we need to develop public-sector audience research and marketing expertise and ways of placing enhanced cultural choice in the hands of individuals and groups, choice which these distribution services would then enable cultural workers to respond to, perhaps helping them to be more nearly self-sufficient. This seems preferable to the current tendency, which is to encourage the overproduction of cultural goods and services for which there is no audience.

5 If we are serious about improving access to cultural production for disadvantaged groups such as women and ethnic minorities, then we need to negotiate with the major companies in the cultural industries over their training and recruitment policies in collaboration with the relevant trade unions. But this raises an issue we cannot dodge. No one has the *right* to be a cultural worker. Their numbers will always be limited. The illusion of free access is at present sustained only by the high levels of unemployment and marginal employment. The price that would have to be paid for better terms and conditions is limitation on access. This applies as much to existing publicly funded cultural activities as it does to the private sector. How, then, is such access to be controlled, on what criteria and by whom?

6 Are there certain cultural trends we cannot buck, in particular the trend to concentrate cultural consumption in the home? The GLC has to decide how to respond to the dramatic decline in cinema attendances and the resulting prospect of widespread cinema closure in Greater London. Should those cinemas be taken over and, if so, for what purpose, if cinema-going cannot be re-created? Perhaps resources would be better spent ensuring that the choice people received at home was enhanced.

7 Should we campaign for a cultural levy on advertising? Advertising, for reasons I have outlined, is a crucial and growing source of cultural funding. It is a course of funding which structures cultural production and distribution in specific ways which are not directly responsive to the demands of audiences. In particular it subsidizes more heavily the cultural consumption of the better-off. There is, therefore, a powerful case for adopting on a national and cultural sector-wide basis the strategy adopted within the IBA system, through differential rentals and the Channel 4 levy, of redistributing advertising expenditure to support cultural provision which advertising would not support. The problem is to construct appropriate mechanisms to this end.

Reference

Williams, R. (1958) *Culture and Society*. London: Chatto and Windus.

11

The Economics of the US Motion Picture Industry

The report that follows was written in 1979 as an early contribution to the development of European policies towards the audiovisual industry within the context of the European Community and the Council of Europe.

Since the rise to international dominance of the US film industry in the 1920s, in the wake of the extensive economic damage suffered by national European industries during the First World War, all western European governments developed a range of interventions in an effort to sustain a viable domestic film industry for both economic and cultural reasons.

Against this background, the problem facing European institutions and national governments in the 1970s was whether and how to replace national systems of intervention with a Europe-wide system compatible with the free-trade principles enshrined in the Treaty of Rome. The search for an appropriate policy faced the problem that existing national systems of intervention had failed to stem growing US dominance of European cinema screens. The search was also made more urgent by the dawning realization that this dominance might well be translated into a similar dominance over TV programming as Europe's public service TV systems were undermined by a wave of so-called deregulation created by the arrival of the new distribution technologies of satellite and cable and the plethora of new channels those technologies made potentially available. In particular at the time the main imminent danger to European audio visual production was seen as stemming from uncontrolled cross-frontier broadcasting via satellite.

Within this context, therefore, the purpose of this report was to show how and why the international market for motion pictures had come to be dominated by a small oligopoly of US companies, the so-called 'majors', grouped in the Motion Picture Export Association of America (MPEAA); whether current industry trends indicated that this dominance was likely to continue in the absence of countervailing policies in Europe; and what types of intervention might be appropriate.

The report provides a snapshot of the industry's structure in the late 1970s and a historical analysis of how it came to be that way. Its essence lies in a broad general analysis of the structure and dynamic of the industry and the ways in which that structure and dynamic determine what films can be made by whom and what films can be viewed and by whom. The statistics are used to support the general analysis. Given the continuing problem of obtaining accurate economic statistics on the industry, figures for any one year should not be fetishized and should be taken as indicative of broad trends and general structural relationships.

It is for this reason that, although the statistical details have dated, I have chosen not to update them in the body of the report, but rather to add a postscript at the end, which both poses the question of the adequacy of the analysis in the light of subsequent developments and current figures, and relates it to subsequent European policy developments.

THE STRUCTURE OF THE US MARKET AND ITS POSITION IN THE WORLD MARKET

The film industry in the United States is dominated by a small group of production/distribution companies, the so-called 'majors': Columbia, 20th Century Fox, MGM, United Artists, Warner Bros, Paramount and Universal, all of whom are member of the Motion Picture Association of America (MPAA). In addition there are four so-called mini-majors: Allied Artists and Avco Embassy, who are members of the MPAA and Disney (whose distribution arm is called Buena Vista) and American International Pictures (AIP), who are not.

The extent of their domination of both the US domestic market, but also of the world market is illustrated in Tables 11.1a and 11.1b.

The concentration of control is even greater than these figures show, since MGM films are distributed in the US market by United Artists and internationally by Cinema International Corporation, which is a company that combines the international distribution business of Paramount and Universal, while outside the US Columbia–Warner operates as a joint company and in several territories distributes with Fox, for example, in Australia. The result is that internationally the market is dominated by four distribution companies.

When we talk of the US film industry we must think not only of feature films for cinema exhibition, but of the production and distribution of filmed entertainment. All the majors are now heavily involved in production for TV (see Table 11.2).

The structure of the world market

At this point it is necessary to present in broad outline the structure of the world market for filmed entertainment and to attempt to quantify the position of the US industry and of the majors in particular within it. In so doing I shall at the same time outline the general problems relating to economic data in the international movie industry which must be taken into account when reading this study.

Table 11.1a　*Major company percentage of US–Canadian market receipts for films earning rentals of $1 million or more, 1970–8*

	1970	1971	1972	1973	1974	1975	1976	1977	1978
Columbia	14.1	10.2	9.1	7.0	7.0	13.1	8.3	11.5	11.6
MGM	3.4	9.3	6.0	4.6	a	a	a	a	a
Paramount	11.8	17.0	21.6	8.6	10.0	11.3	9.6	10.0	23.8
20th Century Fox	19.4	11.5	9.1	18.8	10.9	14.0	13.4	19.5	13.4
United Artists	8.7	7.4	15.0	10.7	8.5	10.7	16.2	17.8	10.3
Universal	13.1	5.2	5.0	10.0	18.6	25.1	13.0	11.5	16.8
Warner Bros	5.3	9.3	17.6	16.4	23.2	9.1	18.0	13.7	13.2
Total top seven	75.8	69.9	83.4	76.1	78.2	83.3	78.5	84.0	89.1
Buena Vista	9.1	8.0	5.0	6.5	7.0	6.0	6.7	5.6	4.8
American International					3.8	3.4	3.8	3.4	1.4
Total top nine	84.9	77.9	88.4	82.6	89.0	92.7	89.0	93.0	95.3

a Distributed by United Artists since 1974.
Source: Guback (1979) based on *Variety* editions – 15 January 1975, 11 February 1976, 18 January 1978, 10 January 1979.

Table 11.1b　*Major company percentage share of foreign rentals earned by MPAA companies*

	1972	1973	1974
Columbia	12.0	10.5	14.0
MGM	14.0	14.0	8.5
Paramount	14.5	14.0	10.0
20th Century Fox	16.5	16.0	12.0
United Artists	21.0	22.5	16.0
Universal	9.0	10.5	17.0
Warner Bros	13.0	12.5	22.5
Total	100.0	100.0	100.0

The difficulty of obtaining accurate financial data is notorious among those who have studied the US film industry. As David Gordon has put it 'Facts are scarce; the absence of government assistance to the American film industry means that there is no government agency that collects figures on it and the trade association, the MPAA, is secretive.' As Thomas Guback has remarked:

> The industry exercises a monopoly of knowledge and therefore is in a position to impose selective ignorance. The federal government collects and publishes data, but that is done less to give an investigator a view of the industry's structure and operation, and more to show how the industry fits in the general economy on the national, state and local levels. Furthermore, the privacy of private enterprise is preserved because no single company data are published by the government and no companies are identified by name.

We can illustrate the problems this raises if we attempt to examine the major sources of income from filmed entertainment of the major US

Table 11.2 *Proportion of earnings from film and TV for the ten major companies, 1970–6*

| Financial year ending | Receipts ($ million) | | | TV receipts as a percentage | | Proportion of TV receipts to each dollar of theatre receipt |
	Theatre distribution	TV distribution	Total	Of TV and theatre	Of total revenue	
Allied Artists						
2 Apr. 1976	11.3	5.3	16.5	32.1	32.1	0.47
1975	10.5	0.5	11.1	4.5	4.3	0.05
30 June 1974	22.4	0.6	23.4	2.7	2.6	0.03
1973	13.5	1.1	15.3	7.3	6.9	0.08
1972	7.3	0.6	8.3	7.6	7.3	0.08
1971	1.9	0.6	2.7	22.5	20.5	0.29
1970	5.9	0.7	6.8	10.9	10.5	0.12
American International						
26 Feb. 1977	41.8	7.4	51.1	15.0	14.5	0.18
1976	44.5	5.5	51.0	11.0	10.8	0.12
1975	40.4	5.5	46.9	12.0	11.7	0.14
1974	28.7	2.8	32.2	9.0	8.8	0.10
1973	21.8	2.5	25.3	10.0	9.7	0.11
1972	18.9	1.9	21.8	9.0	8.7	0.10
1971	17.6	3.4	22.4	10.0	15.3	0.19
Columbia						
26 June 1976	152.2	87.1	332.1	36.4	26.2	0.57
1975	170.3	84.3	325.9	33.1	25.9	0.50
1974	111.3	80.6	256.6	42.0	31.4	0.72
1973	101.5	44.6	211.5	30.5	21.1	0.44
1972	110.0	72.2	242.2	39.6	29.8	0.66
1971	113.0	63.1	222.6	35.8	28.3	0.56
1970	137.9	58.7	242.1	29.9	24.3	0.43
Disney						
30 Sept. 1976	100.3	18.8	583.9	15.8	3.2	0.19
1975	98.8	13.7	520.0	12.2	2.6	0.14
1974	78.5	11.9	429.9	13.2	2.8	0.15
1973	66.5	9.6	385.1	12.7	2.5	0.15
1972	61.7	9.1	329.4	12.8	2.8	0.15
1971	57.1	8.0	175.6	12.3	4.6	0.14
1970	55.9	7.4	167.1	11.7	4.4	0.13
MGM						
31 Aug. 1976	47.6	57.4	266.0	54.7	21.6	1.21
1975	51.5	49.2	255.0	48.9	19.3	0.96
1974	66.1	65.7	234.2	49.8	28.1	0.99
1973	85.0	53.9	152.8	63.4	35.3	0.63
1972	91.1	43.0	148.2	47.2	29.0	0.52
1971	111.1	38.3	155.6	25.7	22.6	0.35
1970	98.5	50.9	170.7	34.1	29.8	0.52

Table 11.2   *contd.*

Financial year ending	Receipts ($ million)			TV receipts as a percentage		Proportion of TV receipts to each dollar of theatre receipt
	Theatre distribution	TV distribution	Total	Of TV and theatre	Of total revenue	
Paramount						
31 July 1976	152.0	65.0	451.4	30.0	14.4	0.43
1975	175.0	52.0	368.3	22.9	14.1	0.30
1974	103.0	63.0	298.1	38.0	21.1	0.61
1973	120.0	50.0	277.5	29.4	18.0	0.42
1972	142.0	43.0	291.0	23.2	14.8	0.30
1971	139.0	44.0	278.7	24.0	15.8	0.32
1970	101.0	54.0	240.9	34.8	22.4	0.53
20th Century Fox						
25 Dec. 1976	205.7	49.2	355.0	19.3	13.9	0.24
1975	188.7	53.4	342.7	22.1	15.6	0.28
1974	144.5	42.2	281.9	22.6	15.0	0.29
1973	144.3	35.7	250.4	19.9	14.3	0.25
1972	99.6	45.1	198.7	31.2	22.7	0.45
1971	120.7	49.5	222.5	29.1	28.0	0.41
1970	155.7	39.3	246.5	20.2	19.4	0.25
United Artists						
31 Dec. 1976	229.5	55.5	377.7	19.5	14.7	0.24
1975	187.4	29.6	319.7	13.6	9.3	0.16
1974	142.7	40.6	289.4	22.2	14.0	0.29
1973	163.8	51.7	327.5	24.0	15.8	0.32
1972	152.7	50.6	317.2	24.9	16.0	0.33
1971	97.2	19.1	205.1	16.5	9.3	0.20
1970	118.0	18.4	211.0	13.5	8.7	0.16
Universal						
31 Dec. 1976	213.4	249.7	802.9	53.9	31.1	1.17
1975	289.1	189.6	811.5	39.6	23.4	0.65
1974	205.1	158.5	641.9	43.6	24.7	0.77
1973	87.5	119.9	417.8	57.8	28.7	1.37
1972	61.9	127.3	345.9	67.3	36.8	2.06
1971	57.8	124.2	333.7	68.2	37.2	2.15
1970	96.7	110.0	333.5	53.2	33.0	1.14
Warner						
31 Dec. 1976	221.6	63.5	826.8	22.3	7.7	0.29
1975	202.3	53.6	669.8	26.5	8.0	0.26
1974	275.5	43.5	720.1	13.6	6.0	0.16
1973	152.7	56.7	549.6	27.1	10.3	0.37
1972	144.3	49.0	498.6	25.4	9.8	0.34
1971	86.3	38.0	377.1	30.6	10.1	0.44
1970	64.2	50.7	295.1	44.1	17.2	0.79

Source: Guback, 1978.

companies, and also to work out the US share of the total world market. The figures available are difficult to interpret and are often incompatible even when they are from the same source because:

1 Different methods of accounting in different companies means that one can never be sure when TV revenue includes both sales of feature films to TV and material specially made for TV, or conversely when film rental revenue in fact includes sales to TV.
2 When foreign earnings are in question one does not know whether the earnings referred to are only repatriated earnings or the total earnings abroad of foreign subsidiaries; nor is it clear whether foreign revenue is earnings on exports, that is films made in the US, or earnings on material produced abroad by US companies.

If we look at the way in which world income of the majors is divided between film and TV and its total dimension, it is convenient to take 1976, because for that year we have a variety of different sources that we can compare. As can be seen from Table 11.2, Guback, on the basis of company reports, computes total MPAA world revenue from TV at 632.7 million dollars for 1976.

In evidence to a Senate Committee in 1977, Jack Valenti, head of the MPAA, gave the following figures for MPAA members' earnings:

700 million dollars for total export receipts of which more than two-thirds came from cinema exhibition. Thus foreign cinema market produces 49.5 per cent of the total cinema rental income. The foreign TV market represents 23.4 per cent of the total TV market.

Thus on the basis of Guback's figures, 23.4 per cent of the total TV market would give us 146 million dollars for foreign TV receipts and 485 million dollars for US TV sales. Since the figures reported by the MPEAA to the US government for the same year, and published in *US Industrial Outlook*, give 152 million dollars for foreign TV receipts, we can assume that MPAA foreign TV receipts were of the order of 150 million dollars.

In the same MPEAA report total foreign earnings are given as 531 million dollars compared with Valenti's figure of 700 million dollars, while foreign cinema rental receipts are given as 399 million which, added to their figure of 152 million for TV, does not add up to their total of 531 million dollars.

Let us therefore approach the figures for the cinema receipts from another direction. *Variety* reported MPAA figures for 1976 film rental as 1,147 worldwide split between US 576 million dollars and foreign 571 million dollars. So far as one can tell this refers only to cinema receipts, and since the proportions roughly tally with those given by Valenti, and furthermore if we add 150 million for foreign TV to 571 million we arrive at a figure of 720 million dollars, which is near enough to Valenti's total figure for foreign earnings, we can arrive at the overall breakdown shown in Table 11.3 as the best available educated guess.

Table 11.3   *World-wide earnings of MPAA companies in 1976*
($ million)

	Film	TV	Total
US	576	485	1,061
Foreign	571	150	721
Total	1,147	635	1,782

Table 11.4   *US earnings in top ten markets in 1979 ($ million)*

	US earnings	Total distributors gross
Canada	64	
Germany	52	81
Japan	49	
France	46	137
Italy	40	138
UK	36	58
Spain	29	80 (1976 figure)
Australia	26	
Brazil	21	
Mexico	17	

What proportion is this of the world market? Once again we can only make an educated guess, and this time the guess must be based on even less firm foundations. In 1969 the *Film Daily Year Book* estimated the world box-office at 3.75 billion dollars and the share of US films at 2 billion dollars. Although they did not say so, this almost certainly refers to the non-socialist world.

Another source in 1973 in the ACTT Nationalization Report (ACTT, 1973) estimated world theatrical rental receipts at 1.28 billion dollars, of which US films received 763 million, that is roughly 60 per cent and in the same year Valenti claimed in an MPAA publication over 50 per cent of world screen time for US films.

Since we know that in Europe, which outside Canada is the major US market, in recent years US films have been taking an increasing proportion of the box-office receipts, this proportion is likely to have increased. At any rate for 1979 we have figures for the top ten foreign markets from which the US majors receive 65 per cent of their foreign earnings (see Table 11.4). As can be seen where we have figures to compare, the US earnings represent a proportion ranging from 66 per cent in Germany to 29 per cent in Italy. However, if we take the Canadian market first, which represents the largest foreign market, since in the joint figures for the US/Canadian market the majors plus Disney receive 94 per cent of the film rental income, we can assume that the figure for Canada alone is in the region of 90 per cent. Similarly, while Table 11.4 gives US earnings in Britain as 62 per cent of the total, in fact in 1977 foreign films, mostly US, took 87 per cent of the box-office and as the US majors also now distribute most British films as well, so the quoted earnings figure almost certainly only represents repatriated earnings. Similarly, for France, as Degand has shown, while US films only take around 40 per cent of the box-office, US distributors take around 60 per cent. Thus it would seem to be a safe assumption that the US majors and mini-majors account for over 70 per cent at a conservative estimate of non-socialist world gross film rentals from the cinema.

It is also important to note that the production and distribution of filmed entertainment now only represents a part of the business of the dominant companies. Either the major film companies were taken over or merged with larger industrial and financial groups in the late 1960s (for reasons and with consequences that we will examine later) or they have themselves diversified, and are increasingly diversifying, in order to lessen their dependency on the film and TV sector.

Warner was taken over by Kinney in 1969 and the resulting conglomerate changed its name to Warners Communications Inc. in 1971. Filmed entertainment now only represents about 32 per cent of Warner's turnover. Paramount merged into Gulf and Western in 1966 and is now part of the Leisure Time Division of that conglomerate along with book and music publishing, race-tracks, Canadian cinemas, an electronic games manufacturing company and Madison Square Gardens. The entire division contributed only 22 per cent of Gulf and Western's operating income in 1978.

United Artists was merged into the Transamerica Corporation in 1968, an insurance and financial giant. Over the past decade MGM has rapidly shifted its financial base from films to hotels and casinos so that in 1978 revenue from filmed entertainment represented less than 50 per cent of total revenue. At the same time three companies which still remain predominantly filmed entertainment companies MCA (Universal), Columbia and 20th Century Fox, have been using their high cash flow from the recent film boon to finance rapid diversification (see Table 11.5).

Thus control of the production and distribution of filmed entertainment is now closely integrated, often as only a minority and dominated partner, into a wider and deeper pattern of concentration, not only within the media and leisure industries in general, but within the wider financial and industrial sectors of a world economy increasingly dominated by large, multinational enterprises (see especially Mattelart, 1980; Guback, 1979).

The film industry is commonly regarded as a risky business, a reputation that is not entirely unwarranted. The main purpose of this chapter is to establish how, in such a business, a small group of companies established an oligopolistic dominance, not only over their US market, but also in the world market, and have retained that position for over half a century, during which they have not only withstood the slings and arrows of both the US Anti-trust laws and the rise of TV, but have

Table 11.5 *Film income as a percentage of sales and net operating profit of the eight major motion picture production companies in the US, 1972–6*

	1972		1973		1974		1975		1976	
	S	P	S	P	S	P	S	P	S	P
Columbia	75	N/A	68	N/A	61	N/A	52	N/A	52	N/A
Disney	24	60	22	37	21	41	22	40	20	36
MCA	59	64	54	48	60	57	63	68	63	67
MGM	94	80	95	80	61	43	46	34	46	30
Paramount	64	N/A	66	N/A	56	N/A	89	N/A	87	N/A
20th Century Fox	70	35	60	N/A	66	50	71	73	72	64
United Artists	64	94	65	98	N/A	N/A	N/A	N/A	N/A	N/A
Warner Bros	38	32	38	43	44	62	38	46	34	33

S = sales; P = profit. N/A not available.
Source: Sterling and Haight (1978). Based upon Standard and Poor, *Industry Survey: Leisure Time, Basic Analysis*, for the relevant year.

Table 11.6 *Market concentration among the major film distributors in the US, 1948–67*

	Estimated total US film rentals from theatres ($ million)	Estimated share of seven 'majors'	
		($ million)	(%)
1948	378	288	76
1954	371	317	85
1958	415	272	66
1963	412	236	57
1967	503	354	74

Source: Sterling and Haight (1978) from Crandall (1975) p. 60, using data from Census of Business.

survived to experience in the past two or three years greater prosperity than ever. As a New York journalist said of the major film financiers, 'Gamblers they may be, fools they are not.'

The continuity of the majors' dominance is graphically illustrated by Table 11.6 and the fluctuations of their profitability by Tables 11.7a and 11.7b.

Before recounting the historical development of that dominance and of its defence in order to see what lessons can be learnt from it, we need to look at the overall structure of the US domestic film industry today. As is the case in other sectors of the culture industry, the leading firms maintain a dominating, but necessary and valuable relationship with a large number of fragmented so-called 'independents' in both production and distribution. Not only do these myriad 'pilot fish' give the industry an appearance of diversity and competition, thus helping at least to

Table 11.7a   *Motion picture industry corporate profits and dividend payments selected years, 1930–77 ($ million)*

| | Corporate profits | | |
	Pre-tax	Post-tax	Net dividend payments
1930	51	42	33
1931	2	(2)	26
1932	(82)	(86)	10
1933	(40)	(43)	5
1934	2	(2)	7
1935	13	8	6
1940	51	37	18
1945	238	99	35
1950	112	60	38
1955	124	61	26
1960	49	1	22
1965	104	39	3
1970	93	8	10
1971	15	(29)	24
1972	1	(50)	17
1973	94	46	13
1974	190	116	31
1975	226	131	30
1976	426	311	53
1977	514	377	57

Figures in parentheses indicate losses.
Source: Encyclopaedia of Exhibition, 1978 reprinted in Guback (1979).

Table 11.7b   *Net profits and losses of the eight major motion picture production companies in the US, 1932–76 ($ million)*

	Columbia	Loew's/ MGM	Paramount[a]	20th Century Fox	United Artists[b]	Universal	Warner Bros	Disney
1932	0.6	8.0	–	N/A[c]	N/A[c]	N/A[c]	(14.1)	N/A[c]
1933	0.7	4.3	–	1.7	N/A	(1.0)	(6.3)	N/A
1934	1.0	8.6	–	1.3	N/A	(0.2)	(2.5)	N/A
1935	1.8	7.5	–	3.1	N/A	(0.7)	0.7	N/A
1936	1.6	10.6	4.0	7.7	N/A	(1.8)	3.2	N/A
1937	1.3	14.3	6.0	8.6	N/A	(1.1)	5.9	N/A
1938	0.2	9.9	2.8	7.2	N/A	(0.5)	1.9	N/A
1939	0.0	9.5	2.8	4.2	N/A	1.2	1.7	N/A
1940	0.5	8.7	6.4	(0.5)	N/A	2.4	2.7	N/A
1941	0.6	11.0	9.2	4.9	N/A	2.7	5.5	(0.8)
1942	1.6	11.8	13.1	10.6	N/A	3.0	8.6	(0.2)
1943	1.8	13.4	14.6	10.9	N/A	3.8	8.3	0.4
1944	2.0	14.5	14.7	12.5	N/A	3.4	6.9	0.5
1945	1.9	12.9	15.4	12.7	N/A	4.0	9.9	0.4
1946	3.5	17.9	39.2	22.6	N/A	4.6	19.4	0.2

Table 11.7b *contd.*

	Columbia	Loew's/ MGM	Paramount[a]	20th Century Fox	United Artists[b]	Universal	Warner Bros	Disney
1947	3.7	10.5	28.2	14.0	N/A	3.2	22.0	0.3
1948	0.5	4.2[d]	22.6	12.5	N/A	(3.2)	11.8	(0.1)
1949	1.0	6.0	20.8[e]	12.4	N/A	(1.1)	10.5	(0.1)
1950	1.9	7.6	6.6	9.5	N/A	1.4	10.3	0.7
1951	1.5	7.8	5.5	4.3[f]	0.3	2.3	9.4	0.4
1952	0.8	4.6	5.9	4.7	0.4	2.3	7.2	0.5
1953	0.9	4.5	6.7	4.8	0.6	2.6	2.9[g]	0.5
1954	3.6	6.3	8.1	8.0	0.9	3.8	3.9	0.7
1955	4.9	5.0	9.4	6.0	2.7	4.0	4.0	1.4
1956	2.6	4.6	4.3	6.2	3.1	4.0	2.1	2.6
1957	2.3	(0.5)	5.4	6.5	3.3	2.8	3.4	3.6
1958	(5.0)	0.8	4.6	7.6	3.7	(2.0)	(1.0)	3.9
1959	(2.4)	7.7	4.4	2.3	4.1	4.7	9.4	3.4
1960	1.9	9.6	7.0	(2.9)	4.3	6.3	7.1	(1.3)
1961	(1.4)	12.7	5.9	(22.5)	4.0	7.5	7.2	4.2
1962	2.3	2.6	3.4	(39.8)	3.8	12.7	7.6	6.6
1963	2.6	(17.5)	5.9	9.1	(0.8)	13.6	5.7	7.0
1964	3.2	7.4	6.6	10.6	9.3	14.8	(3.9)	7.0
1965	2.0	7.8	6.3	11.7	12.8	16.2	4.7	11.0
1966	2.0	10.2	N/A[h]	12.5	13.6	13.6	6.5	12.4
1967	6.0	14.0	N/A	15.4	15.5	16.5	3.0	11.3
1968	10.0	8.5	N/A	13.7	19.5[i]	13.5	10.0	13.1
1969	6.0	(35.0)	N/A	(36.8)	16.2	2.5	(52.0)[j]	15.8
1970	6.0	(8.2)	(2.0)[k]	(77.4)	(45.0)	13.3	33.5	22.0
1971	(29.0)	7.8	(22.0)[k]	6.5	1.0	16.7	41.6	21.7
1972	(4.0)	9.2	31.2[k]	6.7	10.8	20.8	50.1[l]	40.3
1973	(50.0)	2.1	38.7	10.7	14.0	25.6	47.4	N/A
1974	(2.3)	26.8	18.7	10.9	9.9	59.2	48.5[m]	48.5
1975	10.5[n]	31.8	29.9	22.7	11.5	95.5	9.1[o]	61.7
1976	11.5	31.9	49.6	10.7	16.0	90.2	61.2	74.6

Losses are in parentheses. Net sums are after taxes and write-offs, before special credits.
a   In reorganization until 1936.
b   Not a listed corporation until 1950.
c   Editorial insertion; does not appear in the original table.
d   Divorcement: Loew's Theatres hived off.
e   Divorcement: United Paramount theatres hived off, with profits of $16.7 million in
    1948 and $17.6 million in 1949.
f   Divorcement: National Theatres hived off.
g   Divorcement: Stanley Warner hived off.
h   Bought by Gulf and Western; financial figures burned.
i   Bought by Transamerica Corporation.
j   Warner Bros bought by Kinney Services, which changed its name to Warner
    Communications in 1971.
k   Operating loss profits.
l   Breakdown of profits: records and music – $23.8 million; films – $15.8 million;
    publishing – $2 million; cable TV – $1.8 million.
m   Percentage breakdown of profits; 38 per cent from theatrical films and 6 per cent from
    TV films.
n $5.2 million gain on exchange of debentures; total is net with deferred income tax.
o   Includes reduction in carrying value of investment in National Kinney Corporation.

Sources: Sterling and Haight (1978). Based for 1932–72 data on Jowett (1976) pp. 483–4
using data from company reports and *Moody's Industrial Manual*. 1973–6 data: *Moody's
Industrial Manual* and for United Artists *Moody's Bank and Finance Manual*.

Table 11.8   *Total receipts and expenditures of the US motion picture industry ($ thousand)*

	No. of establishments	Total receipts	Total expenditure
Production			
Theatrical	1,392	238,517	N/A
TV	1,138	464,471	N/A
Distribution			
Theatrical	877	1,381,491	509,045
TV	151	319,648	190,136
Services	855	389,419	318,957

mitigate public concern and pressure against oligopolistic control, but they also fulfil a valuable economic function by attracting risk capital and creative talent which the majors can then exploit through their control of distribution. The independent but junior sector fulfils the vital function of research and development, the overheads of which the majors thus do not have to bear.

Thus the 1972 Government Census of Selected Service Industries gives a breakdown of the total receipts and expenditures of the US motion picture industry (see Table 11.8). Similarly if one looks at the number of films released each year in the US, the majors have been consistently responsible themselves for less than 50 per cent, and in recent years nearer 40 per cent (see Tables 11.9a and 11.9b).

However, to understand the position of the majors within the US market, a number of factors need to be taken into account.

1 The majors as production companies themselves produce and wholly finance a very small number of films each year; for example, Columbia's inventories for 1978 show $17 million tied up in current releases and approximately the same amount in current production, while they released twenty-five films in 1977/8 and planned to release twenty-three in 1978/9. If one takes Columbia's own figures of an average of $5 million per picture, they themselves could only be fully financing a maximum of seven pictures.

2 In addition they wholly or largely finance a range of 'independent' productions which they then distribute. This financing is done by means of debt guarantees in return for which they receive the first share in any profits while not having to bear any excess overheads and while taking their 30 per cent or more distribution fee off the top. Thus the independence of this independent production should not be exaggerated. As *Variety* has put it:

> The latter-day independent producer is typically dependent in the financial sense, receiving full financing from a distributor. Tax concepts and vanity combined in approximately equal measure to create the myths of the 'independent' producer. (21 February 1973)

Table 11.9a   *Motion pictures released by national distributors, 1930–77*

	New	Reissues	Total
1930			355
1935	388	3	391
1940	472	3	475
1941	497	7	504
1942	484	8	492
1943	426	6	432
1944	409	6	415
1945	367	8	375
1946	383	17	400
1947	371	55	426
1948	398	50	448
1949	406	85	491
Average 1940–9	421	25	446
1950	425	48	473
1951	411	28	439
1952	353	33	386
1953	378	36	414
1954	294	75	369
1955	281	38	319
1956	311	35	346
1957	363	19	382
1958	327	25	352
1959	236	18	254
Average 1950–9	338	36	374
1960	233	15	248
1961	225	15	240
1962	213	24	237
1963	203	20	223
1964	227	15	242
1965	257	22	274
1966	231	26	257
1967	229	35	264
1968	241	17	258
1969	241	10	251
Average 1960–9	230	20	250
1970	267	39	306
1971	281	32	313
1972	279	39	318
1973	237	38	275
1974	229	45	274
1975	190	40	230
1976	187	30	217
1977	154	32	186
Average 1970–7	228	37	265

Source: MPAA as reprinted in Guback (1979).

Table 11.9b   *Motion pictures rated by
the classification and rating
administration, 1965–77*

	Total	MPAA companies
1965	191	175
1966	168	149
1967	215	206
1968	230	201
1969	325	171
1970	431	181
1971	513	177
1972	540	208
1973	584	185
1974	523	151
1975	459	123
1976	486	119
1977	378	95

Source: MPAA as reprinted in Guback (1979).

3 There is then a further sector of independent production that gets picked up by the major distributors after completion, or at least after production finance has been raised and while production is in progress, for distribution either within the US or for distribution abroad after having been distributed independently in the US market.
4 There is a further complication as regards imported films. Not only are the statistics inconsistent owing to the different reporting methods used, but we need to distinguish in a way no available statistics do, between so-called 'runaway' production, that is US financed films made abroad, and films produced abroad by foreign companies and subsequently imported into the US. Within the 'runaway' production we need to distinguish between those films financed abroad by the majors and those made by the independents (see Tables 11.10 and 11.11).
5 Then there is a further sector of independent production for specialized markets which, owing to the size and competitiveness of the US exhibition sector, is truly independent of the majors, for example, nature films, soft porn, etc.

When all these factors are taken into account, *Variety* estimated in 1976 that the independent production/distribution sector, that is excluding the majors and mini-majors, involved a production investment of $100 million, produced 300 films, but was struggling for 10–15 per cent of the box-office.

Table 11.10   *Major/minor share of feature productions, 1968–72, US made and imported*

	1968	1969	1970	1971	1972
Major/minor					
US made	90	87	73	66	74
Foreign made	110	84	62	42	52
Independent					
US made	20	31	64	77	107
Foreign made	13	24	37	71	63
Total US	169	118	137	143	181
Total foreign	123	108	99	113	115

Source: Variety, January 1973.

WHY THE MAJORS DOMINATE

The movie industry as an economic system

The reason for the dominance of the majors lies in the nature of the movie business and in the strategic position in that business occupied by distribution. It is easy to overlook and misunderstand the nature of distribution because to ordinary members of the public (as well as to many specialist writers on film who should know better), film is mainly associated either with the experience of watching films in a cinema (or increasingly on TV) or with all that the word Hollywood represents in popular mythology, the glamour of the stars, big-name directors, flamboyant producers, etc., that surrounds production, while distribution appears to be a mundane and mechanical function of linkage. Nothing could be further from the truth. If we want to examine 'the real relations' of the movie business rather than 'its phenomenal form' it is upon distribution that it is necessary to focus.

Although competition is one of the essential mechanisms of capitalist reproduction, that very mechanism, precisely because it is in the interest of each individual capital to suppress competition, produces, as is well known, a tendency to monopoly. This tendency is exaggerated in the movie business because of its specific characteristics. In order to understand those characteristics it is first useful to examine schematically the circuit of capital specific to the cinema industry (excluding for the moment TV) upon which historically the existing structure of the international film business is based.

The problem in this circuit is how to establish a viable linkage between production on the one hand and exchange (exhibition) on the other. Production involves high levels of investment (relative to the cost to the ultimate consumer, the ticket price) in a heterogeneous, highly perishable product, for which demand (for each individual unit of production) is uncertain. Exhibition involves the projection of that product to relatively small numbers of people in geographically scattered locales paying

Table 11.11 *Number, percentage and distribution source of imported feature films released in the US market, 1927–72*

	No. of films imported	Percentage of all releases in US	Source of imported films	
			Major US distributors	Independent US distributors
1927	65	8.7	9	56
1928	193	21.8	83	160
1929	145	20.5	14	181
1930	86	14.5	6	86
1931	121	19.5	17	104
1932	196	28.6	18	178
1933	137	21.3	21	116
1934	182	27.5	11	171
1935	241	31.5	16	225
1936	213	29.0	14	199
1937	240	30.8	15	225
1938	314	40.8	16	298
1939	278	37.0	21	297
1940	196	29.1	15	181
1941	106	17.7	11	95
1942	45	8.4	12	33
1943	30	7.0	10	20
1944	41	9.3	8	33
1945	27	7.2	6	21
1946	89	19.1	13	76
1947	118	24.3	10	108
1948	93	20.3	23	70
1949	123	25.7	10	113
1950	239	38.1	21	218
1951	263	40.2	43	220
1952	137	34.5	26	113
1953	190	35.6	16	174
1954	174	40.7	28	146
1955	138	35.2	26	112
1956	207	43.2	27	180
1957	233	43.7	48	185
1958	266	52.5	63	203
1959	252	57.4	41	211
1960	233	60.2	65	168
1961	331	71.6	64	267
1962	280	65.6	60	220
1963	299	71.2	56	243
1964	295	71.9	58	303
1965	284	61.2	69	230
1966	295	65.4	56	239
1967	284	61.5	70	214
1968	274	60.4	74	195
1968[a]	123	–	–	–
1969	108	43.0	–	–

Table 11.11   *contd.*

| | No. of films imported | Percentage of all releases in US | Source of imported films | |
			Major US distributors	Independent US distributors
1970	99	32.4	–	–
1971	111	35.5	–	–
1972	103	33.0	–	–

[a] The different sources for pre- and post-1968 data are the probable explanation for the marked drop in import totals beginning with the second set of 1968 figures.
Source: Sterling and Haight (1978) drawn from 1927–68 data: *Film Daily Yearbook* 1969; 1968 (second) – 1972 data: *Variety* estimates, quoted in Office of Telecommunications Policy, *Analysis of the Cause and Effects of Increase in Same Year Programming and Related Issues in Prime-Time Network Television* (1973), table 15.

individually small sums that bear no necessary relationship to either the cost or the quality of the film. Beyond a certain point economies of scale and increases in productivity could not be attained in production. Moreover, historically they could only be maximized within these limits, as they were in the heyday of the studios in the 1930s and 1940s, when control over exhibition ensured a steady and predictable flow of product and thus allowed the utilization of the techniques of classic, mass, factory production.

However, because of this limit on productivity in production, there was and is always a premium on expanding the audience to the maximum possible for each unit of production and in making the flow of money from the widely scattered box-offices back into production as efficient (in terms of the overhead costs of the distribution/exhibition system) and as rapid as possible (thus accelerating the turnover time of capital). This explains the very early oligopolistic control over the world market established by the US industry and also the tendency, similarly established earlier, to amortize production investment over a very short release period.

As Strauss put it in the *Harvard Business Review* in 1930:

Once the original expenditures connected with the production of the picture have been incurred, no further costs other than those of distribution and exploitation must be met, whether the picture is exhibited in ten, or ten thousand playhouses . . . .

When a producer of motion pictures therefore increases his customers for any given film from two thousand theatres to four thousand theatres of the same grade, he may increase his net revenue a dozen times or more; for there is a reduction of 50 per cent in the costs of production that must be charged against the revenue from each of the theatres in which the picture is shown.

It follows that in the motion picture industry, more perhaps than in any other, there is no factor so important as wide distribution. . . . This is not only true within the domestic market but holds with equal force in considering the advisability of attempting to obtain world-wide distribution for the pictures produced by any company, whatever the nationality of the producing company itself. . . . In the absence of legislative restrictions on the importation of motion pictures, therefore, or of differences in civilizations and customs which would make a film unsuitable for certain markets, the natural tendency in the industry is to obtain world-wide distribution for all pictures produced.

The result of this tendency allied to the natural advantages of the US industry led, as Strauss himself pointed out, to the US industry capturing between 75 and 85 per cent of the European market in the 1920s.

As to the second point, Howard Lewis stated, in his study of *The Motion Picture Industry* published back in 1933, that:

It is claimed that 40 per cent of the total revenue of all pictures is secured from the first run showing in 100 key centres and that about 50 per cent of the total revenue of a picture is obtained within the first 90 days.

Thus the characteristics of the contemporary industry that we shall be examining are deeply rooted historically in the specific nature of the movie business.

We can present the resulting capital flow in Table 11.12 based upon a presentation made by A. H. Howe when he retired as Vice President of the Bank of America in Los Angeles, after a career as one of the leading bankers to the US movie industry. This presentation was in 1971.

Table 11.12   *Distribution of box-office revenues, 1971 and 1979*

	1971	1979
Annual world-wide box-office	2 billion	6.3 billion
Film rental share 30 per cent	600 million	1.9 billion
Distribution fee deducted 30 per cent	180 million	(570 million)
Amount left to cover distribution costs (e.g. prints and advertising) and negative costs	420 million	(1.3 billion)
Distribution costs (30 per cent of film rentals)	180 million	(570 million)
To cover negative costs	240 million	(730 million)

While the growing importance of TV revenue and revenue from spin-offs such as books, records and merchandising complicates this picture increasingly, the unsentimental bankers' view of the industry clarifies the nature of the problem, especially because it is not concerned with the type or quality of the films produced. This subject understandably occupies a great deal of attention, but is of marginal relevance to the operation of the movie business as an economic system; to concentrate on it actually obstructs our understanding of the modalities of the present system and thus of the ways in which one might intervene with the aim of affecting the type or quality of film produced.

The problem for the system is to match production investment to box-office revenue for any given state of the costs of collection. The problem for individual firms is to exert sufficient control over the total capital flow to ensure that investment and revenue are in profitable balance, and (if possible) to extend that control so that excess profits can be extracted by them from other parts of the total system.

The lessons of the history of the movie industry are two-fold:

1 That in a competitive system it takes the participants time to work out the optimum means for achieving these ends;
2 That as the characteristics of the system are changed by exogenous pressures (for example, the intervention of the US Justice Department or the rise of TV), so the optimum means will themselves change.

The historical rise of the majors

The first attempt to control the movie business was based upon production and upon control over patents in the technology needed for production and for projection. The reign of the Motion Picture Patents Company, as this cartel was called, lasted from 1908 to 1917, when it was finally dissolved by a Supreme Court decision that the licensing procedures upon which its powers were based were illegal.

Even prior to 1917, however, a rapidly expanding market and the possibility of importing equipment from abroad had led to the development of an aggressive independent industry outside MPPC control. It was out of this independent sector that the present majors developed during a battle for control of the nascent industry in the 1920s, during which the essential structure and modes of operation of the movie business as a mature economic form were discovered and put into operation by individual competitive entrepreneurs in the heat of commercial battle. This form, which it retains to this day, included feature-length films, licensed to exhibitors on a variable scale linked to box-office receipts rather than outright sale, the star system as the preferred mode of product differentiation with its linked publicity machine, and the distribution/exhibition practices of zoning, block booking and blind booking, road shows, etc.

Whether starting from a base in production and moving into distribution and exhibition, like Zukor with Paramount or Warner Bros with Vitagraph and First National, or whether from a base in exhibition and distribution and moving into production like Fox and Loew's (MGM) or whether on the basis of its control of sound patents and the backing of Rockefeller banking finance building much a combine from outside the industry, like RKO, *all* those involved discovered that, in the competitive conditions then reigning, the only way to run a profitable film business was to control all parts of the capital circuit.

Thus by 1930 the US industry was controlled by five vertically integrated combines – Warners, Paramount, Fox, Loew's and RKO. Alongside were three mini-majors – Universal and Columbia who owned studio and distribution facilities and United Artists which uniquely was a distribution company for independent producers.

This oligopolistic structure not only controlled the US industry, it also already dominated the world industry and drew a significant proportion of its revenue and profits from the non-US market. One contemporary analyst reckoned that in 1930

> American distributors received about 200 million dollars in gross revenue annually out of the total annual world gross revenue of approximately $275 million and that between 75% and 85% of the pictures shown throughout the world in recent years have been films of American origin.

Although European opposition to this dominance led between 1925 and 1928 to some small reduction in the proportion of American films shown in world markets, a growing total box-office meant that foreign revenues going to US producers and distributors rose from $50 million in 1925 to $70 million in 1928. This dominance was based upon the position of the US domestic market which produced over 60 per cent of world revenue, thus enabling US producers and distributors to undercut foreign competition with products of superior quality. Although the balance within the world market somewhat shifted away from the US domestic market in the 1950s and 1960s, because the US experienced the impact of TV upon cinema attendances earlier than the rest of the world, the situation has now reverted to the position of the 1920s. It is interesting to note that contemporary analysts of the US industry, such as Strauss and Lewis, could not believe that European interests would allow such a situation to continue and Strauss himself argued that it was 'folly to believe that, no matter what developments take place in the industry, the American producers and distributors will be able to maintain as a mere matter of course, the commanding position which they at present possess'.

Strauss envisaged the creation of a European production/distribution cartel, backed by the State on the model of German law in the 1920s, and based upon the ability to exclude the Americans from the European market and thus to bargain a guaranteed access to the US market against a limited US access to Europe. It is also interesting and relevant to note that he considered it 'probable that production throughout the world could in this way be cut nearly 35% and such a development as this would tend considerably to increase the net revenue obtained both by American and by European companies'. As we shall see the US majors have used their oligopolistic position to impose such a situation in recent years to their undoubted revenue advantage.

Anti-trust in the movie industry

Thus it was against an industry controlled by five major vertically integrated combines that the US Justice Department launched its anti-trust actions. The battle between the Anti-Trust division of the Justice

Department and the US majors is a long saga beginning with the first case against Paramount in 1922 and continuing at present with action, for example, to restrain Kerkorian of MGM gaining control of Columbia. Since 1976 there have been Federal suits against Fox on block booking and against Warners on 'four-walling'. In addition, numerous private suits have been brought by exhibitors against distributors alleging restraint of trade and the infringement of the consent decrees. Even the majors themselves have, as we shall see, joined in the act and are now involved in anti-trust suits against the US TV networks.

However, for our purposes we are concerned with a process that effectively began in 1938 with the anti-trust case, US v Paramount Pictures Inc et al., and culminated in consent decrees with Loew's in 1948, Paramount in 1949, 20th Century Fox in 1951 and Warners in 1953, by which the majors agreed to divorce themselves of their holdings in exhibition and to refrain from distribution practices in restraint of trade, such as block booking (for details see Conant, 1960). While, as I have indicated, there is evidence that, especially in the recent boom period, and for reasons which I shall explain, the major distributors have resorted to some of these outlawed practices, I think one can assert for the purposes of this chapter that the exhibition market in the United States is as competitive as it reasonably could be, given the specific nature of film as a marketable commodity. Or at least for our purposes what we have to explain is how the majors have maintained their dominance and profitability without control over exhibition.

Initially divorcement created severe problems for the majors for two reasons:

1   As Heutig showed, the financial structure of the majors was based upon theatre ownership, upon the high fixed capital investment involved and upon the need to service the long-term debts incurred in the acquisition of theatre chains. The majors were fundamentally real-estate companies.

As Heutig puts it: 'The production of films, essentially fluid and experimental as a process, is harnessed to a form of organization which can rarely afford to be either experimental or speculative because of the regularity with which heavy debt charges must be met.'

This meant that since accounting between divisions of the vertically integrated combines was a purely internal matter arranged to present the best picture to bankers and investment analysts, film rental charges were so arranged as to take the profits in the exhibition division, while investment capital for production could at the same time be raised against the security of the fixed assets of the theatres (see Tables 11.13 and 11.14).

There are some industry analysts today who would argue that as a result the share of box-office revenue going to film rental was too low in the period following divorcement, and that the rise in this share that the majors as distributors have been able to squeeze out of the exhibitors

Table 11.13   *Investment in the US film industry prior to divorcement*

| | Investment | |
Sector	($ million)	(%)
Production	125	6.1
Distribution	25	1.2
Exhibition	1,900	92.7
Total	2,050	100.0

Source: Conant (1960).

Table 11.14   *Income from domestic film rentals as a percentage of total volume of business: five major motion picture companies, 1939*

	Domestic film rental ($ thousand)	Volume of business ($ thousand)	Film rental as percentage of volume of business
Loew's	43,227	112,489	38.4
20th Century Fox[a]	33,150	53,752	61.0
Warner Bros	28,917	102,083	28.3
Paramount	28,227	96,183	29.3
RKO	18,190	51,451	35.3
Total	151,711	415,958	36.4

[a] The case of 20th Century Fox differs somewhat from that of other majors. During a complicated reorganization in 1933, control of Fox Theatres changed hands, ending up eventually in General Theatres Equipment Corporation. This company, in turn, was controlled by Chase National Bank. Fox merged with 20th Century in 1935, possessed a 42 per cent stock interest in General Theatres Equipment Corporation. The company's income from theatres takes the form of dividends on the stock interest and is therefore not comparable to the amounts listed as income from theatres for the other majors.
Source: Heutig (1944).

in recent years by using their oligopoly powers merely restores a proper balance (however questionable under the terms of the consent decrees the methods used to do this).

What is undoubtedly true is that this shift in the balance between the share of revenue going to exhibitors and that going to film rental has made a contribution to the renewed prosperity of the majors after a prolonged period of slump.

The divorcement of the exhibition divisions left production divisions that had often been running at break-even or at a loss in accountancy terms, with a problem of how to raise funds for investment in production without the security of theatres. This problem was only finally solved satisfactorily by the absorption of the film companies into larger conglomerates or their own diversification to form more widely based conglomerates.

2   The second problem caused by divorcement was in part economic
and in part psychological. That is to say the production arms of the
majors had high fixed investments in studios with high overheads in the
form of permanent staff and contract stars, which depended for their
economic viability on a large and steady production throughput. Moreover, the men running these studios had become habituated to a form of
production behaviour and associated expectations about both the product
and the audience that derived from the economics of the vertically
integrated combine. It was not until the profound crisis of the late 1960s
and 1970s that this generation was finally removed, and the majors learnt
not only to live with but to actually enjoy the new situation in which
they found themselves.

The extent of their basic strength can be gauged by the fact that they
survived between 15 and 20 years of delusion. Until the almost terminal
crisis struck, the majors continued as though their problems stemmed not
from a fundamental shift in the economic structure of the industry, but
from the loss of their audience to TV. They continued to believe, and
any minor upsurge within the steady downward trend or any single
smash hit (*The Sound of Music* being the straw that nearly broke the
camel's back) confirmed them in that belief, that bigger and better and
more expensive films involving new processes such as Cinemascope or
Cinerama would bring the audience back and restore their prosperity (see
Tables 11.15a and 11.15b).

However, hindsight shows us that divorcement was in fact a blessing
in disguise, and that the growth of TV, far from threatening the produc-
tion/distribution majors, has been a key element in their renewed
strength. Why is this the case?

Divorcement took place at precisely the moment when cinemas were
becoming a declining asset. They represented a large fixed investment in
an inflexible form (cinemas were not easy to convert to other uses and
as a result to sell at their value as cinemas) attracting a rapidly declining
revenue. Moreover, the initial move by the majors into exhibition was
only necessary for producer/distributors in a competitive situation in
order to stop rivals freezing them out of the market. Once access to the
key US domestic cinema market was policed by the Justice Department,
this motive was removed and a concentrated production/distribution
oligopoly faced a fragmented exhibition sector within which no single
exhibition chain was strong enough to exert real competitive pressure.

Moreover, although for the psychological reasons already outlined, it
took a considerable time for the industry to realize this, exhibitors
needed them more than they needed the exhibitors. The reason for this,
especially once the majors had rationalized their production arms and cut
the fixed investments in studios and studio staff to the bone, was that
the exhibitors were running a business with high fixed investment and
continuous overheads which they needed to operate all the year round,
while the producer/distributors, once they no longer needed to keep their

Table 11.15a   *Total admissions income of US motion picture theatres,
with admissions expenditures as a percentage of selected consumer
expenditures, 1921–75*

	Admissions to film theatres ($ million)	Constant 1972 dollars ($ million)	Admissions as percentage of:		
			Personal consumption expenditure	Recreational expenditure	Spectator amusement expenditure
1921	301	703	–	–	–
1923	336	824	–	–	–
1925	367	876	–	–	–
1927	526	1,267	–	–	–
1929	720	1,760	0.9	16.6	78.9
1930	732	1,816	1.1	18.4	82.1
1931	719	1,975	1.2	21.8	84.2
1932	527	1,617	1.1	21.6	83.5
1933	482	1,155	1.1	21.9	84.1
1934	518	1,619	1.0	21.2	82.9
1935	556	1,695	1.0	21.1	82.7
1936	626	1,891	1.0	20.7	82.5
1937	676	1,971	1.0	20.0	82.6
1938	663	1,967	1.0	20.5	81.3
1939	659	1,985	1.0	19.1	80.3
1940	735	2,194	1.0	19.5	81.3
1941	809	2,298	1.0	19.1	81.3
1942	1,022	2,627	1.2	21.6	84.9
1943	1,175	3,087	1.3	25.7	87.6
1944	1,341	3,185	1.2	24.7	85.8
1945	1,450	3,372	1.2	23.6	84.6
1946	1,692	3,623	1.2	19.8	81.9
1947	1,594	2,985	1.0	17.2	79.6
1948	1,506	2,619	0.9	15.5	78.5
1949	1,451	2,546	0.8	14.5	77.5
1950	1,376	2,893	0.7	12.3	77.3
1951	1,310	2,110	0.6	11.3	76.3
1952	1,246	1,965	0.6	10.3	75.3
1953	1,187	1,858	0.5	9.3	73.9
1954	1,228	1,913	0.5	9.4	73.4
1955	1,326	2,072	0.5	9.4	73.6
1956	1,394	2,145	0.5	9.3	73.4
1957	1,126	1,673	0.4	7.3	68.0
1958	992	1,436	0.3	6.3	64.5
1959	954	1,369	0.3	5.6	60.7
1960	956	1,350	0.3	5.4	57.9
1961	955	1,336	0.3	5.1	56.7
1962	945	1,307	0.3	4.7	53.8
1963	942	1,287	0.3	4.4	51.8
1964	951	1,283	0.2	4.0	49.5
1965	1,067	1,434	0.3	4.1	50.3
1966	1,119	1,442	0.2	4.0	48.4

Table 11.15a *Contd.*

	Admissions to film theatres ($ million)	Constant 1972 dollars ($ million)	Admissions as percentage of:		
			Personal consumption expenditure	Recreational expenditure	Spectator amusement expenditure
1967	1,128	1,414	0.2	3.5	46.9
1968	1,294	1,555	0.2	3.7	48.8
1969	1,400	1,598	0.2	3.7	48.2
1970	1,521	1,639	0.3	3.7	48.4
1971	1,626	1,680	0.2	3.7	48.4
1972	1,644	1,644	0.2	3.4	47.2
1973	1,965	1,850	0.2	3.6	50.8
1974	2,264	1,920	0.3	3.7	52.2
1975	2,274	1,767	0.2	3.5	49.5

Source: Sterling and Haight (1978). Based upon US Department of Commerce data.

own cinemas full of product on a year-round basis were in a position to create a seller's market by cutting back the number of their releases and, as we shall see, to match their release pattern to the box-office peaks. Thus hardly was divorcement complete than the very exhibitors who shortly before had been calling for the creation of a competitive market were back asking the government to allow the majors back into exhibition (see US Senate, 1953, 1956).

The strategic position of distribution

Divorcement revealed the truly strategic position occupied by distribution, a function which, within a vertically integrated combine, can appear as though it is merely a matter of physically distributing film prints and of book-keeping. But exhibition was fragmented, not only by divorcement, but also by the creation of a new exhibition market in TV. At the same time, the economic rationale of the major production studios having been removed, the rise of the so-called independent producer had fragmented the production sector as well, distribution was left as the key linkage between production and exhibition, a narrow funnel through which the capital circuit of the movie industry had to pass.

Why was the funnel narrow? Why was distribution too not fragmented? Here we see the crucial importance of the control of worldwide distribution networks, a control which the US government, while fighting anti-trust within the US, actually encouraged by its support for the external cartel of the MPEAA. The maintenance of a worldwide distribution network is expensive (approximately $20 million per year currently), thus barriers to entry are high. After divorcement the majors retained control over these networks which they had built up in parallel with the

Table 11.15b   *Average weekly motion picture attendance in US,*
1922–65

	Average weekly attendance	Attendance index
1922	40,000	44
1923	43,000	48
1924	46,000	51
1925	46,000	51
1926	50,000	56
1927	57,000	63
1928	65,000	72
1929	80,000	89
1930	90,000	100
1931	75,000	83
1932	60,000	67
1933	60,000	67
1934	70,000	78
1935	80,000	89
1936	88,000	98
1937	88,000	98
1938	85,000	94
1939	85,000	94
1940	80,000	89
1941	85,000	94
1942	85,000	94
1943	85,000	94
1944	85,000	94
1945	85,000	94
1946	90,000	100
1947	90,000	100
1948	90,000	100
1949	70,000	78
1950	60,000	67
1951	54,000	60
1952	51,000	57
1953	46,000	51
1954	49,000	54
1955	46,000	51
1956	47,000	52
1957	45,000	50
1958	40,000	44
1959	42,000	57
1960	40,000	44
1961	42,000	47
1962	43,000	47
1963	42,000	47
1964	44,000	49
1965	44,000	49

Weekly attendance figures are in thousands. Index figures calculated on a base of 100 for
the years 1946–8.
Source: Historical Statistics, 1975, Series H-873, p. 400, as reprinted in Sterling and
Haight (1978).

development and operation of vertically integrated combines in the US market. It was control of these networks that alone allowed access to the worldwide market, a market which, as the US market declined, represented in the 1950s around 50 per cent of total film rental revenue to the US industry.

Thus the major distributors alone controlled access to enough of the market to spread their investment risk in production over a large enough programme of films to return a regular and reasonable profit. Only they were in a position to ensure the necessary match between production investment and box-office revenue upon which the economic viability of the total system rests. (This does not mean they always did so. The crisis of the late 1960s was caused by their massive over-investment in production.) As Howe (1971) put it:

> Pictures are not bankable risks. No sane banker can make loans for the production of a picture where the sole source of payment is revenue from that picture. Producers agree, they won't risk *their* funds in such a project. So for twenty years it has been the major American motion picture companies who have taken the risk.

As a study by Kobi Jaeger, based upon the analysis of 300 US features, showed in 1973 (as reported in *Variety*, 16 January 1974) 'Out of 9 pictures, one is a hit, 3 break even and five are "ambivalent".'

Thus the major distributors are also, indeed primarily, film financiers. Their distribution charge covers not just the cost of physically distributing that film but the risk of distributing the majority of films that do not even make enough to cover the actual cost of distribution. At the same time, since without the access to the world market that these majors control there is little hope of a viable return on any single production investment, the majors are in a position to invest in a range of productions on the most favourable terms to themselves, terms which in general include the valuable right to amortize their investment out of the first slice of revenue before capital repayment or profits (if any) are paid to the other participants. Moreover, the distributors' necessary book-keeping function puts them alone in a position to monitor costs efficiently and control production investment in relation to those costs, while at the same time giving them the opportunity for those 'metaphysical' accounting practices so often commented upon, which lead occasionally to the courts, and which undoubtedly give them the opportunity of allocating to themselves the favour of every accounting doubt.

The majors and TV

This control over worldwide distribution would have given the majors dominance in the role of distributor/financiers even if cinemas had remained the only form of cinema exhibition. The rise of TV, while initially seen as a threat, merely reinforced this dominance. As I have pointed out above, the aim of distribution is to make the collection of box-office revenue as efficient, in overhead cost terms, and as rapid (for reasons of capital turnover time) as possible. From this point of view network TV presents significant advantages, namely access to a major share of the domestic US market instantly by means of a single transaction. The disadvantage from the majors' point of view was that access to this market was controlled by even larger and more powerful monopolies than themselves.

Hollywood initially came to terms with TV in two ways:

1 The sale of its film libraries to TV. This represented a significant contribution during the 1950s and early 1960s to staving off the moment of reckoning for the majors, since it provided a source of funds for current production investment against assets that had already been amortized in the cinemas and written down in the books.

2 The production of TV series. Universal moved earliest and with most vigour into this field, and their rise from the second rank can in part at least be attributed to this fact. Their annual accounts continue to show, alone of the majors, a higher annual revenue from TV than from film. Such production was a means of continuing factory studio production, originally designed to supply block-booked cinemas, in order to supply a new exhibition outlet with an even more voracious need for a continuous flow of product.

However, the relationship with TV has evolved significantly in recent years and is both one of the key elements accounting for the prosperity of the majors and also an illustration of the continuing strategic importance of control over a world distribution network. Because of the monopoly control that they exercised over access to the major TV audience, the networks were able to drive a very hard bargain, so that in general the production of series for the networks was not profitable on its own, since the networks, operating in a buyers' market, could keep prices low. Thus profits depended upon exploiting the publicity gained from a network showing through US domestic TV syndication, foreign TV sales and (in the case of made-for-TV movies) even subsequent cinema exhibition. Thus profitable operation in this field required both the financial muscle to sustain the original production investment and access to an efficient international distribution network.

On the other hand, so far as films were concerned, while you could not make enough from a network sale to cover production costs, you could make enough to represent a significant extra profit on a production already amortized in the cinema worldwide. Moreover, success at the cinema box-office, access to which was increasingly controlled by the majors, in its turn raised the price that would be paid by TV.

In the case of TV series and made-for-TV movies the position of the majors has recently been significantly assisted by the Justice Department and the FCC. Because a network sale was so important to the subsidiary marketing possibilities of such product, the networks had been exploiting their oligopolistic position in order to insist upon a share of all subsequent non-networks receipts. This practice has now been outlawed, thus putting the majors in a stronger position vis-à-vis the networks.

The case of the sale of cinema films to TV illustrates graphically the power that the majors draw from their control of distribution. Until the mid-1960s the majors had sold their old films to the networks in packages for comparatively low sums, sums that represented apparent windfall profits to the sellers who still remained primarily concerned with production and distribution for cinemas. In the mid-1960s this changed dramatically. In September 1966 the TV showing of *Bridge on the River Kwai* demonstrated the immense TV ratings potential of major feature films. The result was that shortly afterwards ABC paid $2 million for two showings of a film and the Ford Motor Company $1,800,000 for one showing. The rush was on. Within days MGM announced a $53 million deal with CBS for 51 films, Paramount sold ABC 32 films for $20 million and ABC paid 20th Century Fox $19.5 million for 17 films.

This situation produced two results. First, the film companies suddenly became very vulnerable to take-over, because the sudden rise in the inventory value of their film libraries meant that their assets were significantly undervalued in their books. As a result United Artists executed a defensive merger with Transamerica and Paramount with Gulf and Western. This started the rapid trend towards conglomeration and diversification which, as I have outlined, is now the economic form that the majors have assumed.

More importantly for our present purposes the sudden dramatic rise in the cost to the networks of feature films inspired an attempt by two of them to use their control of TV exhibition as a base for a move into film production and distribution. The fact that the film majors were able decisively to defeat this challenge to their dominance on the part of among the most powerful corporations in the United States clearly illustrates the continuing strength that they draw from their control of world distribution. (As a safety measure the majors also lodged a suit in 1970 under the anti-trust laws and under the terms of their own consent decrees claiming that the networks, as exhibitors, should not be allowed to participate in production or distribution. They were joined in this action by the Justice Department in 1972. In 1977 NBC agreed an out-of-court settlement. CBS and ABC are still fighting.)

Thus in 1967 ABC started ABC Picture Holdings, and CBS started Cinema Centre Films distributed through National General. By 1970 they had between them succeeded in gaining 10 per cent of the US film rental market. When ABC pulled out of film production in 1974, however, it announced accumulated losses of 47 million dollars. CBS also announced losses of tens of millions of dollars when it too pulled out at around the same time.

THE MAJORS TODAY: STRATEGIES OF DOMINATION

Let us turn to look now in more detail at the ways in which the existing majors use their dominant position. A new breed of managers entered the industry with the conglomerates in the late 1960s and early 1970s. Their great advantage is their rational approach to the business free from the hype and mythology associated with Hollywood. The business philosophy that guides them, and which has brought the majors from the brink of bankruptcy to their present prosperity, is well expressed in the *Gulf and Western Handbook* for 1971.

> At the time of its late 1966 merger with Gulf and Western, Paramount Pictures Corporation was a declining force in the motion picture business. Like most big movie companies Paramount was suffering losses on its feature productions. With Gulf and Western encouragement and capital support, Paramount moved seriously into TV production, becoming the second largest supplier of prime-time network TV shows, such as 'Mannix'. Paramount also stepped up leasing of its feature films to TV. And as the new economics of the movie business began to exert itself at the end of the 1960s, Paramount led the industry into a much needed revitalization. It trimmed production schedules to meet the realistic conditions of the market place, moved a major portion of its film production off the Hollywood studio lot and onto location and streamlined its world wide distribution network.

The effect of reducing the costs of distribution has been, as we have seen, mergers between the majors in both US domestic and foreign distribution; a further effect we will examine when we look at the role of advertising.

The effect of 'trimming production schedules to meet the realistic conditions of the market-place' has meant a steady decline in the number of pictures released annually by the majors (see Table 11.9a).

The 'stepping-up leasing' of feature films to TV has meant that, having driven off the competition from the networks themselves, the majors have been in a position to accelerate the turnover time of their production investment capital by planning network sales from the start as an integral part of their investment and marketing strategy, often receiving payment from the network before production starts (and also thus able to shoot special or extra footage for the TV showing).

For example, in early 1978 Alan Hirschfield, at the time President of Columbia Pictures Industries, gave the figures in a talk to Wall Street security analysts for a typical Columbia project (see Table 11.16). From these figures it can be seen that TV revenue is higher than, and is regarded as more certain than, cinema revenue.

Nonetheless, cinema revenue, both in the US and worldwide, still represents the largest proportion of the majors' income from filmed entertainment and, as we have seen, it is also success in the cinema that keeps up the price of TV sales. It is crucial, therefore, in order to understand the way in which the majors operate and in particular in order to understand recent trends towards the reinforcement of the

Table 11.16 *Network sales ($ million)*

Cash negative cost	5.6
Less: outside finance	2.0
	3.6
Plus: initial release costs	3.0
Cash break-even point	6.6
Network TV	2.3
Syndication	0.6
Pay-TV and other	0.6
	3.5
Net to be cleared from cinemas	3.1
Minimum sales target	6.6

majors' dominance and their associated prosperity, to understand how the majors use the strategic position they have won as distributor/financiers to manipulate the relationship between production and cinema exhibition to their continuing advantage. This involves managing the relationship, as distribution alone can, between two functional hierarchies, one in production and the other in exhibition.

The hierarchy of production

A distributor has to balance two factors. These are the higher return to be obtained from a production in which he is the sole investor and the need to spread the investment risk over a range of product wide enough to ensure an average profit and to keep the distribution network fully occupied. Obviously, his total investment must not exceed his total potential revenue.

The majors achieve this by involving themselves in production at a number of levels; levels arranged in a descending hierarchy of importance when it comes to the effort made to sell them to the public. The first level is one on which production is fully financed and controlled by themselves. They must therefore bear all the risks and must incur all expenditures prior to any returns from the box-office.

The second level takes in so-called independent productions, which are in fact fully financed by the distributor in the sense that all immediate production costs are paid for by him, offset against the first slice of future revenue after his own distribution fee has been deducted, but where risks are spread because other production participants defer fees against future profits.

At the third level, films are independently financed and the distributor guarantees loan repayment against a share of the profits and upon whose distribution guarantees further risk capital can be raised by the immediate producers. Here the distributor has lower risks but also a lower share of the profit.

At the fourth, final, level, films are fully independently financed while the distributor picks them up for distribution either for a flat percentage fee or for a fee plus profit participation.

It is crucial here to remember that, in all cases except the first, the distributor is charging a distribution fee of at least 30 per cent, which is taken off gross rentals before profits are calculated. In addition, the distributor charges the independent producers for the cost of prints and publicity which is, as we shall see, an increasingly important item. Thus control over distribution ensures the ability both to spread and to minimize that risk by extracting the cost of maintaining the distribution network from gross receipts prior to the contribution to the amortization of any production investment. Moreover, where the distributors' capital is at risk in production, it is in general amortized before that of other participants. Thus distributors make profits out of loss-making movies.

The hierarchy of exhibition

The aim of the distributor is to extract for his product the highest possible proportion of the available box-office revenue. There is a hierarchy of access to that revenue. A film is a highly perishable commodity. It earns a high proportion of its cinema receipts in the first few weeks of its release in any market. This concentration of the earning period of a film is being reinforced, by the profits to be gained by accelerating the turnover time of capital invested in production, especially when interest rates are high, and by the rise in advertising costs (see AIP amortization breakdown, in Guback, 1979: 74).

The US and Canadian markets, figures for which are usually lumped together as the US domestic box-office, represent the largest single market and so a high proportion of a film's earnings is drawn from its first few weeks of release in the US market.

Within the US market a high proportion of total box-office receipts is collected in a small number of key urban first-run cinemas in three short periods of peak cinema attendance – Christmas, Easter and the summer months. MGM, for instance, has declared that seventeen weeks provide 40–50 per cent of its theatrical rentals (MGM preliminary prospectus, 25 September 1973). One-third of US admissions comes from nine major metropolitan areas, and territories served by film exchanges in four cities typically generate a third of all revenue.

The top five cinema chains in the US control 16% of screens and these major groups do the most business with the major distributors. 'Thus in the 5 years up to 1978 General Cinema was the largest customer for each of the five major distributors except United Artists. In fiscal 1978, for example, General Cinema contributed about 12 million dollars in film rental to Columbia or about 8.5% of the distributors' total domestic rentals. Probably in second and third places were United Artists Theatre Circuit and ABC Theatres, each contributing about 6 million dollars in rentals. Thus 3 chains provided about 17% of Columbia's domestic theatrical revenue.' On the other hand the effect of one smash-hit on a chain's revenue not only from ticket sales, but from concession stand receipts ($0.20 for each box-office dollar) can be considerable. 'Jaws' grossed over $20 million in General Cinema's houses and represented $13 million in extra business for the company (see Guback, 1979).

Their ability profitably to exploit the world cinema market thus depends first upon controlling access to a temporarily and geographically restricted market segment: a few key US first-run cinemas during about twenty weeks per year.

This control is achieved by concentrating both production and, more importantly, marketing investment on these key markets, a concentration reinforced by imposing within the seller's market created by strictly limiting production, blind bidding and splitting, by long runs thus excluding rivals from these key periods, by extracting advances from exhibitors and by four-walling. Although many of these practices have been challenged by exhibitors as violations of the consent decrees, there is, as shown above, an element of mutual interest ensuring collusion between the major chains and the major distributors, since the cinemas also earn the major proportion of their revenue from the same periods and from the kind of blockbusters backed by the publicity expenditure that only the majors can ensure.

Promotion

Advertising expenditure has always played an important role in the oligopolistic control of markets. It stimulates demand and maintains market shares where price competition is mutually disadvantageous to the firms involved. It further serves to defend the market against new entrants by raising the price of entry. It is increasingly playing this role in the movie industry and is at the same time reinforcing tendencies to concentration of control.

Data on advertising and promotion expenditure are patchy, but they all point to its rapid escalation in relation to the costs of production. In 1977 Standard and Poor reported the entire industry as spending $200 million. Norman Levy, President of distribution for Columbia Pictures, claimed that it cost a minimum of $2 million to market a film domestically and estimated that Columbia would spend about $70 million to push twenty releases in 1979. *Variety*, on 5 February 1975, reported TV Bureau of Advertising figures showing a 100 per cent increase in expenditure on film advertising in the first nine months of 1974 compared with the same period in 1973, from $27,931,900 to $56,324,900. In 1974 the 'Trial of Billy Jack' was released to 1,000 theatres in one week supported by a $3 million advertising campaign; 50 per cent spent on TV resulting in a $11 million box-office gross. Broadcasting Advertising Reports Inc. reported in 1973 an increase of TV advertising for film by 33 per cent from $32.3 million in 1972 to $43.1 million in 1973.

In 1977 Barry Diller, Chairman of Paramount, was quoted by *Variety* as saying 'In the last three years the cost of producing the negative has risen by 50%. The cost of marketing may have risen by 100%.'

This increased advertising expenditure is concentrated on fewer and fewer pictures, in particular upon the films wholly financed by the majors themselves. The reasons for this are as follows:

1 Shrinkage of media outlets and the rising cost of advertising.
2 Reduction in the advertising staff employed by distributors as part of their cost-cutting. The reduced staff can thus devote themselves effectively to fewer pictures.
3 The fact that the film rental terms are often renegotiated weekly depending upon box-office returns and so in a falling market distributors do not want to send good money after bad.
4 The majors derive one-third of their product from independents and do not spend so much pushing those films, with the result that in 1971, for instance, one out of twelve of the top box-office grosses was a 'pick-up', while sixteen out of the bottom fifty-four grosses were.

However, the role of advertising and publicity in the reinforcement of the majors' control has entered a radically new phase with the development of these companies into multi-media conglomerates. For once these companies control under one corporate umbrella music publishing, record production, book publishing, theme parks, toy and electronic game manufacturing and so forth, such that the spin-off effect can be exploited across a range of media, it becomes increasingly difficult to tell what is promotion for what.

That is to say a film becomes only one ingredient in a multi-media package in which each element is not only profit-earning in its own right, but serves as publicity for every other part of the package. Thus a film may only need hardly to break even in cinemas if its mere exhibition and associated publicity can generate sufficient book, record and merchandising sales, while at the same time the distribution of books, records, T-shirts and toys can create an atmosphere of 'want-to-see' for the film. In Italy, for instance, in 1978 one-quarter of the toy market was captured by film and TV spin-offs. 'Star Wars' produced $100 million in merchandising sales in one year. Over the years Disney has been both the pioneer and the most successful exponent of this general strategy.

This new phase represents, of course, a massive rise in the barriers to entry since it is now necessary to be a conglomerate large enough to have a significant simultaneous stake across a whole range of leisure markets.

Because of the hierarchy of the majors' production involvement they will, as we have seen, concentrate their marketing strength behind their own product as first priority, since it is from those films that they stand

Table 11.17   *Market domination by six leading distributors of theatrical films*[a]

	1978	1979
Number of:		
Top ten films handled	10	9
Rental revenue ($ million)	434.5	344.8
Films with $10 million or more in North American rentals	25 of 27	23 of 28
Rental revenue ($ million)	642.9	622.6
Films with $2 million or more in North American rentals	66 of 82	53 of 78

[a] Columbia, Paramount, 20th Century Fox, United Artists, Universal, Warner Bros.
Source: Guback (1979) based on *Variety*, 4 January 1978, 3 January 1979, 10 January 1979. Does not include reissues.

to make the highest return. However, the majors cannot ensure success for their most-favoured films, so that the US market is used as a test market, the majors ruthlessly pulling films out of release at the first sign of lack of box-office success, while from their range of independently financed pick-ups they are able, at the first sign of box-office appeal, to send in replacements to fill the gaps in the favoured market segments with the necessary promotional support. Furthermore, using the pre-publicity and the rolling 'want-to-see' effect of US box-office success, the majors strictly select for international distribution the most successful pictures. Thus in 1979 Columbia planned to release twenty-three films in all, thirteen world-wide, three only in the US and Canada, and seven only outside the US and Canada. The results of all these strategies of control are graphically illustrated in Table 11.17 and in Tables 11.1a, 11.1b, 11.4 and 11.6.

The power and prosperity of the majors is based upon control of worldwide distribution networks which give them alone the possibility to balance, on world scale, production investment with box-office revenue. From that base they alone, helped by the limits placed upon the US TV networks by the Federal Government, have been able to expand with maximum efficiency into the new markets for filmed entertainment, broadcast TV and now pay-TV, as well as into associated spin-off markets such as records, books and toys.

This market control has been rapidly strengthened in recent years through raising barriers to market entry involving interrelated modes of publicity and merchandising.

Michael Conant, in his classic study of the effects of anti-trust action on the US movie industry published in 1960, raised the following question:

Should distribution and production departments also have been divorced from one another? On the basis of the available evidence on the cost structure of the industry, the answer to this question must be no. Indications are that a least-cost distribution system with full market penetration throughout the United States would have to distribute many more than the 25 to 40 pictures distributed by each of the leading distributors today. For this reason if distribution departments were divorced from production, there is a great probability that these separate distribution firms would merge and consolidate in order to lower costs. This would make for monopolies on the distribution level able to exploit their input markets in dealing with producers and their output markets in dealing with exhibitors. Such firms, able to bottleneck the flow of films into the market would increase monopoly in the industry not decrease it.

As we have seen, this was in fact a remarkably accurate prophecy of what has happened without benefit of government intervention.

What lessons can we learn from all this for European film policy? To compete in the world market would now require the control of one of the international distributors and their associated entertainment interests. At a price this could presumably be purchased. Columbia, for instance, would seem vulnerable to take-over. However, since the prosperity of such a company depends in the end on satisfying the taste of the US cinema-going and TV-watching public, control of such a company might produce money for Europe, but it would do little to foster indigenous European production, unless of course the profits were channelled into subsidizing such production. The alternative is to create a siege economy for filmed entertainment in Europe, denying entry to the product of the majors to the European market and building a rationalized production and distribution system to service European cinemas and TV networks. This system would have the power in Europe, similar to that given to the majors in the world market by the historical play of market forces, to match production investment to revenue from whatever source that revenue might come.

POSTSCRIPT

In the decade since this report was written the market and industry structure it analyses had experienced four significant major developments: (1) the rapid rise to maturity of the US cable TV industry and its associated pay-TV channels; (2) the explosive worldwide growth of the videocassette market; (3) a significant growth in investment in cinema exhibition and an associated rapid rise in the number of US cinema screens – a process now being exported to Europe; (4) the expansion of the private TV sector in Europe. What policy significance do these developments have in Europe? In particular has the overall structure of the industry significantly altered, undermining the oligopolistic dominance of the US majors?

The best available recent estimate of global US movie revenues, produced in a report by the US investment bank, Goldman Sachs, is shown in Table 11.18.

The key points to note about these figures are:

Table 11.18   *Distribution of US movie revenues, 1983–8 (estimated revenues, $ million)*

	1983	1984	1985	1986	1987	1988
Exhibition						
Domestic	1,700	1,800	1,635	1,650	1,830	1,920
Foreign	910	900	795	850	940	1,100
Total	2,610	2,700	2,430	2,500	2,770	3,020
Pay-TV						
Domestic	550	600	625	600	575	630
Foreign	0	0	0	35	70	110
Total	550	600	625	635	645	740
Videocassettes						
Domestic	400	950	1,335	1,630	1,810	2,300
Foreign	350	450	625	885	1,150	1,425
Total	750	1,400	1,960	2,515	2,960	3,725
Television						
Domestic	410	410	450	450	425	425
Foreign	125	135	145	175	250	550
Total	535	545	595	625	675	975

Source: Goldman, Sachs.

1   In global terms theatrical rentals exhibit very low growth in dollar terms and a marked decline in real terms, since the late 1970s, of around 45 per cent. Within these figures we can see a relative decline in foreign earnings at the beginning of the 1980s as the US box-office responded to aggressive investment in new multi-screen complexes and the blanket release of a small number of new blockbusters with associated advertising expenditure. As this trend has spread abroad, especially to Europe, the share of foreign revenues is swinging back to the position occupied at the beginning of the 1980s.

2   A dramatic shift in the structure of the revenue stream as between 1983 and 1989 video grew from 17 to 40 per cent of revenues and all TV from 10 to 27 per cent. Video has in fact grown explosively from 2 per cent in 1980. Within the TV market US pay revenues have almost peaked in dollar terms and are now declining in real terms, while foreign pay revenues mainly from Europe have started a dramatic climb from 1986. At the same time revenue from US 'free' TV is static in dollar terms and declining sharply in real terms, while foreign TV revenues have climbed sharply, again from 1986. The result has been an increased dependence on foreign earnings, up from 31 per cent in 1983 to 41 per cent in 1989 and a marked shift from dependence on theatrical to TV and video, especially video earnings. Between 1980 and 1989 the theatrical share of US foreign film revenues fell from 87 to 33 per cent.

Have these shifts entailed any change in the structure of control of the international audiovisual market since the late 1970s? Two trends can be observed. First a continuation of previous trends towards concentration. MGM bought United Artists in 1981 before in 1985 being bought by Turner Broadcasting and dismembered. Columbia has been bought by Coca-Cola, and 20th Century Fox by Murdoch's News International, while at the time of writing Warner and Time are fighting to merge into the world's largest media corporation in the face of a rival move by Paramount to take over Warner. Internationally Paramount, Universal and MGM/UA's non-US distribution activities have been merged in United International Pictures with global rentals in 1983 of $375 million or 27 per cent of all US foreign film earnings.

The number of majors has been somewhat increased by the addition of two so-called mini-majors, Orion and Tri-Star, which have benefited from the expansion and fragmentation of the market, in particular the growth of the US syndication market and the development of strategies of pre-sale on the international market. The relative weight of these mini-majors can be judged by comparing the 1985 filmed entertainment revenues of Orion at $223 million and Tri-Star at $258 million with 20th Century Fox's of $617 million and MCA's of $1,081 million or MGM/UA's pre-break-up revenues of $598 million. In the early 1980s Cannon and the Dino de Laurentis Group both attempted to join the majors, but rapidly fell by the wayside.

These changes have not significantly altered the nature or extent of the majors' control of both US and foreign markets. Indeed in certain respects, as we shall see, they have been reinforced. They have continued to limit the supply of feature films and use expensive marketing campaigns and release schedules as barriers to entry. Thus in spite of a growth in cinema screens in the US from 11,402 in 1975 to 18,327 in 1985 the number of films rated by the Classification and Rating Administration has remained static at around 350 per annum since 1977. Of this total, as has been their regular habit, the majors produced for instance in 1986, 105 or under 30 per cent, while distributing, for instance in 1985, 47 per cent.

In 1985 the MPAA reported the majors' average negative costs at $16.78 million and average marketing costs at $7.21 million. In order to break even on the approximately 130 films they produced that year, therefore, the majors needed a worldwide rental income of $3.1 billion from a total world market of approximately $5.6 billion. In pursuit of this revenue they have not only adopted saturation release patterns, backed by expensive TV advertising, which exclude the smaller independent distributors, but have themselves increasingly moved, with the Justice Department's blessing, back into exhibition. MCA, Paramount, Tri-Star and Columbia have all made this move, first in the US and now in Europe. This strategy has enabled them to maintain their stranglehold on the all-important US domestic market. Market shares for 1986–8 are shown in Table 11.19.

Crucially this control of US cinema exhibition, because of the continuing importance of the publicity and word-of-mouth generated by release

Table 11.19   *US domestic box-office market shares, 1986–8*

	1988		1987		1986	
Distributor	No. of films	Share (%)	No. of films	Share (%)	No. of films	Share (%)
Buena Vista	18	19.4	15	14.0	12	10.1
Paramount	19	15.2	17	19.7	19	22.2
20th Century Fox	14	11.6	15	8.7	21	8.1
Warner	31	11.2	21	12.5	21	1.0
MGM/UA	21	10.3	14	4.2	15	4.4
Universal	20	9.8	18	7.2	16	8.5
Orion	20	6.6	15	10.5	14	7.0
Tri-Star	17	5.8	17	6.2	18	7.1
Columbia	19	3.5	12	4.5	17	9.5
Total, top nine	179	93.4	144	87.5	153	77.9

Source: *Variety*, 25–31 January 1989.

in the few key weeks of the year in the world's largest and richest cinema market, has reinforced the majors' penetration of the European cinema exhibition market. There the same marketing strategy, the blanket release of a few highly boosted blockbusters, has had the same result, namely an ever-greater concentration of box-office revenues on a smaller number of high-grossing films. For instance in France in 1988 the top three films took 85 per cent of the total box-office revenue. The result has been that, for example, between 1983 and 1988 Spanish admissions fell 45 per cent while MPEAA rentals increased 65 per cent. Over the same period MPEAA rentals in West Germany increased 30.7 per cent and in the UK 50 per cent. In 1988 nowhere in Europe did US films have less than a 45 per cent market share.

But more crucially yet, control of the US cinema market has enabled the majors to maximize their returns from the dynamic global video-cassette market. The majors learnt their lesson. At the start they ignored and thus lost control of the pay-TV market. They have ensured by their handling of release schedules and by moving directly into videocassette publication and duplication that they extract the maximum return from consumers in this new market. For instance 20th Century Fox is a part-ner with CBS in a company which duplicates and distributes video-cassettes with a market share of 13.5 per cent. In 1985 it was the most important videocassette publisher in the US. Importantly the growth of the videocassette market has meant a return to a direct financial relation-ship between film viewer and the film's copyright owner similar to that existing in the cinema. This has changed the balance of power between the majors and the TV industry in its various forms.

First, the majors can now extract revenue for their films directly from domestic viewers, long since lost to the cinemas, without depending upon broadcasters or cable operators. Second, the growth of videocassettes has itself weakened the growth of pay-TV.

Furthermore the rapid growth in video distribution channels, first in the US and now in Europe has meant a growing shortage of product for transmission with proven popularity. The majors control access to this product. In particular the main motive for the purchase of MGM/UA by Turner and 20th Century Fox by Murdoch was to get their hands on what they saw as an undervalued film library. The massively increased valuation placed upon such stocks of audiovisual product has meant a significant rerating for long-established film production and distribution companies. At the same time the increasing importance of the non-US market has given a significant advantage to companies with established expertise in international marketing.

The European policy response to the continuing domination of world, and especially European audiovisual markets by the US majors, has been two-fold, and has focused on the TV market where, because of Europe's tradition of public service broadcasting, it has been felt possible to build from strength and lock the stable door before the horse has bolted. Through the European Commission's MEDIA programme, support has been given to making the structure of the European industry both more European and more competitive, building European-wide film and TV programme finance and distribution structures and, through training schemes, moving production away from its traditional artisanal base towards a more industrial and 'market-oriented' mode of production – in for instance, the production of TV series by teams rather than the making of 'auteur' cinema.

On the other hand, following the circulation and discussion of a paper prepared by the European Commission on Television Without Frontiers, the Commission has prepared a Directive which includes a quota of European programming to be carried on all European TV channels. The question of quotas imposed from Brussels has been intensely controversial in Europe. Many European governments, such as Denmark, Belgium and Germany, oppose interference from Brussels in what they regard as 'cultural' affairs as a matter of principle, arguing that it is a field excluded from the Treaty of Rome. Britain is against both from free trade principles and because its broadcasters and programme makers argue that it would cause US retaliation which would especially damage their access to the US market. At the time of writing it would now seem as though the European Commission Directive imposing quotas will not be accepted. As a result Europe will be left virtually defenceless with only the weak protection of the voluntary quotas under the Council of Europe Convention on Television. Meanwhile France is proposing, as an alternative, to move to a system which concentrates on ensuring that all broadcasters spend a given proportion of their revenues on original production. As 1992 and the unified internal market in the European Community approach, what to do about US domination of the audiovisual sector is likely to remain a subject of intense policy debate, controversy and diplomatic negotiation. Unless and until European productions have adequate access to the US market, protectionism is certainly justified on both economic and cultural grounds, and it is hard to see how some form of protectionism can be avoided.

Meanwhile the economic and cultural conflict between the US and Europe over the production and distribution of audiovisual material will move to GATT (General Agreement on Tariffs and Trade) and the current negotiations on an international agreement on Trade in Services.

These battles will be intense because the US majors are, as we have seen, becoming more dependent upon foreign and especially European revenues, as the US cinema and TV market stagnates. This relatively rare export success for a US industry in recent years against the background of the continuing massive US trade deficit also means that the US industry has the full and enthusiastic backing of the US government in international trade negotiations. On the other hand the very dependency of the US majors on European revenues gives the Europeans a powerful bargaining weapon.

References

ACCT (1973) *Nationalizing the Film Industry*. London: Association of Cinematograph Television and Allied Technicians.

Conant, M. (1960) *Antitrust in the Motion Picture Business*. Berkeley: University of California Press.

Crandall, R. W. (1975) 'The postwar performance of the motion-picture industry', *Antitrust Bulletin*, 20(1).

Guback, T. (1978) 'Les relations cinéma-TV aux Etats-Unis aujourdhui', *Filme Echange*, 2 (Spring).

Guback, T. (1979) 'Theatrical film', in B. M. Compaine (ed.), *Who Owns the Media*? New York: Harmony Books.

Heutig, M. D. (1944) *Economic Control of the Motion Picture Industry*. Philadelphia: University of Pennsylvania Press.

Howe, A. H. (1971) 'A banker looks at the picture business', *Journal of the Screen Producers Guild*, June.

Jowett, G. (1976) *Film: The Democratic Art*. Boston: Little, Brown.

Lewis, H. (1933) *The Motion Picture Industry*. New York: Van Nostrand.

Mattelart, A. (1980) *Multi-national Corporations and the Control of Culture*. Brighton: Harvester.

Sterling, C. and Haight, T. (1978) *The Mass Media: Aspen Institute Guide to Communication Industry Trends*. New York: Praeger.

US Senate (1953) *Hearings before the Select Committee on Small Business*. US Senate, 83rd Congress, 1st Session. Washington: Government Printing Office.

US Senate (1956) *Hearings before the Select Committee on Small Business*. US Senate, 84th Congress, 2nd Session. Washington: Government Printing Office.

Index